"At a time when writers in urban citadels have turned again to describing rural Americans as stupid, lazy, and even as bad people, it is refreshing to see a book that takes the strengths and weaknesses of rural America seriously. Here, we find a balanced discussion of the heterogeneity of rural America as well as valuable insights about the values, dispositions, and needs of its citizens."
Robert Wuthnow, professor, Princeton University

"As we face unprecedented rates of suicide, addiction, and behavioral health issues in rural America, Dr. Boilen's focus on this issue is timely and crucial. As I work with organizations serving rural areas in Montana and beyond to plan their future strategies and services, I see the real-life implications of the trends Dr. Boilen references in action: the challenge of attracting and retaining trained providers of behavioral health services leaves many undiagnosed, untreated, and isolated. Our communities are suffering because of this gap. While we can be proud of our go-it-alone, independent streak, rural Americans can also teach all of us how much we need each other to survive and thrive (as evidenced by the bars, pie socials, and church potlucks that still survive in otherwise struggling towns). I urge practitioners with any connection to rural America to explore and respond to the ethical and treatment considerations in this book; healing and support from providers who understand the unique needs and strengths of rural America, especially as telehealth brings this 20% of the country more in contact with our existing secondary and tertiary treatment systems. Rural America needs you now more than ever."
Ned Cooney, MSW, facilitator and consultant to organizations and community groups, Bigfork, Montana

Ethics in Rural Psychology

Ethics in Rural Psychology provides readers with theoretical underpinnings, practical applications, and empirically based knowledge of the practice of psychology in rural communities.

Dr. Boilen explores the similarities and differences within and across rural American communities to provide a framework for understanding this vast and varied population. Focusing on the ethical considerations unique to these communities, chapters use illustrative case examples, useful exercises, and personal anecdotes to highlight obstacles unique to rural areas. Finally, the book emphasizes the opportunity to be innovative and creative in rural practice, demonstrating how rural practices hold promise for cutting-edge advancements in the field of psychology.

This book will serve practitioners, students, and researchers as a primer, handbook, and road map for the challenging and rewarding clinical work that awaits in rural America.

Sara Boilen, PsyD, is the owner and chief psychologist at Sweetgrass Psychological Services, a community-minded group practice in Northwest Montana. She serves on the Montana Board of Psychologists.

Ethics in Rural Psychology
Case Studies and Guidance for Practice

Sara Boilen

NEW YORK AND LONDON

First published 2021
by Routledge
52 Vanderbilt Avenue, New York, NY 10017

and by Routledge
2 Park Square, Milton Park, Abingdon, Oxon, OX14 4RN

Routledge is an imprint of the Taylor & Francis Group, an informa business

© 2021 Taylor & Francis

The right of Sara Boilen to be identified as author of this work has been asserted by her in accordance with sections 77 and 78 of the Copyright, Designs and Patents Act 1988.

All rights reserved. No part of this book may be reprinted or reproduced or utilised in any form or by any electronic, mechanical, or other means, now known or hereafter invented, including photocopying and recording, or in any information storage or retrieval system, without permission in writing from the publishers.

Trademark notice: Product or corporate names may be trademarks or registered trademarks, and are used only for identification and explanation without intent to infringe.

Library of Congress Cataloging-in-Publication Data
Names: Boilen, Sara, author.
Title: Ethics in rural psychology : case studies and guidance for practice / Sara Boilen.
Description: New York, NY : Routledge, 2020. | Includes bibliographical references and index.
Identifiers: LCCN 2020007670 (print) | LCCN 2020007671 (ebook) | ISBN 9781138542938 (hbk) | ISBN 9781138542990 (pbk) | ISBN 9781351007603 (ebk)
Subjects: MESH: Rural Health Services | Community Mental Health Services—ethics | Rural Population | Cultural Characteristics | United States
Classification: LCC RA771.5 (print) | LCC RA771.5 (ebook) | NLM WA 390 | DDC 362.1/04257—dc23
LC record available at https://lccn.loc.gov/2020007670
LC ebook record available at https://lccn.loc.gov/2020007671

ISBN: 978-1-138-54293-8 (hbk)
ISBN: 978-1-138-54299-0 (pbk)
ISBN: 978-1-351-00760-3 (ebk)

Typeset in Baskerville
by Apex CoVantage, LLC

Contents

List of figures ix
Foreword by Emily M. Selby-Nelson x
Author's Note xii

Introduction 1

SECTION ONE
Rural America 5

1 What Is Rural? 7
2 Cultural Competence and Rural America 13
3 Rural Americans 23
4 The Psychological Landscape of Rural America: Values, Culture, and Norms 42
5 Health in Rural America 55
6 Healthcare in Rural America 70

SECTION TWO
Ethics in Rural Communities 77

7 An Ethical Framework 79
8 Ethics in Rural Practice 84
9 A Road Map for Managing Ethical Dilemmas in Rural Practice 90

10	Dual Roles, Multiple Relationships: No One Is a Stranger Here	107
11	Confidentiality and Privacy: Small-Town Secrets	121
12	The Generalist: Competencies and Necessity	128
13	Life as a Rural Clinician: Isolation, Impairment, and Self-Care	135

SECTION THREE
Innovations and Opportunities: Practical Applications in Rural Communities — 149

14	Clinical Practice in Insular Communities	151
15	Recruitment and Retention	154
16	Defining Rural Mental Healthcare	159
17	From Collaboration to Colocation: Integrated, Whole-Person Care in Rural America	173
18	Telehealth: Advances, Advantages, and Limitations	180
19	Creating a Culture: Decreasing Stigma, Increasing Wellness	188
	Closing Thoughts	191
	Appendix: Recommended Readings and Resources	193
	Index	195

Figures

1.1	US Counties and County Equivalents	8
3.1	Rural Lands in America	23
3.2	Poverty Rates by Region and Metro/Nonmetro Status, 2013–2017	27
3.3	2015 American Deprivation Index	29
3.4	Race and Ethnicity in Rural and Small Town America, 2010	30
3.5	Mortality Disparity Rates: American Indian and Alaska Natives, 2009–2011	36
4.1	Rural Values	42
4.2	Urban-Suburban-Rural Divide in Politics	47
5.1	Illicit Drug Use	58
5.2	Suicide Rates, by Sex and Age Group, United States (1999–2017)	61
5.3	Age-Adjusted Suicide Rates by Urbanization Level, United States (1999–2017)	62
5.4	Factors Contributing to Suicide	66
7.1	Professional Behavior	82
7.2	Ethical Guidelines	82
8.1	Primary Ethical Issues in Rural Mental Healthcare	85
9.1	Resolving Ethical Dilemmas	94
9.2	The Nature of Ethical Dilemmas	96
10.1	Types of Multiple Relationships	108
10.2	Multiple Relationship Flow Chart	111
10.3	Multiple Relationships With Client B	113
11.1	Small Town Woes	121
13.1	Essential Elements of Self-Care	140
16.1	Peer-to-Peer Service Requirements	166

Foreword

Individuals living in rural and remote regions are known to face significant and challenging barriers to treatment and, consequently, experience higher rates and complexity of both physical and mental health disparities. With ever-increasing national attention on substance use and mental health issues in rural America, the call for improved access to quality mental health services in rural and remote settings has been shouted loudly across our nation. This call climbs from the depths of valleys, over mountains, and across plains, hoping to fall upon the ears of competent, committed, and compassionate mental health practitioners.

Rural residents deserve the same quality and evidence-based treatments available to individuals living in more urban settings but are often isolated from such services. Workforce development issues in rural areas are well known and include insufficient cultural competence, recruitment and retention barriers, challenging practice and practical issues, and clinical and ethical nuances that can add to professional isolation, stress, and burnout. Unfortunately, psychology as a field has historically exhibited an inequity in education and research when it comes to rural psychology training and expertise. Knowledge gained from clinical psychology research and education has historically been obtained from information discovered in more urban settings, which often cannot consistently be applied in rural contexts. Rural communities need expert rural mental health champions to advocate for the needs of these typically underserved populations. All these issues are thoroughly addressed in this book.

Few clinical psychology or other mental health training programs offer rurally focused training to meet the needs of rural, remote, and underserved communities. It is this author's mission to provide culturally specific expertise to supplement generalist training for those either considering entering, or attempting to maintain, a successful rural practice. Without a sustainable rural mental health workforce, the needs of rural communities will never be met. With the right expertise and support, psychologists and other mental health professionals are well equipped to work together and build practices that can reach into valleys, across plains, and over mountains to meet those most in need right in their own communities.

Mental health practitioners who are a good fit to answer the call to rural practice are passionately invested in serving the underserved, have or will develop a clear and deep understanding of rural living (including the beauty and hardship that can be characteristic of that life), and are resilient and tolerant of the ambiguity and challenges that can be inherent in rural practice. If a rural mental health practice is to be successful, it must be designed in unique ways that truly meet the specific needs of each rural community; must balance the implementation of evidence-based practice while translating those services to the specific needs of rural patients or clients; and should integrate provider-focused interventions to address practitioner wellness, burnout, and sustainability of service.

This book effectively and thoroughly addresses the aforementioned aspects of rural practice. The author inspires learners, practitioners, trainers, supervisors, and administrators to answer the call and address the inequity in rural mental healthcare by equipping mental health professionals with the insight, knowledge, and skills needed to build sustainable and culturally relevant mental health practices in rural and remote settings. From a personal and professional point of view, the author offers uniquely engaging, practical, and interactive guidance on the diverse and complex issues that arise in rural practice while passing on the skills and perspectives needed to infuse resilience and commitment into a sustainable and successful rural practice. This book offers a more intimate and experience-based perspective to the already-growing knowledge base that offers guidance to rural mental health professionals. This author goes further by providing specific scenarios and evidence-based recommendations for navigating the nuances of rural practice.

As a psychologist who has dedicated my entire education, training, and professional career to rural mental health practice, research, teaching, and administration, I am motivated and inspired by the idea of the potential improvements this book may contribute to the rural mental health workforce. I have observed trainees and early career rural practitioners struggle with the very issues addressed in this text. I am confident that after reading this book, rural mental health students, trainees, practitioners, educators, and administrators will be better equipped to answer the call of rural mental health practice with enhanced courage, compassion, and creativity.

Emily M. Selby-Nelson, PsyD
—Director of Behavioral Health
Cabin Creek Health Systems
—Clinical Assistant Faculty
West Virginia University School of Medicine-Charleston Division
Marshall University
Emily.selby-nelson@cchcwv.com

Author's Note

In early 2020, while this book was in press, a global pandemic—caused by a novel coronavirus—swept through the world. One of the primary responses used by communities to stop the spread was known as social distancing. Since the virus spreads through droplet transmission, scientists encouraged people to stay in their homes whenever possible and avoid public places. Many therapists, psychologists, and social workers, in a matter of days, closed their offices and pivoted to telehealth.

In Chapter 18, I combined my personal experience, colleagues' anecdotes, and research to write about the practice of telehealth. In the months since I wrote that chapter, much has changed, some of it, perhaps, forever.

Today, May 5, 2020, I operate a fully telehealth practice. Like many practitioners in the United States, and globally, in the spirit of observing the scientific community's recommendations, I have not sat in my office with a client in over seven weeks. I have conducted all of my recent therapy sessions, weekly consultations, and supervision meetings through face-to-face video conferencing, and have supported my staff in the abrupt transition to working from home. I have read countless articles and engaged in dialog with colleagues near and far. I humbly share what we have learned.

All told, it is hard to connect over video conferencing. I mean this in two ways. First, as rural providers, several members of my team have struggled with the reality that our home internet is insufficient for the heavy requirements of a secure telehealth platform. The same is true for our clients. It has not been uncommon to experience significant delays, buffering issues, and a phenomenon one client describes as "robot head," where the poor connection results in my face becoming distorted and pixilated on the screen. One of my therapists informed me that three weeks into using telehealth exclusively a client asked, "Have none of your other clients mentioned how blurry you are?" Several providers in our clinic live rurally and have faced significant connectivity issues resulting from the lack of broadband internet access in our region. Our clients are no different. We have resorted to phone calls, typically not covered by insurance companies (though they have made exceptions during this time), as a means of remaining in touch with our most remote clients and those who do not have wifi at their homes. Several clients have simply dropped off, indicating that they will return for therapy when in-person sessions become available once again.

Second, as many writers before me have surmised, face-to-face video conferencing is a close approximation but most definitely not an exact replica of in-person contact. Video delays, screen blurriness, and computerized voices all confound our unconscious processing, making it hard for our brains to pick up on the subtle cues of the human experience. Mirror neurons seem to have a hard time functioning in such situations. I may miss a wince or mistake a blur in the screen for a tear. These oddities of virtual connections may short circuit my neural connections, making it hard for me to empathize. Even with the best internet connection, we miss body language and the felt sense of a person in the room, and our brains must work harder to perceive the same amount of data we might get when sitting with someone. My clinicians report greater fatigue, a decreased sense of fulfillment, and a lot more frustration with their work.

Ironically, I have found (and this is anecdotal, of course) that individuals with more avoidant attachment styles have fared better with telehealth. Clients have reported that whereas they may feel tremendously vulnerable and exposed during an in-person therapy session, they feel a bit more protected in a telehealth session, which actually enables them to open up more. I have yet to come across any research regarding attachment styles and telehealth outcomes, but I suspect it would be interesting.

Since the pandemic hit, I have personally completed three new intakes for clients seeking therapeutic services. I initially believed it would be hard to build rapport without actually sitting face-to-face with a client but have found it to be far less challenging than I had imagined. The thing that I have learned, however, is that because subtleties are harder to notice through video conferencing means, I have found our work remains in the realm of the presenting problems and have found it harder to dig into the meatier clinical material that I know lies just below the surface. The one exception, I will note, is with a new couple I started seeing a few weeks into the pandemic. Perhaps because they are in the same room, it seems easier to note their interpersonal dynamics, and I am able to pick up on subtleties better than with individual clients.

Despite this one small victory, more generally, it has proven very difficult to serve children and families through telehealth. Our practice was roughly 25% children and families prior to the shelter-in-place orders that led us to close our offices. During the pandemic, the percentage dropped significantly, with only one in five families choosing to continue services remotely. Much of our work with children is focused on play, art, sand-tray manipulation, and bibliotherapy, and many of these modalities are difficult, though not impossible, to recreate in a telehealth session. While telehealth platforms may create barriers to engagement with children, it also opens up new possibilities, such as allowing children to show their therapists exciting or interesting things in their homes. I have gotten to actually be in one of my client's safe spaces, which is a nook in her bedroom closet that she has arranged, with the help of her parent, based on our work together. I have also had the insight afforded by overhearing casual conversations in the household in which my child lives or seeing his home. In the past, our fields have debated whether or not it is ethical to research our clients on the internet; now we must decide what to do with the information inadvertently gleaned from our video conferences.

While this is incredibly true for children (whose therapy sessions may make the provider nauseous, given the sudden and continuous movements of the camera held by the little one), it also holds true for adult clients who may provide their therapist with information about themselves without realizing it. Colleagues have met their client's children when they barged into the room and piled on their mother. I have been "in bed" with clients who have been too depressed to emerge from their cocoons for our sessions. Sessions have become incredibly intimate, with the details no longer just found in the words spoken but also available in the backgrounds observed.

While clients seemingly have less privacy over what they reveal, so too does the therapist. Initially, I set up a makeshift home office in our small house in the guest room, with a blank wall behind me and my computer propped up on a couple of old research textbooks. I soon realized that the blank background was, as one client called it, "creepy," and hung some non-descript photographs. The therapist who I see for my own self-care sits in front of a bookshelf displaying photos of people I can only assume are her children. What's more, it can feel as if my clients are in my home, which, depending on the countertransference, can feel safe, neutral, or threatening and quite troublesome.

Privacy is not only compromised by the presence of the therapist in the home of the client and vice versa, but also for the client who may struggle to find a safe space to speak without being overheard. I have had clients sit in their cars for the entire therapy hour and others bundle up in blankets so that they can sit under a tree in their yard. Still others have driven to our office and sat in the parking lot so that they might not only have privacy but also the sense that they actually "went" to therapy. One of my providers set up an office in her camper to ensure her small children wouldn't interrupt her therapy sessions. Meanwhile, my colleague, who works largely with victims of domestic violence, has noticed a significant decline in new client calls because the victims are no longer able to separate from their abusers long enough to safely and securely access help.

Domestic violence victims are not the only group experiencing difficulties accessing services. Mental health professionals who routinely perform evaluations and assessments largely ceased providing such services at the onset of the pandemic. While distributors of testing materials scrambled to provide online access and virtual administration methods, most professionals agreed that the normative data, which is almost entirely based on in-person administration methods, does not support the use of telehealth and testing through virtual means, and the validity and reliability of the resultant findings may be called into question. That has meant that individuals seeking disability determinations and requiring an evaluation, courts waiting to make decisions on sentencing, those needing presurgical screens, and families hoping to finally understand if their child has autism or ADHD or anxiety have had to wait.

Obviously, the sharp pivot to telemental health gave providers and clients little time to prepare. Further, the heightened levels of anxiety and distress caused by the pandemic have likely tainted our experience of virtual therapy, serving as a confounding variable in this informal assessment of efficacy and comfort. All of that said, during this time of great uncertainty and cultural change, we have learned a great deal about what it means to provide services remotely. Nearly every professional reading this book, I suspect, will have tried telehealth for themselves. Despite the frustrations or resistance, we, as a profession, have shifted, rather seamlessly, to this virtual model. We have continued to provide services and have demonstrated the ability to reach those who cannot step into our offices. While we have perhaps swapped physical accessibility issues for technological accessibility issues, we have certainly demonstrated our ability to provide services to those who cannot step into our offices. We may not like it and it may prove challenging for those in rural reaches with poor connectivity, but we now, as a collective profession, have no lingering doubt that it is possible. It remains to be seen, however, what we as a society will carry forth from this time. Perhaps more urban providers will extend their service reach to rural communities and telehealth will continue to break down the traditional barriers of accessibility. And, based on what we learned during the global pandemic, we as a profession will face new obstacles to connectivity and access, including those I have referenced here and many, I suspect, we have yet to understand. I trust we will rise to the challenge, though, I must admit, I am very much looking forward to sitting with my clients, in person, again soon.

Introduction

> There are some significant differences in factors that affect rural people's mental health, as well as in the manner in which we can most effectively provide mental health services to them. It is not only psychologists working in rural areas who need to attend to the differences, since rural people are often referred to urban areas for secondary and tertiary health care. If you work in a large medical center or a specialized psychology service, you are likely to assess and treat people from outside your city.
>
> (Slama, 2004, pp. 9–13)

The mountains fill the horizon on the drive from Browning to Babb on the Blackfeet Indian Reservation in Northwest Montana. The snowy, jagged peaks of Glacier National Park are like a beacon in the distance, in direct contrast to the dreary isolation on the periphery. Stray dogs and free-range cattle occasionally command the driver's attention; their focus, suddenly pulled back to the present landscape: trailer home roofs layered with old tires (a strategy for combatting the ever-present wind that whips down from the mountains and clears the prairie all the way to Minnesota); the plastic bags stuck to deteriorating fence posts, thrashing against the breeze; slender horses grazing on grass struggling to grow in the infertile soil. I was 20 when I first drove this stretch of highway, simultaneously rattled by the despair and awed by the beauty.

The distance to Babb was profoundly far, both physically and metaphorically, for me. I grew up in a suburban area just beyond the limits of one of the largest cities in the country. I was living there when my father died, and my mother, struggling with her own despair, dutifully brought me to see a therapist (Joan) who aimed to help me with my grief. Ineffective and perhaps inexperienced with childhood grief, she somberly explained to my mother that there was little known about childhood grief and how to treat it. After a few sessions, we stopped going, the grief unresolved, my pain combined with shame and hopelessness. Some years later, at a conference in New York, just 30 miles from my childhood home, I met a therapist in her 60s who had been working with childhood grief for nearly 40 years. She and I had lunch, and she explained that my therapist was mistaken; they (the collective psychological helpers of the day) did know and understand childhood grief and had been implementing best practices for decades. Somehow, Joan was uninformed or ill equipped and my connection to her—a fluke of a referral made by a caring friend of my mother's—destined me to enduring pain that I would only come to resolve in my 20s. My heart sank with the overwhelming awareness that if I had had access to a different professional, if my mother had driven west toward Manhattan instead of east toward Joan's office, the course of my grief—my life—might have been different. Profoundly different. Though I grew up in a populated suburban region with access to a wealth of cultural experiences and opportunity, by chance, I simply did not get the very thing I needed. Years later, when I would move to an Indian reservation in Northwest Montana, the realities of this hit me hard: there were places in our country, even in an era of Google and Uber, where it wasn't simply about not finding the *right* therapist; it was about there being no therapist at all. Of course, this anecdote not only fueled my journey to become a competent and skilled therapist but is also at the heart of my passion to ensure equity in accessibility of mental health services, regardless of where someone lives, who they know, or what their health literacy status is.

Indeed, the town of Babb, Montana, my landing point after launching from the New York suburbs as a college student, has no mental health workers. Provider density is usually proportionate to population density, and so we simply see more providers living in suburban and urban areas. The proportions, however, are not equivalent, and those living in rural landscapes have even less access due to provider shortages. Utilization issues are not limited to numbers alone. Stigma, values, and other cultural factors influence the availability and acceptability of mental health treatment usage. Further, those providers who have elected to practice in a rural area face numerous threats to efficacy and sustainability, including inadequate training, burnout, and limited resources.

By the end of this book, you will know what is required of you to become an ethically sound provider of services to rural populations. Ethical service provision requires practitioners to develop and maintain cultural competence and understand and apply their ethical codes of conduct in such a way as to assure virtuous action and individualized care (Allen-Meares, 2007). Perhaps you are an individual provider living in, or aspiring to live in, a rural community; an urban-based provider exploring or expanding telemental health services to rural areas in your state; or a graduate student aiming to become culturally and ethically competent with this unique but heterogenous cultural group. As you may know, or will quickly come to learn, the need is tremendous, and our training often overlooks rural Americans as a culturally distinct group worthy of our attention, internships and fellowships rarely occur in rural communities (Association of Psychology Postdoctoral and Internship Centers, n.d.), and rural America is frequently neglected on the whole (Wuthnow, 2019).

Despite rural Americans making up nearly 20% of the nation's populace, they remain an under-studied, misunderstood, and underserved group (Smalley, Warren, & Rainer, 2012). Though struggling at rates similar to their urban counterparts, rural Americans receive services with significantly less frequency (Rural Health Quarterly, 2017), and rurality is often associated with poorer overall psychological outcomes (Reschovsky & Staiti, 2005).

Most professionals also do not receive training in cultural competence—the ability to understand, appreciate, and interact with people from cultures different from our own (DeAngelis, 2015)—as it pertains to rural Americans. As Slama (2004) beseeches us, it is our task—as psychologists, social workers, psychiatrists, mental health counselors, and researchers—to get to know rural America and, ultimately, to serve them well.

Of course, rural America—including, but not limited to, the idyllic rolling hills of Southern Appalachia, the cornfields of the Midwest, and the rugged desert of the Southwest—is a diverse place. It is homogeneous neither in its landscape nor in its peoples. It is beyond the purview of this book to provide you with all you need to know about each subset of the rural population to adequately ensure your cultural competence. Rather, I aim to have this book serve as a foundation for knowledge upon which each of you, based on your locale and your clientele, can build a culturally competent and ethical practice. Drawing on my own experience in the Rocky Mountain region, I hope to provide you with a sense of what culturally competent practice looks like in rural America and some recommendations for deepening your own.

With a heightened awareness of the cultural elements that make rural Americans unique, we will then move to a discussion of ethical challenges unique to, or amplified by, rural practice.

Finally, we will review the various barriers to the more equitable provision of rural services and solutions to the problem of rural access in the spirit of ensuring that this long-underserved group may finally begin to gain some traction.

In this book, I aim to educate those who might be working with rural Americans in the spirit of improving the mental wellness of a marginalized and at-risk group. Follow me as I wander down the country roads, belly up to bars in Podunk towns, and meet the locals on an Indian reservation. By the end, I suspect you will agree not only that rural Americans are an overlooked minority worthy of your attention, but also that it is your ethical responsibility to serve them.

References

Allen-Meares, P. (2007). Cultural competence: An ethical requirement. *Journal of Ethnic & Cultural Diversity in Social Work, 16*(3–4), 83–92. https://doi.org/10.1300/J051v16n03_06

Association of Psychology Postdoctoral and Internship Centers. (n.d.). *Membership directory*. Retrieved November 13, 2019, from https://membership.appic.org/directory

DeAngelis, T. (2015). In search of cultural competence. *Monitor on Psychology, 46*(3). Retrieved August 10, 2019, from www.apa.org/monitor/2015/03/cultural-competence

Reschovsky, J. D., & Staiti, A. B. (2005). Access and quality: Does rural America lag behind? *Health Affairs, 24*(4), 1128–1139. https://doi.org/10.1377/hlthaff.24.4.1128

Rural Health Quarterly. (2017). RHQ's 2017 rural health report card: Grading the state of rural health in America. *Rural Health Report, 1*(4), 11–111. Retrieved October 10,

2019, from http://ruralhealthquarterly.com/home/wp-content/uploads/2017/12/RHQ.1.4_U.S.-Rural-Health-Report-Card.pdf

Slama, K. (2004). Rural culture is a diversity issue [PDF file]. *Minnesota Psychologist*, 9–13. Retrieved July 1, 2019, from www.apa.org/practice/programs/rural/rural-culture.pdf

Smalley, K. B., Warren, J. C., & Rainer, J. P. (Eds.). (2012). *Rural mental health: Issues, policies, and best practices*. New York: Springer Publishing Company.

Wuthnow, R. (2019). *The left behind: Decline and rage in small-town America*. Princeton, NJ: Princeton University Press.

Section One
Rural America

1 What Is Rural?

Before we begin our efforts at achieving some degree of understanding of rural America, we must start by understanding where rural America is. I have no intention of this being an exhaustive analysis of every group that makes up the vast and heterogeneous rural America. Instead, readers will come away with a newfound appreciation for the distinct characteristics of rural Americans and, I hope, a hunger to learn more.

Rural America is not a uniform construct, and it is evolving. One hundred years ago, "rural" was synonymous with "farming." Individuals living outside the city were typically engaged in one of four jobs: mining, farming, ranching, or logging. Identities and landscape intertwined. Rural Americans were farmers, ranchers, loggers, and miners. Nowadays, the association between one's economic livelihood and one's geographic location is looser. Indeed, dentists can live near forests and lawyers in the pastoral countryside. As a result, rural Americans today are not necessarily wholly different from their urban counterparts. With the advent of the automobile, individuals were no longer limited to dwelling in cities centered around railcars as a means of transport. Similarly, half a century after the Industrial Revolution, the internet allowed individuals to maintain connection to their urban centers while living miles from them. The lines between rural and urban blurred, and their definitions grew fuzzy.

Strictly Defined

Rural America, surprisingly, is not easily demarcated, and many institutions tasked with managing resources for, tallying up, or providing representation to rural areas do not share a common definition. The Census Bureau relies on three categories in its classification of defining areas in which people live: urban, urban clusters, and rural. Urban areas are defined as those that are home to more than 50,000 people. Urban clusters are areas with populations greater than 2,500 and less than 50,000. And finally, "the U.S. Census Bureau defines rural as what is not urban—that is, after defining individual urban areas, rural is what is left" (Ratcliffe, Burd, Holder, & Fields, 2016). The Census Bureau's system designates 19.3% of the population (59.5 million people) and

8 *Rural America*

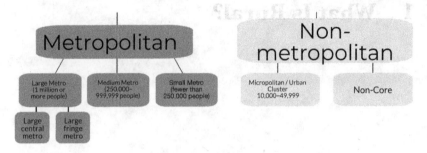

Figure 1.1 US Counties and County Equivalents

95% of the landmass of the United States as rural (Ratcliffe, Burd, Holder, & Fields, 2016).

Many of the agencies tasked with helping us draw such distinctions rely on a process of elimination rather than a practice of designation. That is, rural is often defined by what is not metropolitan (including suburban and urban): that which is a remnant. No wonder rural Americans feel overlooked. Indeed, when counted, tallied, or classified, they are of a leftover status. (See Figure 1.1.)

The Office of Management and Budget has a similar system of designation, though the terminology varies slightly. The OMB designates metropolitan and nonmetropolitan areas and then makes further delineations based on population. Using this designation system, 15% (46.2 million) Americans are considered rural, and 72% of the total landmass comprises rural America (Ingram & Franco, 2014).

Finally, the Federal Office on Rural Health Policy (Health Resources and Service Administration, n.d.), in an attempt to deal with some limitations of the aforementioned designations, assesses rurality based on something called the Rural-Urban Commuting Area (RUCA) codes. These codes aim to account for the distance one must travel to access services and the sparseness of populations. By their estimates, rural America consists of 57 million people (18% of the national population) and 84% of America's landmass.

Between 1983 and 2013, 447 counties were re-designated from nonmetropolitan to metropolitan, according to the Department of Agriculture's Economic Research Service, owing to urbanization. Urbanization is the phenomenon by which areas experience such significant increases in population that their status is officially changed by the federal government (Ratcliffe et al., 2016).

Rurality

The US Census Bureau, in an effort to make it easier to understand the rural landscape, further divides it up into designations based on the "level of rurality": completely rural, mostly rural, and mostly urban designations. The level of rurality is a figure based on percentages of populations, in any given county, living in a rural setting. "Mostly urban" counties are defined as counties in which less than 50% of the population lives in a rural setting. "Mostly rural" counties have between 50% and 99.9% of their population living in a rural setting. Finally, "completely rural" counties are those in which 100% of the population is in a rural area. There are 704 such counties in the United States, housing approximately 5.3 million Americans. All told, approximately 29.9 million Americans live in either mostly rural or completely rural regions (American Community Survey Office, 2016).

Glacier County, Montana, serves as a good example of how the level of rurality may mask some important elements pertinent to our discussion. Glacier County's eastern border is the Continental Divide, the nation's spine, which, in Glacier County, sits at a high point of approximately 10,000 feet and a low point closer to 5,000 feet. From the highest point on the Divide, just a few miles into the county itself, it seems as if I can see North Dakota, the prairie laid out before me. With just under 14,000 residents, Glacier County is also home to the Blackfeet Indian Reservation. Canada is just to the north, the county's landscape brutalized by fierce winds and harsh, cold, snowy winters. Residents of Glacier County have been plagued by ferocious weather events that left their homes barricaded by 14 feet of snow, transported by the fierce squalls of winter, for days, if not weeks, at a time. Cut Bank, the county seat, home to approximately 3,500 residents, and Browning, the Blackfeet government seat, with 1,300 residents, make up two of the larger incorporated towns in the county.

Driving from Browning toward the Divide, one sees craggy mountains looming on the horizon with names reminiscent of the original inhabitants of the region: Going to the Sun, Chief Mountain, Otokomi, and Napi. Dogs run alongside the car as it pulls out of the gas station, their ownership or residences unclear and uncertain. Dotting the road, if one is able to pull one's eyes off the brilliant landscape in the distance, are trailers and small shacks. There is a large casino, a sign of financial hope to many Native communities, although, because gambling is legal throughout Montana, the draw is not so great. The parking lot, only a quarter filled, speaks to the economic insecurity plaguing the region. A hospital in Browning provides behavioral health services as well as well-child exams, obstetrics, emergency care, and some other specialties. Recruitment of professionals is extraordinarily difficult. The 13,000 or so residents of Glacier County who live outside of the established communities of Browning or Cut Bank may be a one- or two-hour drive from those services and from the grocery store. There are roughly four people per square mile in Glacier County. There is no industry aside from tourism, which the harsh climate wipes out every October when the snow begins to fly. Despondency overshadows its beauty; unemployment and a lack of resources define its existence ("Glacier County, Montana," 2019). And yet, for reasons I cannot explain, Glacier County is labeled, per the 2010 census, as a "mostly urban" community. This designation might suggest a county peppered with services. Instead,

Glacier County is one of the most desolate, depressed areas I have seen, lacking profoundly in services. The designation, by some oddity of calculations, belies an underlying desolation and lack of resources more commonly found in rural areas. Consequently, it is important to take these statistics as suggestive but not wholly revealing of the landscape or its people. Indeed, "counties in the West generally had larger land areas than counties in other regions, increasing the likelihood that even metro county residents may be far from an urban center" (Meit et al., 2014, p. 1).

Accordingly, many government and nongovernment agencies struggle to define what is "rural" and, consequently, who lives in a rural area. What's more, counties tend to be used as a unit of measurement, and counties are neither uniform nor appropriate for comparison. Glacier County is just over 3,000 square miles. Its neighbor, Pondera County, is a mere 1,640 square miles with 5,960 residents. It is designated "mostly rural." Realizing this, at times, the US census defines rurality based on the degree to which openness dominates the landscape and there are only settlements with fewer than 2,500 people. Through such a lens, Glacier County is undoubtedly rural ("Pondera County, Montana," 2019).

The Frontier

Another designation, per the National Rural Health Association Policy Brief, is that of "frontier and remote areas." Frontier America "consists of sparsely populated areas that are geographically isolated from population centers and services" (United States Department of Agriculture [USDA], 2019). In this context, the term "frontier and remote" is used "to describe territory characterized by some combination of low population size and high geographic remoteness" (USDA, 2019). Glacier County, with its seasonally limited accessibility, unpaved roads, and travel-inhibiting weather, might be more accurately described as a frontier area than a mostly urban community (Wilger, 2016). Colorado, Idaho, Montana, Nevada, Alaska, North Dakota, South Dakota, New Mexico, Utah, and Wyoming are designated as frontier states. To understand this designation, it might be useful to think about population density. The average population density in the United States is 72.9 people per square mile. That means, if you were to walk for 20 minutes in a random spot in the country, you'd be likely to pass by the residences of about 73 people. However, in New Mexico, that number would be closer to 35 and, in Alaska, just one (Wilger, 2016).

Because frontier status relates more to distances traveled to urban centers, counties in the rural West tend to qualify more easily because of the nature of travel times in a more expansive landscape. The frontier area designation contains four further classifications based on a metric incorporating travel time and the next nearest community's size (Rural Health Information Hub, n.d.). Babb, Montana, located in Glacier County, receives the highest level (four) designation as a frontier and remote area (FAR).

Frontier states continue to experience population growth at a rate slightly higher than non-frontier states. As we will see later, though, the percentage increase of professionals and highly educated individuals lags behind.

The Economic Research Service has designated both rural-urban commuting areas and frontier and remote area codes as practical ways to apply such designations. The former bases the classification on population density, urbanization, and daily commutes and has a ten-point system that delineates between metropolitan, micropolitan, small-town, and rural commuting areas (USDA, 2019).

Prior to World War II, cities were distinct entities with clear boundaries. What lay outside the city limits was rural. Prior to the proliferation of the personal automobile and Henry Levitt's vision for suburban living (Hales, 2001), cities were tightly packed areas centered around rail lines and often surrounded by waterways and industrial buildings. After World War II and the invention of what is now called suburbia, wealthy idealists moved even further beyond the limits of the suburban into what was previously open space, farmlands, or forests. Distinct boundaries eroded, and the urbanization of the rural landscape began. These blurry lines are what, to this day, make it difficult to define and talk about rural America. If you were to imagine a city, you would likely see some version of vertical dwellings, public transportation, and concrete. If, on the other hand, you were to imagine a "rural landscape," your images might vary dramatically. Some would see silos and wheat fields; others would see forests and hills and still others county roads lined with small shack-like dwellings and churches.

In summary, it is not easy to define *what* is rural simply on the basis of geographical location or population density. I do not wish to try and master a task that government offices have failed at for decades. I will instead offer up the following definition of rural America: rural America is not a uniform construct. It is not just the plains or the mountains, the forest or the prairie; it is not simply farmland, nor is it exclusively pastoral. It is, instead, a collection of cultural pockets that all have this in common: an above-average physical and metaphorical distance to the urban center.

References

American Community Survey Office. (2016, October 27). *2015 data profiles*. Retrieved October 10, 2019, from www.census.gov/acs/www/data/data-tables-and-tools/data-profiles/2015/

Glacier County, Montana. (n.d.). Retrieved November 30, 2019, from https://en.wikipedia.org/wiki/Glacier_County,_Montana

Hales, P. B. (2001). *Levittown: Documents of an ideal American suburb* [PDF file]. Retrieved October 1, 2019, from http://websupport1.citytech.cuny.edu/Faculty/pcatapano/US2/US%20Documents/Levittown%20Documents%20of%20an%20Ideal%20American%20Suburb.pdf

Health Resources and Service Administration. (n.d.). *Defining rural population*. Retrieved October 10, 2019, from www.hrsa.gov/rural-health/about-us/definition/index.html

Ingram, D. D., & Franco, S. J. (2014). 2013 NCHS urban–rural classification scheme for counties. *Vital and Health Statistics, 2*(166), 1–73.

Meit, M., Knudson, A., Gilbert, T., Yu, A. T. C., Tanenbaum, E., Ormson, E., & Popat, S. (2014). *The 2014 update of the rural-urban chartbook*. Bethesda, MD: Rural Health Reform Policy Research Center.

Pondera County, Montana. (n.d.). Retrieved December 1, 2019, from https://en.wikipedia.org/wiki/Pondera_County,_Montana

Ratcliffe, M., Burd, C., Holder, K., & Fields, A. (2016). American community survey and geography brief. *Defining Rural at the US Census Bureau*, 1–8.

Rural Health Information Hub. Health and healthcare in frontier areas. (n.d.). Retrieved August 10, 2019, from www.ruralhealthinfo.org/topics/frontier

United States Department of Agriculture. (2019, August 20). *Frontier and remote area codes*. Retrieved September 9, 2019, from www.ers.usda.gov/data-products/frontier-and-remote-area-codes/

Wilger, S. (2016, February). *National rural health association policy brief: Definition of frontier* [PDF file]. Retrieved September 9, 2019, from www.ruralhealthweb.org/getattachment/Advocate/Policy-Documents/NRHAFrontierDefPolicyPaperFeb2016.pdf.aspx

2 Cultural Competence and Rural America

Culture and Competence

Matsumoto and Juang have defined culture as "a unique meaning and information system, shared by a group and transmitted across generations, that allows the group to meet basic needs of survival, pursue happiness and well-being, and derive meaning from life" (Matsumoto & Juang, 2009, p. 12). Culture is the water in which a particular group swims, the water influencing values, behaviors, and communication.

Cultural competence entails understanding, appreciating, and adeptly interacting with people different from you (DeAngelis, 2015). At a bare minimum, this requires a degree of knowledge about the various cultural groups one serves, as well as an attitude of respect and appreciation for both the similarities and differences between the provider's group and the client's, and the skills to provide such services in a manner consistent with the cultural norms and needs ("Cultural Competence Education for Students in Medicine and Public Health: Report of an Expert Panel," 2012). Additionally, providers must be able to identify cultural elements of provider and client, be sensitive to nuance and differences (within and between cultures), maintain empathy for how one's culture is relevant to the individual and in the professional relationship, and should be adept at understanding how one's interventions may or may not be culturally appropriate (Tseng & Streltzer, 2004). Cultural competence, then, is not a singular set of skills but an adaptable way of being that adjusts based on the needs of those served (Sue, 1998, p. 440).

Cultural competence has been steadily gaining traction among nearly all helping professions. The American Psychological Association (APA) (2003), the National Association of Social Workers (NASW) (2015), and the American Counseling Association (ACA) (Yee, 2019) have all emphasized culturally competent practices as an ethical imperative. Cultural competence is a requirement for graduate training programs to be accredited with the American Psychological Association (2011), and many internships, post-doctoral fellowships, and state licensing boards require it as well.

The *Diagnostic and Statistical Manual of Mental Disorders, Fifth Edition* (DSM-V) is the primary diagnostic tool, published by the American Psychiatric Association

(APA, 2013), utilized by mental health professionals. In its revised form, the authors included a section on cultural formulation. This formulation requires the clinician to consider five elements of functioning and identity to better understand the culture of the client and the implications in regard to mental illness. The five elements are (1) the cultural identity of the individual, (2) cultural conceptualization of clinical distress, (3) culturally related psychosocial factors, (4) cultural elements in the therapeutic relationship, and (5) cultural implications of diagnosis and care (Substance Abuse and Mental Health Services Administration [SAMHSA], 2014).

In 2018, NASW changed the wording of Standard 1.05 from "Cultural Competence and Social Diversity" to "Cultural Awareness and Social Diversity," highlighting the knowledge that it is impossible for any social worker to be competent working with any and all populations. Because competence requires knowledge and such knowledge might be impossible to acquire on any and all cultural groups, NASW shifted toward language that was far more attainable. Cultural awareness requires self-awareness coupled with an awareness of the cultural characteristics of those they serve. Cultural awareness requires both a foundational level of awareness and the ability and effectiveness to practice with such awareness clinically (Barsky, 2018).

Call it what you will: the clinician's knowledge of their client's culture, as well as the intersection and salient features of their own, will be integral to providing ethically sound and effective treatment. Indeed, cultural competence has been demonstrated, repeatedly, to be linked to better outcomes (Tao, Owen, Pace, & Imel, 2015, p. 337).

Current thought reflects a migration from competence toward awareness based on the supposition that it is impossible for any individual clinician to have, or any educational training program to provide, an exhaustive understanding of any and all cultures potentially encountered during the tenure of the clinician.

As a way of not overwhelming students with this particular aspect of their education, many training programs utilize Sue's multidimensional model of developing cultural competence. This model uses a three-dimensional approach, including components of cultural competence (awareness of attitudes/beliefs, knowledge, skills), foci of cultural competence (societal, organizational, professional, individual), and race- and culture-specific attributes of cultural competence (European American, Native American, Latino American, Asian American, African American) (Sue, 2001).

Rurality as a Cultural Dimension

Though rural Americans are often identified as an underserved community, it is rare that rural Americans are considered a distinct cultural group (Thomas, Lowe, Fulkerson, & Smith, 2011). As Smalley, Warren, and Rainer (2012, p. 38) explain, "Despite the abundant evidence pointing to the importance of considering and incorporating cultural themes into mental health treatment, the recognition of rurality as a bona fide multicultural issue has not been embraced by the mental health field." The APA (2003 and most statements of diversity, equity, and inclusion frequently exclude them. The Rural Health Information Hub (n.d.), sponsored by the Federal Office of Rural Health Policy, even fails to define rural Americans as a culturally distinct group worthy of the application of culturally competent practices. The Substance Abuse and Mental Health Services Administration's (SAMHSA) treatment improvement protocol, Improving Cultural Competence, does include a discussion of the implications of geography on one's culture as well as one's proclivity toward substance abuse (SAMHSA, 2014).

As the policy writers at SAMHSA argue, rural Americans certainly have a unique and distinct cultural experience worthy of our attention and understanding. Some years ago, I was walking through the three-block downtown district of our small town with a friend who grew up in a small town in Missouri. I, a New Yorker by birth, made to cross the road against the light once I had established no cars were coming. She was horrified. We chatted about my impulse and her fear in relation to our respective upbringings. In New York, it is customary to cross streets whenever (and perhaps wherever) one sees fit with a sort of odd aggressive respect existing between pedestrian and drivers. In rural Montana, where law and custom require drivers to stop whenever a pedestrian so much as thinks about crossing the road, the norms are different. Given respect freely by most drivers in crosswalks, pedestrians responsibly obey the traffic lights accordingly. Though a rather trivial example, perhaps how one crosses the road says a lot about the culture in which one has been embedded. There is no doubt that her small-town upbringing and my urban past strongly and persistently influence aspects of our behaviors today.

Still, rural Americans, comprising 20% of the general population, outnumber nearly every other ethnic or cultural group typically recognized in diversity, equity, and inclusion policy.

Along with Smalley et al. (2012), Stewart (2018), Slama (2004, pp. 6–13), SAMSHA (2014), and others who have come before me, I argue that rurality should be seen as a distinct cultural factor and that rural Americans should be understood and appreciated as a unique, but ultimately heterogenous, cultural group by those tasked with serving their mental health needs. To this end, I aim to help you on your path toward cultural competence (which most likely would require additional specific work and research on your part) and cultural humility, which tasks the clinician with showing up as an unassuming learner, eager to better understand the cultures of those whom they serve (Barsky, 2018).

Rurality in Policy, Education, and Training

> If the manpower shortage in rural areas is to be successfully addressed, training in graduate school and beyond must be tailored to fit the needs of rural practitioners.
>
> Jameson and Blank (2007, p. 288)

Historically, our professions failed to view rurality as a diversity issue; our research, policy, education, and training have also been rather urban centric (Dyck, Cornock, Gibson, & Carlson, 2008; Imig, 2014). Research, education, and training mainly take place in urban centers, and, accordingly, the field of psychology has been "largely focused on preparing psychologists for working with urban clients in urban centers, thereby inadvertently reinforcing this as the preferred location of practice" (Dyck et al., 2008, p. 239). We need our organizations to support the work we are doing, and rural providers, in particular, need the backing of their professional associations in their movements toward more culturally competent work.

The National Association of Social Workers, in its policy on rural social work practice (2009), stated: "The understanding of rural people and cultures is a pressing issue of cultural competence in professional social work. Rural people, with their diverse cultural backgrounds, occupy and influence the majority of earth's landmass." The NASW (2009) also suggested that "when rural people relocate, by necessity or choice, to take advantage of urban and suburban economic opportunity, their unique cultural values, norms, and conventions go with them." Indeed, "Special skills are needed to work effectively with displaced rural people" (2009).

The American Psychological Association, to its great credit, has formed the Committee on Rural Health, whose mission is "to ensure that the behavioral healthcare needs of rural and frontier America are met" (2001) by addressing a variety of innovative advocacy and accessibility matters. This group has focused on the proliferation of rural health services, research on behavioral health at the community level in rural communities, encouraging collaborative/interdisciplinary models of care, technological advances, prescriptive authority, and professionalism with rural peoples (APA, n.d.).

The American Psychiatric Association includes rural communities on its list of underserved communities and names "Appalachian people" (though no other rural groups) as a "diverse population." Therein, the APA focuses on the disproportionately negative living experiences and social determinants of health, best practices, and telehealth services (n.d.).

The American Counseling Association does not appear to have a definitive statement on rural populations, particularly as a unique cultural group, though it provides a number of articles and continuing education on the topic (American Counseling Association, n.d.).

In short, the regulatory and organizational groups tasked with guiding the mental healthcare needs of America have varying degrees of buy-in to the concept of rural Americans being worthy of designation, study, and competence as a cultural group.

Understandably, then, the corresponding education and training programs are not uniform in their focus on rural populations and the ways in which they prepare students to provide services for rural Americans. According to the NASW (2009), "Most social workers receive little content on rural social work in their professional training."

Research has demonstrated that urban training models are insufficient in their applicability to rural practice. To train rural providers, training cannot merely be the application of an urban model to a rural practice (Dyck et al., 2008). Rural practice is just different. Rural professionals tend to work more hours, spend more time on nonclinical matters, and practice with a broader breadth of scope. Individual practitioners may find themselves providing consultation, community education, health promotion/illness prevention, and program development, tasks not commonly associated with clinical psychology (Dyck et al., 2008).

In my graduate training program, we spent very little time (if any, really) on the nuances of rural practice. When I relocated to Montana to practice clinical psychology, I felt ill equipped, particularly in terms of ethics. It was only later—much later, if I'm honest—that I realized that I had overlooked my cultural competence requirements. I had not even realized that the populace with which I practiced *was* a cultural group. I had looked around and seen a sea of White people (89% of Montanans are Caucasian) and made some assumptions about our similarities and their ethnic and cultural identities. I was armed with an abysmal understanding of rurality and rural values. It wasn't merely that my graduate training had not helped me learn the nuances of rural life and practice, but also that at no point in my training had anyone mentioned that rural *was* a culture.

Further, while many training programs in psychology, psychiatry, and social work aim to create practitioners with expertise in specialization areas, rural practice is decidedly more generalist in nature. This past year, our group practice brought on a psychiatric nurse practitioner. Having trained at the renowned Mayo Clinic, she came to us with rich clinical and practical knowledge about the psychiatric needs of adults. She had received little to no training in children and adolescents because, as she explained, "most nurses pick a population and then focus on that population throughout their training [so] as to develop an expertise." Indeed, in urban environs, it is more than likely that a practitioner may have a specialty or preferred population. In a rural community, however, the demands and size of the community often prohibit the possibility of such a focus. Just the opposite is true: rural practice often favors a generalist model (Daley & Avant, 1999).

For those who know they want to live in and serve rural populations, opportunities for applicable advanced degrees are limited. Fewer than 1% of universities awarding doctoral degrees are located in rural areas (Domino et al., 2018). Later, when we explore the particulars of what defines a rural area, it will become clear that the very nature of having a university is often enough to make an area no longer rural. That is, sheer numbers are often used to define rurality, and if there are enough numbers for a university large enough to have a doctoral program, it is likely there are enough numbers to make that town not rural.

Georgia Southern University (which graduated its first cohort in 2012) places particular emphasis on training culturally competent rural psychologists

(2018). There, in addition to having a rural practicum requirement, students take a course called Rural Mental Health in their first year. Similarly, starting in 2015, Eastern Kentucky University launched a PsyD program specifically designed to prepare practitioners for practice in rural communities. EKU's curriculum includes mental health administration; substance use; suicide; working with disabled, veteran, and underserved populations; and school-based programming, all elements key to a well-rounded training program that equips practitioners with the broad base of knowledge necessary to successfully help rural individuals and communities (Eastern Kentucky University, 2014). PsyD students at Marshall University (n.d.) will take six credit hours in Rural Community Psychology, in addition to two semesters of rural practicum, prior to degree completion. Both EKU's and MU's curricula, with their focus on community interventions rather than the individual emphasis in many doctoral training programs, support the notion that rural psychology is fundamentally different. Likewise, the University of Hawaii, embedded in a very rural state with profound access issues such as distances between islands, not merely towns, has developed a psychiatric training program designed around telehealth interventions. Ola Lāhui is an integrated behavioral health clinic in Honolulu, Hawaii. There, they train pre- and post-doctoral psychology interns in culturally competent, telehealth-dependent psychological diagnosis, treatment, and intervention (I Ola Lāhui, n.d.).

While there are an increasing number of training programs specifically designed for individuals seeking graduate education and training for and with rural populations, there seems to be a lack of integration of rural culture into mainstream doctoral training (Barbopoulos & Clark, 2003; Jameson & Blank, 2007). There are simply not enough rural providers to meet the mental health needs of the rural population. Presumably, then, individuals are either not getting services or are traveling large distances to seek the help they need from urban providers. So it is necessary not only to create pathways for individuals who want to work with rural groups to get the education they need but also to train individuals who aim to practice in urban environs about this historically underserved group. I believe it is the ethical responsibility of all accredited training programs to offer at least minimal competence training for work with this large minority group.

Doctoral training does not end with coursework. As with all clinical practice, direct care hours are required for graduation and licensure. It is perhaps in these arenas where we see profound discrepancies between rural and urban opportunities. In 2019, out of the 771 psychology internship training sites listed in the APPIC directory, 51 were identified as rural. For post-doctoral fellowships, the numbers drop precipitously, with only six of the 219 APPIC post-doctoral sites offering a rural program or rotation (n.d.). Of course, where there is a dearth of providers, there are likely not adequate training opportunities: who would do the training? Later, we will examine how practitioners in rural communities often work more hours with less institutional support and how this all makes the creation of a viable internship or post-doctoral fellowship program impossible (Dyck et al., 2008). Thus, the cycle continues.

What does culturally competent psychotherapy with rural peoples look like? Culturally competent therapy requires us to (1) understand the social and historical context, (2) understand the cross-cultural zone (if one exists) (Lee, 2008), (3) increase our awareness about our own beliefs, biases, assumptions, and stereotypes in an ongoing manner (SAMHSA, 2016), and (4) understand how cultural differences impact one's experience and the client-therapist working alliance.

Growing up just outside New York City, I rode the subway alone as a teenager and saw the ballet, the opera, and countless Broadway shows. I could find my way, eyes closed, through the Metropolitan Museum of Art. I do not wish to live in New York City, but I certainly could. I moved to Montana as a college student, looking for adventure and summer work. I found the mountains of Glacier National Park and was transformed. I lived on the Blackfeet Indian Reservation and worked as a dishwasher, occasionally volunteering at the local Head Start early childhood education center. I have spent nearly two decades in Montana, and this has transformed me, but I would be remiss if I were to think my urban frame of reference had vanished. I grew up believing in the city and all its magic. As a child, I attended a summer camp in the Catskill Mountains—a place one goes for respite and recharge, not real life. I am certain there is some very old part of me that believes some stereotypes about rural people. Some of those stereotypes may be idealized versions of some fantasy life in a small town in the rural West. And, if I am honest, others may be harsher and more critical—unconscious biases about college attendance, the importance of "cultural experiences," and a sense of impoverishment for those living without.

As a clinician striving to provide culturally competent psychotherapy, I must remain vigilant about my lens of urban centrism and my old beliefs about the countryside. I must understand how my status as a well-educated, liberal coastal elite may play out in the consultation room. I should have some sense of how being Jewish is an anomalous identity in my small community and how those differences may produce judgment, on my part or theirs. Might I overlook a cultural demand (for, say, a loosening of boundaries in the spirit of gaining trust) arising from unspoken norms? Might I stand too close or speak too quickly, causing clients to react instinctively and subtly to my behavioral differences? Do I have some idea about what mental wellness looks like that is incongruous with the ideals of my new community?

When I meet clients, I strive to simultaneously see them as individuals embedded in a larger culture—one that is becoming, but is not historically, my own. I work to understand their level of acculturation and their identification with particular subgroups (churches, niches, professional groups, etc.). I do all this knowing that I am still learning about my community, its people, and its history. I work not to assume, though stereotypes often are our brain's shortcut to, and replacement for, deep understanding.

It is also essential that I understand the historical context of my community. I have educated myself, through coursework, readings, and discussions, on the plight of the American Indians of the area while also gaining an understanding of their tribal systems and Indian Health Service's hospitals and clinics. I have had to learn (embarrassingly) the difference between ranching and farming and between logging and forestry. I have also worked tirelessly to understand our community's particular characteristics and its needs, fighting urges at every turn to come in as an outside expert, here to save the day.

Again, it would be impossible to ensure that every reader learned here the nuances of their communities. Indeed, for me to come in as an expert in communities I have never lived would be quite the opposite of culturally competent. But I hope that this serves as a starting point for individuals practicing in rural communities or with rural people on their path toward their own cultural competence.

Given that rural Americans do make up a large, underserved, heterogenous cultural group, I will aim to provide you with a foundational understanding of this group, with offers at direction for future research. By the end, you will have at least a preliminary understanding (far better than the newly graduated version of myself) of what it means to work with rural Americans, what they need, and how you might go about it.

References

American Counseling Association. (n.d.). *Search*. Retrieved December 18, 2019, from www.counseling.org/search/#/rural/page=1

American Psychiatric Association. (2013). *Diagnostic and statistical manual of mental disorders* (5th ed.). Washington, DC: American Psychiatric Association.

American Psychiatric Association. (n.d.). *Diversity & health equity education: Appalachian people*. Retrieved December 18, 2019, from www.psychiatry.org/psychiatrists/cultural-competency/education/appalachian-patients

American Psychological Association. (2001). *Caring for the rural community: 2000–2001 report*. Washington, DC: American Psychological Association.

American Psychological Association. (2003). *Ethical principles of psychologists and code of conduct*. Retrieved January 12, 2019, from www.apa.org/ethics/code/

American Psychological Association. (2011). *Benchmarks evaluation system*. Retrieved September 10, 2019, from www.apa.org/ed/graduate/benchmarks-evaluation-system

American Psychological Association. (n.d.). *Committee on rural health vision and mission*. Retrieved December 18, 2019, from www.apa.org/practice/programs/rural/committee/mission

Association of Psychology Postdoctoral and Internship Centers. (n.d.). *Association of Psychology Postdoctoral and Internship Centers*. Retrieved December 18, 2019, from www.appic.org/

Barbopoulos, A., & Clark, J. M. (2003). Practising psychology in rural settings: Issues and guidelines. *Canadian Psychology/Psychologie Canadienne, 44*(4), 410–424. https://doi.org/10.1037/h0086962

Barsky, A. (2018). Ethics alive! Cultural competence, awareness, sensitivity, humility, and responsiveness: What's the difference? *The New Social Worker*. Retrieved October 10, 2019, from www.socialworker.com/feature-articles/ethics-articles/ethics-alive-cultural-competence-awareness-sensitivity-humility-responsiveness/

Daley, M. R., & Avant, F. (1999). Attracting and retaining professionals for social work practice in rural areas: An example from East Texas. In I. B. Carlton-LaNey, R. L.

Edwards, & P. N. Reid (Eds.), *Preserving and strengthening small towns and rural communities* (pp. 335–345). Washington, DC: NASW Press.

DeAngelis, T. (2015). In search of cultural competence. *Monitor on Psychology, 46*(3). Retrieved August 10, 2019, from www.apa.org/monitor/2015/03/cultural-competence

Domino, M. E., Lin, C. C., Morrissey, J. P., Ellis, A. R., Fraher, E., Richman, E. L., . . . Prinstein, M. J. (2018). Training psychologists for rural practice: Exploring opportunities and constraints. *The Journal of Rural Health, 35*–41. https://doi.org/10.1111/jrh.12299

Dyck, K. G., Cornock, B. L., Gibson, G., & Carlson, A. A. (2008). Training clinical psychologists for rural and northern practice: Transforming challenge into opportunity. *Australian Psychologist, 43*(4), 239–248. https://doi.org/10.1080/00050060802438096

Eastern Kentucky University. (2014, October 1). *Doctoral program in clinical psychology addresses rural health care needs.* Retrieved November 11, 2019, from https://psychology.eku.edu/insidelook/doctoral-program-clinical-psychology-addresses-rural-health-care-needs

Expert Panel on Cultural Competence Education for Students in Medicine and Public Health (2012). *Cultural competence education for students in medicine and public health: Report of an expert panel.* Washington, DC: Association of American Medical Colleges and Association of Schools of Public Health.

Georgia Southern University. (2018). *Psy.D. program.* Retrieved December 18, 2019, from https://cbss.georgiasouthern.edu/psychology/psyd/

Imig, A. (2014). Small but mighty: Perspectives of rural mental health counselors. *The Professional Counselor, 4*(4), 404–412. https://doi.org/10.15241/aii.4.4.404\

I Ola Lāhui. (n.d.). *About us.* Retrieved December 18, 2019, from http://iolalahui.org/?page_id=668

Jameson, J., & Blank, M. (2007). The role of clinical psychology in rural mental health services: Defining problems and developing solution. *Clinical Psychology: Science and Practice, 14*, 283–298.

Lee, C. C. (2008). *Elements of culturally competent counseling* (ACAPCD-24). Alexandria, VA: American Counseling Association.

Marshall University. (n.d.). *Graduate courses.* Retrieved December 18, 2019, from www.marshall.edu/psych/graduate-courses/

Matsumoto, D., & Juang, L. (2009). *Culture and psychology* (4th ed.). Belmont, CA: Thomson Wadsworth.

National Association of Social Workers. (2009). Rural social work. In *Social work speaks: National Association of Social Workers policy statements, 2009–2012.* Retrieved November 10, 2019, from www.socialworkers.org/assets/secured/documents/da/da2010/referred/Rural%20Social%20work.pdf

National Association of Social Workers. (2015). *Standards and indicators for cultural competence in social work practice.* Retrieved November 10, 2019, from www.socialworkers.org/LinkClick.aspx?fileticket=PonPTDEBrn4=&portalid=0

Slama, K. M. (2004). Toward rural cultural competence. *Minnesota Psychologist, 53*(2), 6–13.

Smalley, K. B., Warren, J. C., & Rainer, J. P. (Eds.). (2012). *Rural mental health: issues, policies, and best practices.* New York: Springer Publishing Company.

Stewart, E. G. (2018). *Mental health in rural America: A field guide.* New York: Routledge.

Substance Abuse and Mental Health Services Administration. (2014). *Improving cultural competence.* (Treatment improvement protocol series, no. 59.) Appendix E, cultural formulation in diagnosis and cultural concepts of distress. Rockville, MD: U.S. Department of Health and Human Services, Substance Abuse and Mental Health Services

Administration, Center for Substance Abuse Treatment. Retrieved October 10, 2019, from www.ncbi.nlm.nih.gov/books/NBK248426/

Substance Abuse and Mental Health Services Administration. (2016). *Quick guide for clinicians: Based on tip 59: Improving cultural competence*. Rockville, MD: U.S. Department of Health and Human Services, Substance Abuse and Mental Health Services Administration, Center for Substance Abuse Treatment. Retrieved October 10, 2019, from https://store.samhsa.gov/system/files/sma16-4931.pdf

Sue, D. W. (2001). Multidimensional facets of cultural competence. *The Counseling Psychologist, 29*(6), 790–821. https://doi.org/10.1177/0011000001296002

Sue, S. (1998). In search of cultural competence in psychotherapy and counseling. *American Psychologist, 53*(4), 440–448. https://doi.org/10.1037/0003-066x.53.4.440

Tao, K. W., Owen, J., Pace, B. T., & Imel, Z. E. (2015). A meta-analysis of multicultural competencies and psychotherapy process and outcome. *Journal of Counseling Psychology, 62*(3), 337. https://doi.org/10.1037/cou0000086

Thomas, A. R., Lowe, B. M., Fulkerson, G. M., & Smith, P. S. (2011). *Critical rural theory: Structure, space, culture*. Lanham, MD: Lexington Books.

Tseng, W., & Streltzer, J. (Eds.) (2004). *Cultural competence in clinical psychiatry*. Washington, DC: American Psychiatric Press.

Yee, E. (2019, January 3). Retrieved October 23, 2019, from www.counseling.org/news/aca-blogs/aca-member-blogs/aca-member-blogs/2019/01/03/why-cultural-competence-matters

3 Rural Americans

Figure 3.1 Rural Lands in America

At the time of the American Revolution, 90% of US residents resided and worked in rural areas. By 1920, more than half the population was living in metropolitan/urbanized areas (with more than 2,500 people). As of 2016, "Rural areas cover 97 percent of the nation's land area but contain 19.3 percent of the population (about 60 million people)," Census Bureau Director John H. Thompson (2016) said. Approximately 60 million United States residents live in areas designated rural by the US Census Bureau. Like other marginalized groups, rural Americans are not a homogeneous bunch. Statistics are often available for rural America as a whole. And while we've already agreed this is not a homogenous group, and statistics may be limited because of their nomothetic nature, they do serve as a good starting point for conceptualizing this highly diverse group of Americans.

Of late, rural America has been termed "flyover country." The name arises from the experience that many urban and coastal Americans have of seeing the inland and rural states from 30,000 feet out the window of an airplane. Drawing on this metaphor, we will take, first, an aerial view of rural America before touching down in various parts of the country to examine characteristics and struggles specific to particular regions and groups. As you now know, rural Americans are not a homogenous group. In fact, rural Americans are likely more hetero- than homogeneous. As with nearly all cultural groups, even within a particular subset (e.g., region), there are likely to be significant within-group differences. However, I do believe it is important to give you, the reader, some basic understanding of the cultural elements common to particular rural groups so that you have a foundational understanding on which you can build your idiographic knowledge.

Population

> In nearly half of today's nonmetropolitan (rural) counties, more people have moved out than in during every decade since 1950.
> (Cromartie, Von Reichert, & Arthun, 2015)

Rural Americans are older, on the whole, than your average American. The median age for those living in rural areas is 43, compared to 36 years for urban areas. There are a few noteworthy hypotheses to explain this phenomenon. First, Americans on the whole are aging. The baby boomers are outnumbering younger adults, and our nation's birth rate has decreased. While this explains why the median age has risen on the whole, it does not fully account for the discrepancy between rural and urban ages. Rural Americans have historically remained where they were raised. In recent years, younger rural Americans have relocated to urban environs, leaving behind their aging relatives, thus contributing to a higher average age in rural America (Wagenfeld, 2003). Older adults in rural communities have likely spent their entire lives there. In their lifetimes, however, they have witnessed a dramatic increase in urbanization and urban migration. Known colloquially as the "brain drain," young rural Americans tend to migrate to cities for educational and employment opportunities, never to return. Qualitative research suggests that individuals who have left rural areas fail to return for one of three reasons: low wages, career limitations, and a preference for urban life (Wuthnow, 2018). Another reason for a decline of rural population numbers is an increased mortality rate amongst working-age rural Americans. Many researchers cite the increase in opioid- and other drug-related deaths as cause of this statistic (Pope, Loeffler, & Ferrell, 2014).

Additionally, available jobs (or lack thereof) have forced some rural residents to make the move to more suburban or urban residences. Manufacturing and farming, two of the hardest hit industries during the Great Recession, once provided jobs for many rural Americans.

As I mentioned previously, one factor impacting population growth/shrinking in rural communities is how once a rural county exceeds a particular number of members, it becomes metropolitan, and its members are no longer considered amongst the ranks of rural Americans. This fluidity makes it hard to truly measure change and growth in rural communities.

Two rural areas that are seeing steady population growth are the frontier states and the recreation counties. Overlapping in many qualities, these two rural types of land attract retirees and other young professionals with discretionary income who seek a "better life" amongst the trees and open spaces. These counties also have the highest median household incomes amongst all rural communities.

Education

Education is essential to economic vitality. In nationwide studies, increased poverty is linked to lower rates of educational attainment. Similarly, employment rates increase when the workforce is better educated (Bonnie, Stroud, & Breiner, 2015).

Based on the American Community Survey, more urban Americans receive high school, bachelor's, and advanced degrees than rural Americans (Marré, 2014). One confounding variable for these data points is the fact that many educated individuals tend to relocate to urban areas either for their schooling or for employment following their degree. This trend may skew the data to make it seem as if folks born in rural areas are less likely to achieve high rates of educational advancement. Rather, the data simply paints a picture that folks living in rural areas are less educated than their urban peers.

Nationwide, median income rates increase with levels of educational attainment. Data suggest that workforce participation and earning potential are also significantly lower in rural America. At every educational level, graduates earn more in urban areas. Unsurprisingly, counties with the lowest rates of educational attainment maintain higher levels of childhood poverty, poverty, unemployment, and population atrophy. In rural counties with relatively low rates of educational attainment, even compared to other rural areas, unemployment rates were one percentage point higher between 2011 and 2015. As with many indicators in our nation, the gap is widening between rural and urban groups in terms of education and unemployment, with increased rurality leading to decreased academic and employment success.

Economic Indicators

Beyond differences better attributed to educational factors, rural Americans experience a different financial landscape than their urban counterparts. The median income in rural America is approximately $2,000 less than that in urban settings. In some cases, this difference is somewhat offset by lower home prices and mortgages, and more families in rural areas own their homes outright (Marré, 2017). These trends are misleading metrics for understanding the economics of the entirety of rural America because they vary greatly by region, and even county.

In the South and the West, the disparity between rural and urban income is more dramatic. In the South, the disparity is closer to $4,000 and in the West, close to $3,000. In the Northwest and Midwest, the median income for rural households actually exceeds the median income for urban households. We also see a greater wage gap between earnings of males and females in such communities.

Since the 2008 recession, urban America has recovered at a faster pace than rural regions. In fact, job growth in rural America is lower than it was before the economic crisis of 2008. Since agriculture and natural resource extraction have continued to decline and mechanization and technological advances continue to increase, it stands to reason that rural areas will continue to struggle in this way for the foreseeable future (IPUMS USA, n.d.).

Rural areas on the whole experience greater financial instability than cities. Economic instability is often the result of the local industry's dependency on climate and conditions well beyond the control of the average American. Tourism, a major economic driver in frontier towns, can fluctuate based on gas prices, the cost of airline travel, natural disasters, and cultural trends. Likewise, agriculture can be massively impacted by fire, drought, tornadoes, flooding, and more.

Poverty

Nearly any way you slice it, rural Americans are disproportionately poor. For our purposes, poverty is defined as having an income below the federally designated threshold. Poverty in nonmetropolitan areas has historically been significantly higher than in urban centers. Though the Great Depression (1929–1939) struck rather equal blows to rural and urban America, its effects have lingered with greater significance and duration in rural communities. Both wages and employment rates have lagged behind in rural America, despite the rebounds seen in metropolitan areas. This, and other factors, contribute to the unarguable statistic that median household income is significantly lower in rural areas. In 2017, the American Community Survey revealed that 16.4% of Americans living in nonmetropolitan areas were living in poverty (compared to 12.9% of urban dwellers). (See Figure 3.2.)

Rural children experience substantially higher rates of poverty, with 22.8% of rural children, compared to 17.7% of urban children, living in poverty in 2017. Of the 43 counties in the US with the highest child poverty rates, 40 of them were nonmetropolitan. The top three were all in the American rural South. The Economic Research Service found that growing income inequality accounted for much of the net increase in childhood poverty in rural communities in the last few decades (Hertz & Farrigan, 2016).

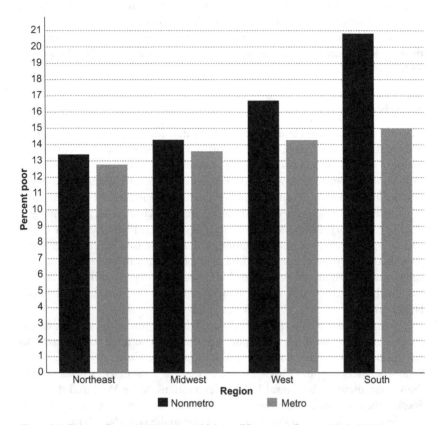

Figure 3.2 Poverty Rates by Region and Metro/Nonmetro Status, 2013–2017

In fact, all age groups have higher poverty rates in rural areas than in metropolitan areas. The smallest discrepancy is found in adults over the age of 65. Perhaps some of this variability is a result of the higher number of federal institutions supporting older adults.

Persistent poverty, a dimension of poverty tracked by the United States Department of Agriculture's Economic Research Service (2019), is characterized by failure to reduce poverty rates in a given area over time. This metric is thought to accurately capture one of the more important elements to consider when contemplating poverty: is there a way out? Of the 353 counties in the US classified by this definition as "persistently poor," 85.3% were in nonmetropolitan counties. A brief scan of the persistently poor counties reveals that the vast majority of those counties are either in the rural South or are counties comprising, at least in part, residents of Indian reservations. Persistent poverty, one might then speculate, may be a lasting systemic force of institutionalized and historical oppression of marginalized groups. Indeed, in 2017, Black/African

Americans had the highest incidence of poverty for a minority group (32%), followed closely by American Indians/Alaska Natives (31%).

Women in nonmetropolitan counties face higher poverty rates as well, particularly if they are single and living alone or serve as the head of a household with children (USDA, 2019).

Deprivation

There is a summative element of rural life that may capture the essence of what makes it so hard: *deprivation*. England and some other countries commonly measure what is known as *indices of deprivation*. Some Americans are beginning to look at this concept as well. Deprivation is a measure of impoverishment that includes income, employment, health and disability status, education, access (or barriers) to services and housing, living environment, and crime (see Box 3.1). Not surprisingly, some research suggests that higher scores of deprivation suggest increased vulnerabilities. And, as evidenced by the information presented in previous chapters, if the US utilized such a measure, rural Americans would undoubtedly experience higher rates of deprivation than those in many urban areas (University of Wisconsin School of Medicine and Public Health, n.d.).

Researchers at the University of Wisconsin have begun analyzing data to better understand how this metric applies to American communities. In researching this book, I used the mapping system through the University of Wisconsin School of Medicine and Public Health to make several maps. I would like to draw your attention to several Indian Reservations in the West and the rural South as having notably high rates of deprivation. Often referred to as the Black Belt (its nomenclature simultaneously referring to the rich, dark, fertile soil and the individuals historically enslaved to work it), the rural South is one of the

---

Box 3.1

Factors of Deprivation

- % with less than HS degree (25 years and over)
- % below poverty level
- % of female-headed households with children under 18
- % in management, science, and arts occupation
- % in crowded households (morethan one occupant per room)
- % with public assistance or food stamps
- % unemployed (16–64 years old in labor force)
- % with less than $30,000 annual household income

Source: University of Wisconsin School of Medicine and Public Health (n.d.)

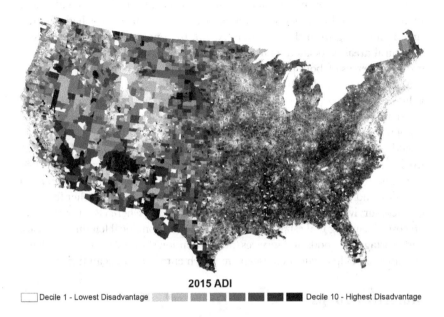

Figure 3.3 2015 American Deprivation Index
Source: University of Wisconsin School of Medicine and Public Health. (2015)

most impoverished areas in the world. Indeed, according to a United Nations special report in 2017, Alabama was named as the "most impoverished state in the developed world" (Ballesteros, 2017).

Figure 3.3 shows deprivation index scores, by county, throughout the United States. Darker areas are associated with higher deprivation scores. The rural South and part of the rural frontier of the West are particularly noteworthy for the presence of significant deprivation.

The Workforce

Historically, rural America's economy was fueled by mining, manufacturing, and farming. Of course, the Industrial Revolution and the technology boom both contributed in their own way to making obsolete the farmer, the factory worker, and the coal miner. While our dependency on oil has contributed to an increase in mining operations (other than coal), the net effect has been a steady loss in jobs typical to rural regions. The more rural an area is, the more likely it is to be dependent on agriculture. In fact, 17% of employment in rural areas is accounted for by agriculture. The closer a rural or mostly rural area is to an urban area, the more likely that region will rely on manufacturing.

It should not be a surprise, then, when I share that unemployment rates in rural communities are higher than we find in urban areas. We know that the demand for jobs typical to rural areas are in decline, lower educational attainment is linked to higher levels of unemployment, and rural areas had a harder time rebounding from the recession. Again, the one exception to this rule is that rural areas associated with recreation are experiencing a slow but steady growth in terms of both population and economic indicators.

While many foundational rural industries are on the decline, rural America is home to a great number of entrepreneurs. The rates for entrepreneurship are significantly higher in rural areas and decline the closer one gets to a metropolitan area. I suspect anyone reading this who lives in a rural community would not be surprised by this. In my community, there are a plethora of small businesses and start-up companies filling niches not otherwise addressed by businesses and government institutions. What's more, entrepreneurs in rural counties tend to fare better than their urban counterparts, with higher five-year business survival rates in the most rural areas than anywhere else. Lower start-up costs, including real estate; availability of loans from local lending agencies; and shortages of goods and services (not to mention slower Amazon.com delivery times) all help create a landscape in which entrepreneurs can thrive.

Minority Groups

Viewed from afar, rural communities appear less diverse, with fewer racial and ethnic minorities than found in cities. (See Figure 3.4.) However, this statistic overlooks some important persons and groups. A majority of American Indian and Alaska Natives (approximately 54%) live in rural areas and small towns.

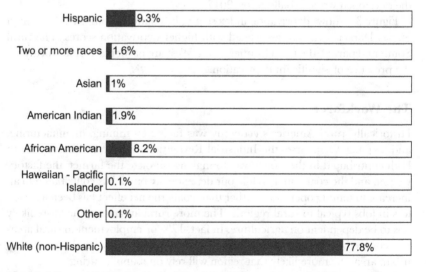

Figure 3.4 Race and Ethnicity in Rural and Small Town America, 2010

As of 2010, Hispanics (9.3%) and African Americans (8.2%) comprise the largest minority groups living in rural America. According to one report, "Many rural minorities are clustered geographically in regions closely tied to historical social and economic dynamics" (Housing Assistance Council, 2012, p. 2). Whereas during the Great Migration, Black Southerners left their rural dwellings to move to cities in the North and East, we are now seeing movement of Hispanic individuals and groups from urban centers to more rural landscapes (Housing Assistance Council, 2012).

Today, African Americans comprise the largest minority group in the rural Southeast. Due to their historical and current experiences of oppression, African Americans are likely to face issues related to intergenerational trauma and persistent effects of interpersonal, systemic, institutional, and internalized racism. Racial discrimination and its effects on socioeconomic status and other aspects of daily living have a profound impact on the mental health of the oppressed. Blacks have been discriminated against by the physical and mental health professions, and the resultant mistrust and stigma may have profound effects on help-seeking behavior and resultant improvements or declines in the overall mental health of a community or its members (Williams & Williams-Morris, 2000).

Here, "Hispanic" will refer to individuals of Spanish descent, including those whose ancestors settled El Norte. "Latino" will refer to anyone with ancestors in Latin America. Mexican Americans are concentrated in Arizona, New Mexico, Colorado, Texas, and California, and 85% of all Hispanic Americans are found in Texas and California. While Hispanics are the fastest growing ethnic group in rural populations, they are still only 6% of the rural population in the US. Their movement is somewhat responsible for lessening the effect of urban migration and population decreases rurally. The growth is occurring nationwide but is most concentrated in the Southeast and Midwest. Those who move to rural areas tend to be young and male, suggesting that they are typically moving for job opportunities (USDA, 2005).

Hispanic and Latino Americans, on the whole, tend to have lower levels of educational attainment than their White counterparts. Hispanic and Latino Americans are more likely to be farmers, foresters, or fisherman than their White counterparts, and they are also more likely to be engaged in the workforce than unemployed. Not all rural Latinos, to be clear, are migrant workers. The limited research on the subject suggests that rural Hispanic and Latino Americans face significant hardship, discrimination, and distress (Saenz & Torres, 2003).

For individuals working in rural regions with racial or ethnic minorities, I encourage you to engage in further training and reading to ensure your cultural competence. Particularly in regions where minorities are small, it remains critical that practitioners familiarize themselves with the group's history, struggles, strengths, and vulnerabilities. Ethnic minorities in rural regions may have an even harder time finding a culturally competent therapist in their small community, and thus it remains our duty to ensure they receive the services they need.

LBGTQ

Individuals, particularly youth, who identify as lesbian, gay, bisexual, transgender, or queer face discrimination and harassment regardless of rurality (Williams, Williams, Pellegrino, & Warren, 2012). Though the experience of LGBTQ individuals can be difficult anywhere in the US, they may face unique challenges in rural America. Rural LGBTQ folks are less likely to be out than their urban counterparts, may experience heightened stigma, and, as a result, are less likely to seek out and receive medical and mental healthcare (Williams et al., 2012).

Many of us know the story of Matthew Shepard. Matthew Shepard was a young gay male attending university in Laramie, Wyoming, not far from his hometown of Casper, in the late 1990s. He was beaten to death by two male peers whose accounts varied from Matthew making sexual advances to robbery. Matthew's funeral was protested by individuals from the Westboro Baptist Church with signs that read "God Hates Fags" and "Matt in Hell." The incident eventually led to the enactment of hate crime legislation specifically addressing protections for sexual identity (Dunn, 2010). While this is but one instance, and tragically, hate crimes against gay individuals happen in urban and rural settings, the circumstances surrounding Matthew's murder speak to the nuances of the gay male in rural America—particularly in the frontier. A year after Matthew's death, *Brokeback Mountain*, a novel by Annie Proulx (1997), was published, depicting two young Wyoming boys who find unexpected love in one another. Their romance, relegated to the privacy one only finds in wilderness, is another reminder of how gender norms, conservative wisdom, and rural life interact, limiting the expression of many. As I recount these anecdotes, let me say that while dated, they both provide a narrative about acceptance and rejection in the rural West that is, I think, demonstrative of a greater trend.

Research on the experience of LGBTQ individuals in rural areas is limited (D'Augelli & Hart, 1987; Connolly & Leedy, 2006). As Wienke and Hill (2013, pp. 1256–1279) explain, much of the literature "is based on the experiences of urban dwellers—as if the gay experience is limited to urban settings and nowhere else." Some research demonstrates that traditional cultural values and norms make the experience of being queer in rural communities more challenging. Some areas, such as Wyoming, may be particularly inhospitable to members of the queer community. As Connolly and Leedy (2006) point out, despite the state motto of "Equal Rights" and the cultural emphasis placed on rugged individualism implying a "live and let live" ethic, queer residents of Wyoming experience significant homophobia. Other studies have found no significant differences, at least in terms of well-being, between urban and rural LGBTQ individuals (Wienke & Hill, 2013). However, some research findings did find differences in affective distress between LGBTQ and non-LGBTQ rural American adolescents. Rural LGBTQ youth may not be significantly worse off than their urban queer peers but may face increased risk of psychological distress than their straight rural counterparts (Cohn & Leake, 2012).

Given the demands for sameness amongst rural dwellers, individuals who are gender nonconforming are particularly at risk for discrimination, judgment, isolation, or ostracization (Gray, 2009). These experiences may, unfortunately, appear in the provider's office as well. (Remember, rural providers are members of their communities and often have similar views, beliefs, and experiences.) Also, given that individuals in rural communities often utilize de facto mental health treatment offerings (e.g., medical professionals or religious institutions), they are even less likely to encounter cultural competence.

American Indians and Alaska Natives

While I do not aim here to provide an exhaustive or expert summary of the historical experience of American Indians and Alaska Natives, it does seem important to highlight this particular cultural subgroup.[1] The approximately three million American Indians make up 573 federally recognized tribes. There are now, reportedly, approximately five million American Indian or Alaska Natives living in the United States. At present, 42% of American Indians live on or near rural areas, with approximately one in five living on Indian reservations (Department of Health and Human Services [HHS], 2001). Whereas they were once spread out throughout the region, most now live west of the Mississippi (Pevar, 1983). For practitioners in rural regions (or urban centers within driving distance of Indian reservations) an important element of your cultural competence will be familiarizing yourself with this historically underserved community.

Twitter user Dani Phantom says, "*goes to therapy*/me: it all started when Columbus set foot on our land" (@datn8vchic, 2019). For some American Indians and Alaska Natives, as Dani Phantom's tweet implies, the historical traumatic experiences of their people will be present in the therapy office. Much has been written about the history of American Indians and Alaska Natives. I will generally leave this topic to the historians and will encourage any reader who suspects they may encounter an American Indian or Alaska Native in their consultation room, or who suspects their lack of cultural sensitivity and awareness may prohibit such a person from entering their room in the first place, to see my recommended readings section and brush up.

In the years that followed Columbus's arrival in what is now known as America, those we have come to know as American Indians experienced a transformation of their land, culture, and way of life. I will summarize here by saying that the cultures that existed in the land now known as America prior to 1492 experienced violence and exposure to previously unknown threats such as the introduction of many new illnesses, guns, and colonialism, and many eventually succumbed to genocide and cultural terrorism. Those who remained demonstrated tremendous resilience, which is present in the rich cultural legacy seen in many tribes today.

This Western approach to civilization, so contradictory to tribes' worldviews, transformed both indigenous economies and, eventually, societies as a whole (Pevar, 1983). Attempts at annihilation and cultural misunderstandings all contributed to profound loss of life, culture, and tradition amongst Native people. American Indians and Alaska Natives continue to struggle in various ways, many of which can be tied to the genocide they endured (Dalal, 2011).

Moving away from the colonial era's annihilation tactics, various governmental policies have oscillated between controlling and affording sovereignty to the American Indians and Alaska Natives (Pevar, 1983). Eventually, the US federal government shifted from a policy that tolerated some sovereignty and separation to one of forced assimilation. In 1887, the Dawes Act was aimed at extinguishing tribal authority and shifting reservation lands from federal oversight to individual membership, the price of which was the elimination of residual aspects of American Indian culture (Pevar, 1983). By offering citizenship, the federal government enticed some American Indians and then sold off the remaining land to White settlers. Eventually, The US Indian Reorganization Act permitted the re-establishment of tribal governments and reservations. All told, the American Indians are, and historically have been, the most regulated ethnic group in our nation. This bit of history is particularly salient to our conversation because the health services industry, which is qualitatively different on Indian reservations, has its roots in this complicated saga of regaining independence.

In 1968, Lyndon Johnson declared, "We must affirm the rights of the first Americans to remain Indians while exercising their rights as Americans. We must affirm their rights to freedom of choice and self-determination" (Pevar, 1983, p. 12). Since that time, the federal government has promoted policies that, at least on the surface, appear to promote tribal sovereignty and autonomy amongst the American Indians. One attempt at autonomy has been the creation of the Indian Health Service (IHS), which is housed under the Department of Health and Human Services. The IHS maintains clinics and hospitals, typically located on Indian reservation land, and is tasked with raising, "the physical, mental, social, and spiritual health of American Indians and Alaska Natives to the highest level" (n.d.) by providing culturally competent and accessible health services to American Indian and Alaska Natives. Given that many American Indian/Alaska Natives do not live on reservations, they may lack access to adequate care. Trust issues, availability of providers, and limitations of care due to inadequate resources also limit the efficacy of the IHS. It wasn't until 1965 that the first mental health office was opened under the banner of the IHS on the Navajo Indian Reservation (HHS, 2001). As is true in the general population, mental health services perpetually lag behind physical health services due to priorities and subsequent funding, language barriers, training, and staffing issues.

Despite the best efforts of the IHS, only one fifth of American Indians and Alaska Natives utilize those services. The IHS, like most medical agencies, struggles to keep up with the demand of its people. Approximately a quarter of American Indians and Alaska Natives are insured through Medicaid, and another quarter have no health insurance at all. Approximately 2,000 facilities exist nationwide, with those American Indians and Alaska Natives living on reservations more likely than their metropolitan counterparts to utilize these services. Reports on the IHS's efficacy vary, with some suggesting that the IHS is only meeting the health needs of approximately half of all Native populations (HHS, 2019). According to the Center for Native American Youth (n.d.), "only 1 in 8 (12.6 percent) of AI/AN adults (24,000 people) in need of alcohol or illicit drug use treatment in the past year received treatment at a specialty facility."

Health in Indian Country

Despite having once exclusively inhabited North America, American Indians today make up less than 1% of the US population. Statistically speaking, American Indians and Alaska Natives are younger (with 32% under the age of 18). This tells us that their life expectancy is shorter or that they are in a period of population growth, with a surge in this younger demographic. Indeed, the population of American Indians and Alaska Natives has grown roughly 27% between 2000 and 2010. (For comparison, the general US population grew at a rate around 10% during that same period.) Researchers speculate that American Indian and Alaska Natives are in a population surge and that their numbers are expected to swell to approximately eight million by 2050 (U.S. Department of Commerce, 2012). Additionally, this group has a lower life expectancy, in part due to lower health status and disproportionately high rates of disease and major illnesses including diabetes, alcoholism, tuberculosis, and heart disease (American Psychiatric Association, n.d.). (See Figure 3.5.)

While American Indians and Alaska Natives tend to have higher incidences of mental and physical illness, their utilization rates (particularly for mental health services) are lower. Specifically, substance use disorders, PTSD, suicide, and attachment disorders are notably high in this community and can be linked back to their historical generations of trauma, violence, and colonization. Depression is pervasive; American Indian and Alaska Natives report the highest rates of any ethnic group in the United States. Culturally competent psychological care continues to be lacking for most American Indians and Alaska Natives (HHS, 2001).

Poverty profoundly affects Native communities with more than a quarter of American Indians and Alaska Natives living below the poverty line. (The rate for the general population is somewhere around 13%.) Their median income is nearly $7,000 less than that of the US general population. Meanwhile, 28.4% of Native people live in poverty (compared to 11.3% for the US as a whole).

Rural America

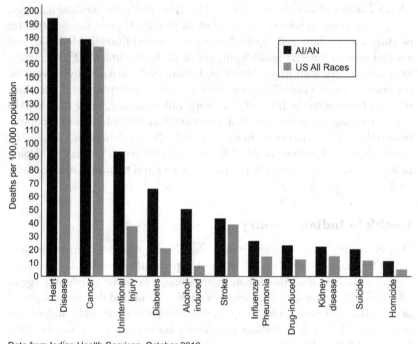

Data from Indian Health Services, October 2019

Figure 3.5 Mortality Disparity Rates: American Indian and Alaska Natives, 2009–2011
Source: Indian Health Service (2019)

Fewer Native families own their own homes than the national average (HHS, 2001).

One in three American Indian women will be raped in their lifetime (Deer, 2009, p. 149–167). Rape, largely unheard of in precolonial native life, is most frequently perpetrated by White men on Native women. The individual assault can be seen as a direct reflection of the systemic and cultural invasion of power, control, and authority perpetrated by White culture onto the American Indian (Smith, 2003, pp. 70–85). American Indian and Alaska Native women are at particularly greater risk. Missing and murdered Indigenous women have received increasing media attention in the past few years, with some states signing laws or assigning task forces to address the issue. The attention, however, does not change their reality: American Indian and Alaska Native women are far more likely than their non-Native counterparts to be the victims of intimate partner violence, sexual assault, kidnappings, and murder (CSVANW, n.d.).

Trauma is pervasive among American Indian people and groups. We know that lower socioeconomic status is linked to an increased likelihood of trauma exposure in one's lifetime (Bradley-Davino & Ruglass, n.d.). As a result, it is unsurprising that American Indians and Alaska Natives experience trauma at higher rates than other ethnic groups in the United States (HHS, 2001). According to one study, over 60% of all individuals surveyed had experienced trauma at some point in their lifetime. American Indians were found to have higher rates of physical trauma than rates found in the general population (Brave Heart et al., 2011, pp. 282–290).

Intergenerational and historical trauma is also widespread amongst American Indians. A study looking at adolescent depression and historical loss found that one fifth of youth ages 11 through 13 reported thinking about the historical loss of their peoples, cultural traditions, and lands on a daily basis. Present-day American Indians have not forgotten the experiences of their language and culture being banned, their families separated while children were forced into boarding schools, and their sacred spaces being demolished or usurped, among other atrocities. American Indians, it would seem, carry with them the history of being the target of ethnic cleansing, and this unwanted, threatened status is embedded in their individual as well as group identity (Whitbeck, Walls, Johnson, Morrisseau, & McDougall, 2009, p. 16).

American Indian and Alaska Natives also enjoy rich cultural and historical traditions and practices that serve as protective factors against mental illness. Values such as family, connection to the past, cultural identification, persistence and resilience, adaptability, and utilization of and connection to elders may all be prophylactic in nature. Additionally, traditional healing systems, which frequently emphasize wellness in a holistic sense, may serve to reduce some of the stigma surrounding mental illness and may offer paths toward healing not found on a therapist's couch (American Psychiatric Association, n.d.).

American Indians have demonstrated, and continue to demonstrate, profound resilience. Their population has rebounded tremendously, growing by over 25% between the 2000 and the 2010 censuses (U.S. Census Bureau, 2012). Various tribes have also, despite generations of assimilation and the desecration of land and culture, carried on their vibrant and robust traditions and cultural celebrations.

As rural providers, or urban providers treating rural Americans, it is essential to be educated on the populations we serve, their needs, and their history. American Indians and Alaska Natives not only make up a significant portion of the rural American population, but they are also disproportionately in need of our services.

Religion

Colonialism was driven in large part by religion. The church often served as a physical and metaphorical center point for new towns and villages. Churches were built as focal points, and towns were built around them. In many rural communities, churches remain at the heart of life to this day (Vidich & Bensman, 2000).

However, rural Americans, as we've discussed, are not a heterogenous group, and their differences when it comes to religion are vast. Rural Southerners tend to be more religious than their rural counterparts in the rest of the nation (Chalfant & Heller, 1991), and since much research of rural America tends to include the entire populace, the data is likely skewed (Dillon & Savage, 2006). The research does suggest that increases in rurality are linked with increases in religiosity. Those individuals living highly rural lives, who place an emphasis on traditional ways of living, are likely to be more fundamentalist than their urban, less-traditional counterparts (Chalfant & Heller, 1991).

Regardless of religiosity, in small communities, the church may serve as a de facto community center, mental health service provider, social epicenter, and even day care provider (Aten, Hall, Weaver, Mangis, & Campbell, 2012). More on this later.

Note

1. After careful debate, I use the nomenclature "American Indian" to refer collectively to the individuals whose ancestors resided in the land region now known as the United States of America. Half of all people who identify as Indigenous prefer the term "American Indian," while 37% prefer "Native American," with the remainder either preferring a different term or not reporting a preference (Bird, 1999, pp. 1–21).

References

@datn8vchic. (2019, October 30). *goes to therapy* me: it all started when columbus set foot on our land [Twitter post]. Retrieved October 30, 2019, from https://twitter.com/datn8vchic/status/1218969538784781 1072

American Psychiatric Association. (n.d.). *Mental health disparities: Diverse populations*. Retrieved December 19, 2019, from www.psychiatry.org/psychiatrists/cultural-competency/education/mental-health-facts

Aten, J., Hall, P., Weaver, I., Mangis, M., & Campbell, C. (2012). Religion and rural mental health. In K. B. Smalley, J. C. Warren, & J. P. Rainer (Eds.), *Rural mental health: Issues, policies, and best practices* (pp. 79–96). New York: Springer Publishing Company.

Ballesteros, C. (2017, December 19). *U.N. officials touring rural Alabama are shocked at the level of poverty and environmental degradation*. Retrieved October 19, 2019, from www.newsweek.com/alabama-un-poverty-environmental-racism-743601

Bird, M. (1999). What we want to be called: Indigenous peoples' perspectives on racial and ethnic identity labels. *American Indian Quarterly*, 23(2), 1–21. https://doi.org/10.2307/1185964

Bonnie, R. J., Stroud, C. J., & Breiner, H. J. (2015). *Investing in the health and well-being of young adults*. Washington, DC: National Academies Press.

Bradley-Davino, B., & Ruglass, L. (n.d.). *Trauma & PTSD in economically disadvantaged populations*. Web-based trauma psychology resources on underserved health priority populations for public and professional education. Retrieved August 23, 2019, from www.apatraumadivision.org/files/58.pdf

Brave Heart, M. Y. H., Chase, J., Elkins, J., & Altschul, D. B. (2011). Historical trauma among indigenous peoples of the Americas: Concepts, research, and clinical considerations. *Journal of Psychoactive Drugs*, 43(4), 282–290.

Center for Native American Youth at the Aspen Institute. (n.d.). *Fast facts on Native American youth and Indian country* [PDF file]. Retrieved December 19, 2019, from https://assets.aspeninstitute.org/content/uploads/files/content/images/Fast Facts.pdf

Chalfant, H. P., & Heller, P. L. (1991). Rural/urban versus regional differences in religiosity. *Review of Religious Research*, 76–86.

Cohn, T. J., & Leake, V. S. (2012). Affective distress among adolescents who endorse same-sex attraction: Urban versus rural differences and the role of protective factors. *Journal of Gay & Lesbian Mental Health*, *16*(4), 291–305. https://doi.org/10.1080/19359705.2012.690931

Connolly, C., & Leedy, G. (2006). Out in the cowboy state: A look at gay and lesbian lives in Wyoming. *Journal of Gay and Lesbian Social Services*, *19*(1), 17–34.

Cromartie, J., Von Reichert, C., & Arthun, R. (2015). *Factors affecting former residents' returning to rural communities*. Retrieved October 23, 2019, from https://www.ers.usda.gov/webdocs/publications/45361/52906_err185.pdf?v=0

CSVANW. (n.d.). *CSVANW: Coalition to stop violence against women*. Retrieved December 19, 2019, from www.csvanw.org/mmiw/

Dalal, N. (2011). The impact of colonial contact on the cultural heritage of native American Indian people [PDF file]. *Diffusion: The UCLA Journal of Undergraduate Research*, *4*(2). Retrieved October 23, 2019, from www.uclan.ac.uk/courses/assets/rcs-dalal.pdf

D'Augelli, A. R., & Hart, M. M. (1987). Gay women, men, and families in rural settings: Toward the development of helping communities. *American Journal of Community Psychology*, *15*(1), 79–93.

Deer, S. (2009). Decolonizing rape law: A native feminist synthesis of safety and sovereignty. *Wicazo Sa Review*, *24*(2), 149–167.

Dillon, M., & Savage, S. (2006). Values and religion in rural America: Attitudes toward abortion and same-sex relations. *The Carsey School of Public Policy at the Scholars' Repository*, *12*. Retrieved December 19, 2019, from https://scholars.unh.edu/carsey/12/

Dunn, T. R. (2010). Remembering Matthew Shepard: Violence, identity, and queer counterpublic memories. *Rhetoric & Public Affairs*, *13*(4), 611–652.

Gray, M. L. (2009). *Out in the country: Youth, media, and queer visibility in rural America* (Vol. 2). New York: NYU Press.

Hertz, T., & Farrigan, T. (2016, May 16). Understanding trends in rural child poverty, 2003-14. *Amber Waves Magazine*. Retrieved December 19, 2019, from www.ers.usda.gov/amber-waves/2016/may/understanding-trends-in-rural-child-poverty-2003-14

Housing Assistance Council. (2012). Race & ethnicity in rural America. *Rural Research Briefs*, *3*, 1283–1288.

Indian Health Service. (2019). *Mortality disparity rates: American Indian and Alaska Natives 2009-2011* [Chart]. Retrieved October 23, 2019, from www.ihs.gov/sites/newsroom/themes/responsive2017/display_objects/documents/factsheets/Disparities.pdf

Indian Health Service. (n.d.). *About IHS*. Retrieved December 18, 2019, from www.ihs.gov/aboutihs/

IPUMS USA. (n.d.). *U.S. census data for social, economic, and health research*. Retrieved December 18, 2019, from https://usa.ipums.org/usa/

Marré, A. (2014, December 1). Rural areas lag urban areas in college completion. *Amber Waves Magazine*.

Marré, A. (2017). *Rural education at a glance* (2017 ed.). Washington, DC: United States Department of Agriculture.

Pevar, S. L. (1983). *The rights of Indians and tribes: An American Civil Liberties Union handbook*. New York: American Civil Liberties Union.

Pope, N. D., Loeffler, D. N., & Ferrell, D. L. (2014). Aging in rural Appalachia: Perspectives from geriatric social service professionals. *Advances in Social Work*, *15*(2), 522–537.

Proulx, A. (1997, October 13). Brokeback Mountain. *The New Yorker*.

Saenz, R., & Torres, C. C. (2003). Latinos in rural America. In *Challenges for rural America in the twenty-first century* (pp. 57–70). University Park, PA: Penn State Press.

Singh, G. K. (2003). Area deprivation and widening inequalities in US mortality, 1969–1998. *American Journal of Public Health*, *93*(7), 1137–1143. https://doi.org/10.2105/ajph.93.7.1137

Smith, A. (2003). Not an Indian tradition: The sexual colonization of Native peoples. *Hypatia*, *18*(2), 70–85. https://doi.org/10.1111/j.1527-2001.2003.tb00802.x

US Census Bureau. (2012). *American Indian and Alaska Native population: 2010* (Report number C2010BR-10). Washington, DC.

US Census Bureau. (2016, December 8). *New Census data show differences between urban and rural populations*. Retrieved October 20, 2019, from www.census.gov/newsroom/press-releases/2016/cb16-210.html.

US Department of Commerce. (2012). American Indian and Alaska Native Heritage Month: November 2012. *Profile America: Facts for features*. Retrieved October 20, 2019, from www.census.gov/newsroom/releases/pdf/cb12ff-22_aian.pdf.

US Department of Health and Human Services. (2019). *Organizational challenges to improving quality of care in Indian Health Service hospitals* (OEI-06-16-00390). Retrieved December 10, 2019, from https://oig.hhs.gov/oei/reports/oei-06-16-00390.pdf.

US Department of Health and Human Services, US Public Health Service. (2001). Chapter 4: Mental health care for American Indians and Alaska Natives. In *Mental health: Culture, race, and ethnicity: A supplement to Mental health: A report of the Surgeon General*. Rockville, MD: U.S. Public Health Service.

United States Department of Agriculture. (2005). *Economic Information Bulletin Number 8* [Chart]. Retrieved December 10, 2019, from www.ers.usda.gov/webdocs/publications/44570/29568_eib8full.pdf?v

United States Department of Agriculture. (2019, August 20). *Rural poverty & well-being*. Retrieved October 20, 2019, from www.ers.usda.gov/topics/rural-economy-population/rural-poverty-well-being/

University of Wisconsin School of Medicine and Public Health. (2015). Area Deprivation Index. *Contiguous Black and White* [Map]. Retrieved December 19, 2019, from www.neighborhoodatlas.medicine.wisc.edu/

University of Wisconsin School of Medicine and Public Health. (n.d.). *Neighborhood atlas*. Retrieved December 18, 2019, from www.neighborhoodatlas.medicine.wisc.edu/

Vidich, A., & Bensman, J. (2000). *Small town in mass society: Class, power, and religion in a rural community*. Chicago: University of Illinois Press.

Wagenfeld, M. O. (2003). A snapshot of rural and frontier America. In B. H. Stamm (Ed.), *Rural behavioral health care: An interdisciplinary guide* (pp. 33–40). Washington, DC: American Psychological Association.

Whitbeck, L. B., Walls, M. L., Johnson, K. D., Morrisseau, A. D., & McDougall, C. M. (2009). Depressed affect and historical loss among North American indigenous adolescents. *American Indian and Alaska Native Mental Health Research (Online)*, *16*(3), 16.

Wienke, C., & Hill, G. J. (2013). Does place of residence matter? Rural-urban differences and the wellbeing of gay men and lesbians. *Journal of Homosexuality*, *60*(9), 1256–1279.

Williams, D. R., & Williams-Morris, R. (2000). Racism and mental health: The African American experience. *Ethnicity and Health*, *5*(3–4), 243–268. https://doi.org/10.1080/713667453

Williams, I., Williams, D., Pellegrino, A., & Warren, J. C. (2012). Providing mental health services for racial, ethnic, and sexual orientation minority groups in rural areas. In K. B. Smalley, J. C. Warren, & J. P. Rainer (Eds.), *Rural mental health: Issues, policies, and best practices* (pp. 229–252). New York: Springer Publishing Company.

Wuthnow, R. (2018). *The left behind: Decline and rage in small-town America*. Princeton, NJ: Princeton University Press.

4 The Psychological Landscape of Rural America
Values, Culture, and Norms

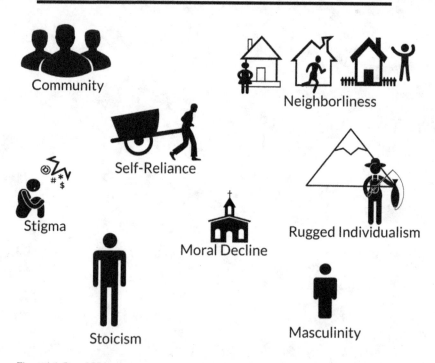

Figure 4.1 Rural Values

We have thus far examined the rural landscape and rural people therein. We have even learned a bit about the problems that plague them. Now, let's turn our attention to what it's like to live in rural America, including some of the cultural elements common among its rural dwellers. To begin, much time has been spent debating if, indeed, there is a particular "rural culture" with specific widely held values (Wagenfeld, 2003). Of course, not every individual living in a rural location will ascribe to these norms, much like every individual living in an urban setting would not. However, given that so few of us learned about the rural life in our graduate training (Jameson & Blank, 2007) and much of our training is urbancentric in nature, it is important that we cultivate a general understanding of rural life so that we know what it is if and when we find it. Figure 4.1 provides a visual overview of some common rural values.

Community

Rural dwellers tend to have a high identification with the **community** (as home, as family). There is often a sense that "everyone knows everyone" (familiarity) and that "we're all the same" (shared identity). Jokes abound about how rural residents can easily spot an outsider simply by their dress, their mannerisms, or their need for directions. Though rural folks rarely *actually* know everyone in their community, their sense of understanding and connection makes it feel that way. I live down a dirt road off a two-lane highway that leads south to Whitefish, Montana, an idyllic mountain town, and north to Canada. When I first moved to this road, some 15 years ago, I noticed that drivers would subtly wave their hands as I drove by. The strategy was fairly predictable—with their hand at 12 o'clock on the steering wheel, a driver could lift a few fingers in a cordial but casual acknowledgment. The "dirt road wave," a phenomenon consistent across the region, was, as far as I could tell, a way for drivers to acknowledge one another, humanizing the driving experience and thanking each other for sharing the road. Ever adaptable, I learned to rest my arm on my steering wheel when driving on a gravel road. I now can identify an outsider by the absence of the dirt road wave. "Out of towners!" I might say as they drive by, much too fast and far too impolitely.

This sense of community has profound effects on several psychological aspects therein: change is slow, outsiders are treated with wariness, and insiders feel an intense connection to those around them, for better (we know the positive impacts of social support networks on one's health) or worse (these connections often encourage folks to remain rooted in their communities, forgoing education or economic advancement) (Bialik, 2018).

Sameness has a profound effect on one's ability to speak up about difficulties, differences, or aberrant experiences. The dirt road wave can teach us a lot about group membership. It is a subtle and yet easily identifiable marker of in-group or out-group status. The underlying premise for the wave originates in friendliness and consideration. It acknowledges we are sharing a small path; we do not drive so fast as to kick up too much dirt to inhibit another's visibility, and we are in this together. If, however, the underlying ideals promoting sameness originate in stigma about mental illness or shame about struggle, the ramifications may be destructive and significant. While many of the other values of rural life can hinder one's ability to achieve mental wellness, the demand for sameness is the glue that holds them all together.

Neighborliness

Neighborliness, which often goes hand-in-hand with the sense of being embedded in a community, is also a prominent element of the psychology of rural Americans (Bushy, 1990). We had lived down the dirt road for nearly five years, and yet I still had not learned her name. She wandered up our driveway, her hair and coat blowing wildly in the windstorm that had, apparently, knocked out power to our area. I opened the door, my dog barking madly, and ushered her into our home, warmed by the roaring wood stove, independent of electricity. With no electricity, we had no internet (and our cellular telephones never work here) and no way of knowing how universal the outage was or how long it was expected to last. Living rurally may mean being independent of city utilities. In our region, we have electric supplied, but, like all of our neighbors, we rely on water dug deep in the Earth. Our well is the sort that gushes naturally, without the need for an electric pump to supply the household. Without second thought, I offered her a shower or to fill a bucket with water, should the outage last longer than their water supply. She was grateful, and we became acquainted as she filled a few water bottles to tide her over. Neighborliness does not require one to be friends with their neighbors. It does, however, demand that we are generous, kind, and helpful to those in need (as long as they are part of the community!).

The flip side of neighborliness, of course, is wariness of outsiders. We know that rural residents are much more likely than urban residents to consider immigrants a threat to, or a strain on, our nation. They are also more likely to be distrustful of "big government," perhaps because they are less likely to see the positive impacts so-called "entitlements" can have on a community or individual (DelReal & Clement, 2017). In his book *The Left Behind: Decline and Rage in Rural America*, Robert Wuthnow (2019) aimed to give voice to the overlooked, writing, "As far as they can see, the federal government hasn't the least interest in trying to understand rural communities' problems, let alone do anything to fix them." He quotes one rural resident as saying, "They're just not listening to us out here" (Wuthnow, 2019, p. 98). This mistrust can affect the rural dwellers' attitudes toward reaching out for and accepting help.

Self-Reliance

Despite neighborliness affording opportunities for connection and interdependency, one of the strongest rural values, particularly salient in the frontier, is that of **self-reliance**. Self-reliance is the concept of (striving for) sustainability of the self/family/community without the need for external support or resources. Upon first glance, it becomes evident why this ethos is prominent in many rural communities—historically, rural towns and villages had little access to metropolitan areas and their many resources and were forced to provide for themselves. When we first moved to Whitefish, we lived on 20 acres, 20 minutes from town, down two miles of dirt road, the last mile of which was privately maintained. On my way to work one morning, as the sun was just rising, I came upon a car stopped at a fallen tree across the road. Together, using our chainsaw, we cut the tree, freed the passage, and carried on, 15 minutes late and covered in sawdust. No one was coming to clear that tree.

Rural dwellers have long been forced to look out for themselves. Self-reliance is a natural byproduct of the isolation common to the rural experience on every level (families often living remotely, rural towns as isolated outposts, and rural communities often feeling forgotten by the government always stationed in urban settings). Indeed, in the days of colonialism and westward expansion, it was necessary for survival.

Now, I might argue, it seems to have become insidious. Self-reliance, of course, impacts people's willingness to seek help. Rural Americans are significantly more likely to use their emergency department than a general practitioner, suggesting that they tend to seek care when necessary rather than prophylactically. Research shows that there are higher incidences of preventable colorectal and cervical cancers and that individuals in rural communities are far less likely to undergo screenings. Indeed, Spleen, Lengerich, Camacho, and Vanderpool (2014, pp. 79–88) found that "residence in a rural area indicates an increased risk for health care avoidance" and that rural individuals were 1.7 times more likely to report medical avoidance of some sort. Whereas we often rightly attribute this finding to a lack of access to medical care, I would also suggest that some of the disparity can be attributed to attitude. Given that privacy and confidentiality are harder to maintain in small communities (more on that in the next section), we can easily understand why rural individuals—striving for self-reliance—may avoid the providers who are available to help them. This finding suggests that our task as rural providers, or providers serving rural people, is not only to make services more widely available, but also to address the cultural characteristics serving as barriers to access to those services (Warshaw, 2017).

Self-reliance is also a prominent cultural value among men in America and, more specifically, men in rural communities (Judd et al., 2006). "Whatever pressure discourages men to ask for help for physical pain is exponentially worse when it comes to psychological pain" (Plank, 2019, p. 245). Plank (2019, p. 245) goes on to explain that "the more you cling to unrealistic definitions of masculinity, the less likely you are to seek the support you need."

Farmers, ranchers, loggers, and miners have had to develop the ability to manage through the tough seasons, the droughts, and the floods, but rarely have they fostered an emotional or psychological resilience. Often survival, for these folks, takes the shape of stoicism. As one logger recently explained to me when I was attempting to get him in for a consultation at his wife's request, "I don't got time for no feelings." Indeed, a strong adherence to traditional masculine traits is demonstrably linked to poorer health outcomes. Unsurprisingly, self-reliance has one of the strongest correlations to this effect (Plank, 2019).

Rugged Individualism

Rugged individualism—frontier-speak for self-reliance—has its roots in the earliest settlers of our country. Every Sunday, our local paper prints photographic announcements of the community's recent births. Photos of adorable tiny babies, wrapped in blankets and adorned with bows and caps, are accompanied by their name, date of birth, and parent's names. This past week, the following babies were born: Brysen Jay Wayne, Blake William, Kaden Scott, Crew Ezekiel, Brighton Mia Dae, Ellis Marie, Marik Joel, and Hadassah Ruth. The children who live in my neighborhood are named Alina, Gracyn, Clay, River, Skyluna, Sonali, Ammirah, and Spiro. Research has shown that individuals striving for individualism are more likely to select uncommon (or even made up) names for their children. Rugged individualism, a phrase coined by Herbert Hoover, has long been associated with the Republican ideals of smaller government and less governmental involvement. Indeed, in areas with greater individualism, there is often greater support for Republican candidates. Rugged individualism champions less government intervention (Bialik, 2018), weighs effort more heavily than luck, and believes in the necessity of self-defense and "manifest destiny" (Bazzi, Fiszbein, & Gebresilasse, 2017).

A brief scan of any electoral map depicts this trend. While rugged individualism is common particularly amongst frontier communities, more conservative political viewpoints have been shown to be consistently pervasive in rural regions. What is even more evident is rural America's dissatisfaction with Washington politics. As a generality, rural Americans tend to feel overlooked and mis- or underrepresented in federal government. They do not feel understood and feel as if, geographically and psychologically, they are far from their representatives. Robert Wuthnow says, "The basis of small-town life is not only that it is 'rural' but that it is small, which means what happens is close enough to witness firsthand and to experience intimately enough to understand and have some hope of influencing" (2019, p. 98). Rural Americans, who are recognized when they go to do their banking and whose kids' soccer coach is also their dentist, were often cited as saying things like "remember the little man." That is not to say that rural Americans have a distorted sense of their own importance, but rather that the experience of living in a small community can create a reality for individuals that is not reflected in the greater American vision. In towns where city hall meetings are attended by regular folk and state representatives are chimney sweeps and schoolteachers, people feel comforted by their engagement and anxious about the overreach of politicians in Washington who don't know them, let alone understand them. So, whereas many urban Americans were scratching their heads, wondering how rural Americans could vote so frequently against their own self-interests, it is the appeal of small government that excites rural voters. (See Figure 4.2.)

Conservative Values

As town size decreases, the likelihood of being pro-life increases. This trend might be partially responsible for the high turnout for Republican politicians as many pro-life individuals indicated that this sole issue would be enough to determine their voting. Similarly, the sparser a community's population is, the more likely they are to support constitutional bans on gay marriage. Both of

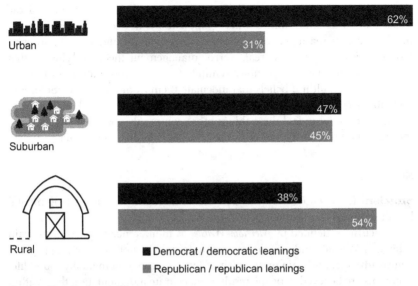

Figure 4.2 Urban-Suburban-Rural Divide in Politics
Source: Parker et al. (2018)

these moral issues are rooted in conservative religious beliefs, which are more common in rural areas. Further, research suggests that knowing someone who is different from yourself helps reduce bias and prejudice. As a Jewish individual who resides in a community plagued by anti-Semitism, I have been struck by how this phenomenon not only manifests but is self-perpetuating. As someone whose last name does not reveal my Jewish identity at first glance, I have refrained from disclosing that aspect of my identity for fear that someone I may confide in holds a very different belief than I suspect. The less I feel inclined to reveal my identity, the less likely someone else would be to have an experience that might actually reduce prejudices. We know this happens with abortion (the numbers of women who have abortions simply don't add up when you survey people about knowing someone who had an abortion) and perhaps with gay individuals who have remained closeted. Of course, we know that rural communities tend to have less diversity (and, anecdotally, that individuals with such differences—e.g., gay or transgender or atheist—might be inclined to move away from their rural roots, toward cities where they may find greater acceptance) (Housing Assistance Council, 2012). Accordingly, individuals living in rural communities are less likely to encounter those who are different from them (or who, say, have had an abortion—or are willing to talk about it) and, as a result, may hold greater prejudice and/or suspicions.

Furthermore, homosexuality and abortion are not both also biblically "wrong"; they challenge the very aspects of life that are required for perpetuation of the species. In rural communities, where population is in decline, severe weather incidents are increasingly common, and people feel misunderstood and overlooked, existential threat is real. Terror management theory teaches us that individuals who have been subtly reminded of their mortality tend to cling more tightly to cultural beliefs that inoculate them from those fears (Solomon, Greenberg, & Pyszczynski, 2015). It is possible that individuals who live in rural communities tend to feel these things more commonly and, consequently, are more inclined to cling tighter to the beliefs that help them feel better.

Stoicism

Stoicism has been demonstrated to be the largest barrier to seeking mental health services (Warbinton, 2019).

"Stoicism" is defined by *Merriam-Webster* as indifference to pleasure or pain (Merriam-Webster, n.d.). Stoicism as a philosophy entails overcoming psychological adversity and pain in the spirit of living a more judgmentally sound life. Emotions are believed to be the result of inaccurate judgment and, thus, within our control. Stoicism underlies many of today's pop psychology mantras such as "happiness is a choice" and lies at the heart of cognitive behavioral therapy's theoretical understanding that individuals can identify, understand the ineffective origins of, and ultimately change one's emotional response. Stoicism is prominent in American culture and hailed as the "ultimate mind hack" by many (Wallace, 2014).

Stoicism, in my experience, is not so much the actual indifference to pleasure or pain as a series of mental gymnastics one might take to convince oneself that the emotionally provoking stimuli has no bearing on thought and logic. Stoicism is noticing the thing that has transpired but refusing to succumb to the feeling it may trigger. Individuals in rural communities are particularly suited to holding stoic attitudes and beliefs. Natural disasters, limited community resources, harsher weather, poverty, underemployment, etc. all make it a challenge to live in a rural community. That is not to say that urban environs don't come with their own set of challenges, but as I've argued up to this point, rural life can be hard. Picture a farmer in Nebraska whose crops have recently been decimated by a pest he believed to have protected them from with chemical deterrents. Imagine a laborer in Eastern Michigan who awakes to three feet of snow and a plow truck that won't start. With no public transportation and county resources that won't get his road cleared until the afternoon, he is without a means of getting to work. What about a family in Mississippi who have dedicated years of work to re-establishing a family tobacco farm hit hard by flooding caused by a recent hurricane? Or the small family logging operation in Wyoming whose forests are destroyed by wildfire? Individuals whose livelihoods depend on natural resources are powerless when it comes to the force of Mother Nature. They have no choice, really, but to accept the consequences of the disaster and rebuild or move on. Stoicism, then, is perhaps adaptive in such situations. Just as someone in a city can do little about frantically running down the stairs to catch the train only to hit the doors as they close, individuals in rural communities are frequently faced with adversity over which they have little control. In rural communities, however, the frequency and intensity with which these issues are faced is thought to be greater.

A combination of a lack of adequate resources to treat struggles, a bootstraps mentality, and some of the other cultural forces (low health literacy, rugged individualism, and self-reliance) all perpetuate the emphasis placed on stoicism and, thus, its continuance as an important element of rural life.

Masculinity

A growing group of theorists are beginning to highlight the ways in which traditional patriarchal standards not only harm women but also have a deeply negative impact on men. In August 2018, the American Psychological Association produced a document titled "APA Guidelines for Psychological Practice with Boys and Men" (2018). In it, authors cited several ways in which boys and men have a harsher reality than girls and women (including higher rates of physical health problems and quality-of-life issues). The APA defines masculinity as adhering to a particular set of norms and value-based behaviors, such as anti-femininity, achievement, eschewal of the appearance of weakness, adventure, risk, and violence (2018, p. 3). Research cited by the APA also demonstrates that individuals who adhere more strictly to masculine codes of conduct are less likely to feel free to explore emotional vulnerabilities in the spirit of creating deep and meaningful adult connections. Despite men suiciding at rates that far surpass their female peers, fewer men report struggles with depression. The more one adheres to traditional masculine roles, one could hypothesize, the more likely they are to suffer in silence. Indeed, health-related help-seeking behavior is negatively associated with masculine ideals. Of course, such values are toxic to women as well as men. Women in relationships that emphasize traditional roles and in which the male adheres to traditional male values are more likely to be depressed. We also know that such ideals are linked to the threat of domestic violence and power imbalances. For younger males, allegiance to traditional masculinity leads to increases in bullying, poor academic performance, and sexual harassment. In short, being aligned with traditional masculinity is bad for everyone's (physical and psychological) health.

Traditional masculinity is, of course, alive and well in America, but it thrives in the frontier (Gurr, 2015, pp. 31–44). That is, of course, the homeland of the Marlboro Man, a quintessentially masculine character if there ever was one. Readers from urban locations may find my discussions of masculinity dated, or even ignorant. Much has shifted for men, particularly in urban regions, in terms of appropriate and acceptable expressions of gender. However, rural culture often lags behind, and gender norms are no exception.

Not only are traditional masculine norms alive and well in the rural West, there is even a term for it: frontier masculinity. Frontier masculinity combines rugged individualism, self-reliance, and a strong work ethic to create profoundly limiting expectations for men and boys (Michelson, 2017).

Suppression of vulnerability is perhaps one of the most devastating elements common to a culture that emphasizes masculinity. And (and this is important) masculinity does not merely apply to men. Women who are taught to value masculine traits suffer the same side effects of this emphasis: a lack of empathy, a lack of vulnerability, and, accordingly, disconnection and less intimacy.

Stigma

Stigma is a "mark of disgrace associated with a particular circumstance, quality, or person" (Oxford English Dictionary, 2019). Stigma is assigning a negative valence to a person based on a particular attribute. Mental health stigma—viewing a person negatively due to their mental health issues or concerns—unfortunately, is not a phenomenon unique to rural communities. Evidence of mental health stigma is easier to note than the stigma itself. Individuals in need of treatment wait, on average, eight to ten years before receiving treatment. Also, only half of the adults in the country in need of mental health services actually receive them. However, rural communities and their members face increased hardship when it comes to experiencing and overcoming mental health stigma.

Given what I have already described about common cultural values of rural Americans, hardships, and the greater incidence of certain afflictions in rural America, it is not hard to see how mental health stigma would be even more relevant in small towns and insular communities than in urban and suburban settings. Stigma can exist in the private or public realm and comprises of stereotypes, prejudice, and discrimination. Stereotypes are collectively agreed-upon notions of what a particular type of person should look, act, seem, or think like. Stereotypes occur as a byproduct of our brains working hard to organize a very confusing world. Prejudice, of course, occurs when a negative valence is assigned to a particular stereotype, and a negative reaction ensues. Discrimination is when negative reactions or behaviors arise from the prejudice. Self-stigmatization occurs when individuals have internalized such societal forces and come to isolate, distort their self-perceptions, or remove themselves from public life as a result of their beliefs. Stigma, inherently, is rooted in shame.

Individuals in rural communities, frequently with lower health literacy, tend not to have information about mental illness. They are also less likely to be exposed, socially or casually, to mental health providers because there are simply fewer of them in their regions. Moreover, they are more likely than their urban counterparts to suffer in silence as a result of these factors. Accordingly, stereotypes are more likely to be rural people's reference points for information about mental illness than firsthand knowledge of someone with such a struggle. Because stereotypes of mental illness and individuals with mental illness are often inaccurate, prejudices are more likely to populate the collective mind-set. Prejudices often include notions that individuals with mental illness are malevolent, unpredictable, and to be feared. Recent narratives in the media regarding mass shootings conflate violence with mental illness and serve to reaffirm societal fears about the mentally unwell despite ample evidence to demonstrate that individuals with mental illness who receive treatment are no more violent than any other person. Mental health stigma not only keeps people from being forthcoming about their struggles but also perpetuates these false beliefs. High levels of stigma are correlated with decreased help-seeking behavior and more shame and subsequent masking of difficulties. It is a rather terrible feedback loop.

One data point that suggests that mental health stigma is a greater force than an individual's need to seek services is the suicide rates in rural communities, particularly among males. I am not picking on men exclusively, but rather highlighting another way in which our anti-vulnerable, stoic society makes it especially hard for men to reach out for help. Men don't ask for directions. They also don't ask for mental health help.

We know that men do not live as long as women. We know that single, widowed, and divorced men don't live as long as married men. We also know that social isolation is associated with increased mortality. That is, the less socially connected one is, the more likely they are to die earlier—regardless of the cause of death. Despite small communities often being a source of neighborliness and communal feelings, ranchers and farmers often work in isolation, with many reporting their wife as their sole confidant.

Ranchers—accustomed to living self-sufficiently and stoically—often struggle with acknowledging they need, and then asking for, help. Older rural Americans may also struggle with the idea that they should even need to ask for help. A study done at the Wake Forest School of Medicine surveyed 478 adults over the age of 60 about barriers to mental health treatment. The most commonly cited personal belief was "I should not need help" (Brenes, Danhauer, Lyles, Hogan, & Miller, 2015, pp. 1172–1178).

Stigma seems to increase as rurality increases. Further, men in the most rural settings have higher rates of depression. Of course, we have reviewed ad nauseum how many additional barriers there are to accessing mental health treatment in rural America. But because of a combination of all these factors, despite having increased symptomology, they are actually less likely to get the help that they need.

Stigma not only serves as a barrier to individuals struggling with mental illness, but it also can distort perceptions about the efficacy and importance of treatment, thus decreasing the likelihood someone will seek services.

Acculturation

"Acculturation comprehends those phenomena which result when groups of individuals having different cultures come into continuous first-hand contact, with subsequent changes in the original cultural patterns of either or both groups" (Redfield, Linton, & Herskovits, 1936, p. 149). Of course, while changes may occur in both groups, the majority of the change is seen in the nondominant group. These changes often come with a biproduct of stress, or perhaps even distress. Rural Americans may undergo acculturation in one of three ways. First, rural-born Americans who have relocated to cities or suburban locales may undergo profound change as a result of their new embeddedness. Second, as a result of urbanization, small-town growth (particularly in the frontier and recreation areas), and suburban expansion, rural Americans are likely to experience pressures to modernize or urbanize themselves and their culture. Finally, individuals living in rural communities may have their origins in cities far away. These individuals ("exurbanites") often flee the city for a different pace of life but may struggle to fully adopt the cultural norms of their new rural communities (Castle, 1995).

Acculturation is a process typically believed to comprise three stages: contact, conflict, and adaptation. Acculturation can have gradients of effect on an individual, in part depending on their response to the dominant culture's permitted influence over them.

I sit on the board of a regional nonprofit in Northwest Montana. The nonprofit's mission is organized around wilderness access and stewardship, and the board is largely comprised of wilderness enthusiasts. At a recent board meeting, a discussion ensued about the benefits of selling our products on Amazon.com. Several board members rejected the proposition vehemently, arguing about the deleterious effects online marketplaces have had on local brick-and-mortar-shops (one board member being an owner of such a business). As tensions flared, one particularly astute board member attempted to reframe the discussion as a philosophical, and perhaps generational, one. She posed a request: can everyone please put their cell phones on the table? Of the 12 members of the board, seven produced smartphones, three produced flip phones, and two produced no phone at all. Cell phones, at least in urban areas of the US, are ubiquitous. Not so in Montana. Or at least not in that board room. I do not have cellular service at my home, and a few miles beyond my house, residents are still relying on dial-up internet service. There are many places in Montana and other rural parts of the country still shielded from cell towers and connectivity. And, of course, there are still holdouts against this form of technological advancement.

In Berry's model of strategies of acculturation, acculturation can be thought of as a dialectic between integration and maintenance of the original and new cultures (2006). The board members without phones were, perhaps, holding tightly to their culture of origin—their rural roots—and rejecting the forces of the urbanization occurring in small towns across America. Such individuals, per Berry's model, are at risk of experiencing separation from those of the dominant culture. These individuals might not be amenable, say, to telehealth or anything even that sounds too modern. Perhaps, one could argue, those with flip phones are striving for integration in which they can maintain their rural cultural values while adapting to the dominant culture overwhelming their neighborhoods. Finally, those of us with smartphones, if we want to see this metaphor through, might have assimilated into the dominant or new culture, letting go of our rural roots entirely.

Levels of, and the process by which one goes through, acculturation are important for any provider working with rural folk. Assessing for the degree to which a person has assimilated to or integrated into the dominant culture or is marginalized or separated from either the dominant culture or their culture of origin is essential in the practice of culturally competent psychotherapy and assessment. This process should be no different when working with people from rural cultures and communities.

References

American Psychological Association, Boys and Men Guidelines Group. (2018). *APA guidelines for psychological practice with boys and men*. Retrieved October 21, 2019, from www.apa.org/about/policy/psychological-practice-boys-men-guidelines.pdf

Bazzi, S., Fiszbein, M., & Gebresilasse, M. (2017). *Frontier culture: The roots and persistence of "rugged individualism" in the United States*. NBER Working Paper No. 23997. https://doi.org/10.3386/w23997

Berry, J. W. (2006). Contexts of acculturation. In D. L. Sam & J. W. Berry (Eds.), *The Cambridge handbook of acculturation psychology* (pp. 27–42). Cambridge: Cambridge University Press

Bialik, K. (2018). Key findings about American life in urban, suburban and rural areas. *Fact Tank: News in the Numbers*. Retrieved December 19, 2019, from www.pewresearch.org/fact-tank/2018/05/22/key-findings-about-american-life-in-urban-suburban-and-rural-areas/

Brenes, G. A., Danhauer, S. C., Lyles, M. F., Hogan, P. E., & Miller, M. E. (2015). Barriers to mental health treatment in rural older adults. *The American Journal of Geriatric Psychiatry, 23*(11), 1172–1178.

Bushy, A. (1990). Rural US women: Traditions and transitions affecting health care. *Health Care for Women International, 11*(4), 503–513.

Castle, E. N. (1995). *The changing American countryside: Rural people and places*. Lawrence: University Press of Kansas.

DelReal, J. A., & Clement, S. (2017, June 17). Rural divide. *The Washington Post*. Retrieved December 19, 2019, from www.washingtonpost.com/graphics/2017/national/rural-america/?utm_term=.a8249a4342b4

Gurr, B. (2015). Masculinity, race, and the (re?)imagined American frontier. In B. Gurr (Ed.), *Race, gender, and sexuality in post-apocalyptic TV and film* (pp. 31–44). New York: Palgrave Macmillan.

Housing Assistance Council. (2012). Race & ethnicity in rural America. *Rural Research Briefs, 3*, 1283–1288.

Jameson, J. P., & Blank, M. B. (2007). The role of clinical psychology in rural mental health services: Defining problems and developing solutions. *Clinical Psychology: Science and Practice, 14*(3), 283–298. https://doi.org/10.1111/j.1468-2850.2007.00089.x

Judd, F., Jackson, H., Komiti, A., Murray, G., Fraser, C., Grieve, A., & Gomez, R. (2006). Help-seeking by rural residents for mental health problems: The importance of agrarian values. *Australian and New Zealand Journal of Psychiatry, 40*(9), 769–776.

Merriam-Webster. (n.d.). Stoicism. In *The Merriam-Webster.com Dictionary*. Retrieved December 22, 2019, from www.merriam-webster.com/dictionary/stoicism

Michelson, C. (2017). *Protectors of hegemonic masculinity: An analysis of gun legislation and masculinity*. (Undergraduate thesis). Retrieved December 19, 2019, from ScholarWorks at University of Montana. (162).

Oxford University Press. (2019). Stigma. In *Oxford English Dictionary*. Oxford: Oxford University Press.

Parker, K., Horowitz, J., Brown, A., Fry, R., Cohn, D. V., & Igielnik, R. (2018). *What unites and divides urban, suburban, and rural communities* [Chart]. Pew Research Center.

Plank, L. (2019). *For the love of men: A new vision for mindful masculinity*. New York: St. Martin's Press.

Redfield, R., Linton, R., & Herskovits, M. J. (1936). Memorandum for the study of acculturation. *American Anthropologist, 38*, 149–152.

Spleen, A. M., Lengerich, E. J., Camacho, F. T., & Vanderpool, R. C. (2014). Health care avoidance among rural populations: Results from a nationally representative survey. *The Journal of Rural Health: Official Journal of the American Rural Health Association and the National Rural Health Care Association, 30*(1), 79–88. https://doi.org/10.1111/jrh.12032

Solomon, S., Greenberg, J., & Pyszczynski, T. (2015). *The worm at the core: On the role of death in life*. New York: Random House.

Wagenfeld, M. O. (2003). A snapshot of rural and frontier America. In B. H. Stamm (Ed.), *Rural behavioral health care: An interdisciplinary guide* (pp. 33–40). Washington, DC: American Psychological Association.

Wallace, L. (2014, December 24). Indifference is a power. *Aeon*. Retrieved December 19, 2019, from https://aeon.co/essays/why-stoicism-is-one-of-the-best-mind-hacks-ever-devised

Warbinton, E. (2019). *Mental health in rural areas: To what extent do stoicism, stigma, and community affiliation predict mental health help-seeking behaviors?* (Doctoral dissertation). Retrieved October 23, 2019, from SHAREOK. (8451)

Warshaw, R. (2017, October 31). Health disparities affect millions in rural U.S. communities. *AAMCNews*. Retrieved December 19, 2019, from www.aamc.org/news-insights/health-disparities-affect-millions-rural-us-communities

Wuthnow, R. (2019). *The left behind: Decline and rage in small-town America*. Princeton, NJ: Princeton University Press.

5 Health in Rural America

In many ways, the cultural values still honored in rural communities are worthy tenets by which to live. However, sometimes the cultural norms valued more commonly in rural America create a bind for its residents, complicating their already difficult lives. Further, many of the quintessential elements of rural life—distance to a major metropolitan area; a more agrarian, rustic, or industrial lifestyle—and factors that frequently accompany those characteristics serve as barriers to the mental (and physical) wellness of its people.

According to the National Alliance on Mental Illness (2019), approximately one in five Americans, regardless of their rurality, will deal with mental illness at some point in their lifetimes. Rurality is not demonstrably linked to higher rates of mental illness. It is, however, associated with poorer overall psychological outcomes. In short, perhaps through some combination of cultural, structural, and practical factors, rural life seems to put more time between the onset of the problem and the resolution of those symptoms through the benefits of adequate treatment (Reschovsky & Staiti, 2005).

It seems several key factors lead to more deleterious effects for rural Americans when it comes to their mental health. First, rural Americans have a higher incidence of chronic disease, disability, alcoholism, and other illnesses that often go hand in hand with mental illness. Second, access issues (such as distance and availability) prevent timely mental and physical healthcare (Gale & Lambert, 2006). Third, socioeconomic barriers such as inadequate insurance, poverty, and instability serve to limit treatment and compliance. Finally, cultural factors play a role in downplaying the importance of mental wellness, lower health literacy rates, and patterns of use.

As I have previously noted, we must also be careful to remember that rural communities are diverse, and rural America is not a homogeneous group. One would be well served to research and understand the community in which one practices, its psychological landscape, rates of incidence and prevalence, rates of usage, needs, and resiliency factors.

Prevalence Rates

Prevalence rates for mental illness appear to be similar in rural and urban dwellers. However, when it comes to severity, suicide, substance use, and outcomes, there is evidence to suggest that rural Americans face harsher effects (HHS, n.d.). There are certain areas in which rural Americans clearly fare far worse than their urban counterparts. Suicide rates amongst rural dwellers are significantly higher, with frontier states (Montana, Wyoming, Alaska) often ranking among the highest. New Jersey, one of the least rural states in the union, has a suicide rate of 8.3 deaths per 100,000 of the total population, whereas Montana, one of the more rural states, has a rate of 28.9. Suicide reflects not only the prevalence of mental health struggles but also access to lethal means and environmental factors. We know that suicide rates fall when living conditions improve. Theorists speculate that "deaths of despair" are often linked to declining economic and social conditions amongst victims (Case & Deaton, 2017). Since living conditions in rural communities tend to be harsher than in urban areas, it is safe to speculate that the harsh realities of rurality impact one's likelihood to die by suicide. What's more, many rural areas, in which people are dependent on hunting for food and fun, allow greater access to guns, one of the most lethal means one can use to attempt suicide.

Though there is variability in findings, rural Americans also appear to have higher rates of drug use and addiction (HHS, n.d.). You would have to have been living under a rock for the past few years not to have heard about the opioid epidemic plaguing rural America, but the drug and alcohol problems didn't start there.

Children in frontier and rural areas fare far worse than their urbanized peers. They have babies earlier, smoke more often, have increased access to illicit drugs, are often under- or uninsured (15%), and are coping with poverty at higher rates (23.2%). Further, children in rural areas face even more obstacles to accessing mental health services based on geographical and supply limitations. While it does not appear to be the case that rural youth have a higher incidence of mental health disturbance, the access issues seem to negatively impact their mental wellness.

Amongst all individuals surveyed for the 2014 update of the Rural-Urban Chartbook, major depression was found to be most common in micropolitan areas (counties with populations of from 10,000 to 49,999) in the West. The highest percentage of men and women who had serious psychological distress in the past 30 days was in the most rural counties of the South. Rates of adolescent depression are higher in urban or non-metro counties. Some researchers suggest that rural rates of depression are significantly higher due to increased isolation and unpredictable incomes, as well as a lack of and limited access to mental health resources.

Where there appear to be some differences in mental illness prevalence rates amongst rural and urban people, the biggest disparity appears in regard to outcomes. Depressed individuals tend to attempt suicide more often in rural areas, and individuals with severe mental illness tend to be more reliant on inpatient treatment options and tend to have greater symptom severity in rural communities. Rural individuals with substance use issues fare worse than their urban counterparts. Additionally, women in rural areas seem to experience (or at least report) more depression than their urban counterparts. Finally, rural elderly persons face many of the same risks and illnesses as their urban counterparts but experience increased barriers to services such as travel distances, lack of affordable options, and lack of services. Despite all of these variables, rural physicians detect fewer cases of depression than urban doctors. This may not only skew the data but also suggests a great need for increased awareness and diagnostic training (HHS, n.d.).

There are a few other concerning elements of rural life that likely impact mental wellness. Individuals in rural areas are more likely to smoke and have sedentary lifestyles. As Mary Wakefield said, "The bucolic myth of the fit, trim farmer is often just that, a myth, because many individuals who live in rural areas are not farmers, and many of them are not trim" (Merchant, Coussens, & Gilbert, 2006). Obesity increases the farther you live from a city. Incidence of chronic illness and disability status rates suggest that those living in rural areas are not only coping with environmental and societal stressors but perhaps individual worries as well.

Nearly 20% of American adults suffer with some sort of mental illness. Approximately 67% of those have received treatment, according to a study conducted by the NIMH in 2017. Women and older adults are more likely to receive treatment for mental health issues. What's more, 17.7% of rural Americans have a disability, compared to an 11.8% rate of disability in urban metropolitan areas. This is striking when we realize that rural areas are far less likely to have the assets required to adequately support a disabled individual.

Drugs

Presently, drug and alcohol misuse appear to be endemic in our society. At press time, opioids are killing more Americans than motor vehicle accidents (Monnat & Rigg, 2016). Opioids are not the only illicit substance threatening the well-being of our communities and our people (rural and urban alike). Methamphetamine use and heroin addiction, in addition to alcohol misuse, have plagued our rural communities for decades. In 2014, research conducted by the Centers for Disease Control showed that rates of overdose by heroin were higher in rural areas than urban ones (Wuthnow, 2019).

Usage can be influenced at three primary levels. On the macro level, social context affects both the availability of drugs and the norms surrounding usage. Institutional and cultural stressors (such as deprivation, poverty, etc.) have an impact on the overall forces affecting availability and standards of behavior. Next, the local context contributes to the vulnerabilities and propensities of the individuals within the group. Family stressors (such as unemployment) and composition (such as single-parent households, young parents, etc.) can all impact one's propensity for use. Peer pressure and one's social status affect individual behaviors on many levels, and drug behavior is no exception. Finally, individual characteristics such as genetic predispositions, attachment status, and personality, combined with the unique characteristics of the actual drug (numbing, stimulating) affect the likelihood that someone will not only use but continue to use (Keyes, Cerdá, Brady, Havens, & Galea, 2014). (See Figure 5.1.)

Despite the increased media attention paid to prescription drug misuse in rural communities, evidence does not support the premise that rural individuals are abusing drugs at rates higher than their suburban and urban peers (Borders & Wen, 2018). Rurality on the whole, as it turns out, is not a reliable correlate to drug misuse, particularly opioids. Economic distress and access to opioids appear to be the key indicators of opioid-related deaths in America (Monnat, 2019). What does appear to be true, notably, is that "the highest drug mortality rates are disproportionately concentrated in economically distressed mining and service sector dependent counties with high exposure to prescription opioids and fentanyl" (Monnat, 2019). Opioids are not used with greater frequency in all rural areas but certainly in some. Individuals who have more physically demanding jobs often suffer from more chronic pain. Individuals with more chronic pain are more likely to be prescribed, and potentially addicted to, opioid pain killers. Accordingly, impoverished areas in which jobs

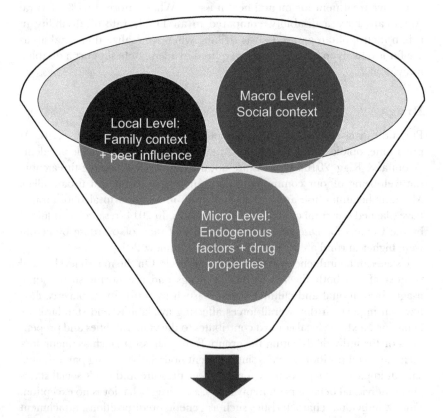

Figure 5.1 Illicit Drug Use

are more likely to be physically hazardous (such as services and mining communities) that also have access to prescription drugs are experiencing higher rates of opioid-related deaths. Specifically, Southwest Pennsylvania, Central Appalachia, Central Florida, and the inland Northwest had higher rates of opioid-related deaths. Marketing campaigns have been demonstrated to be significantly more aggressive in rural communities (particularly in Appalachia) than in other regions. With the one exception being nonrural Florida, the highest rates of opioid prescriptions appear in rural America (Monnat, 2018).

Because many people, and rural more than urban, are apt to only seek services from a primary care provider, emotional pain masquerading as physical pain may be misunderstood, misdiagnosed, and mistreated. If this is the case with individuals whose chronic physical pain is a manifestation of trauma, depression, or despair, it is possible that the treatment—which is aimed at numbing (an avoidance strategy)—will produce dependency in much the same way that individuals who avoid their psychological pain through video games or exercise may fail to develop coping strategies to effectively manage (rather than simply eschew) their distress. The difference, of course, is that individuals who utilize opioids to numb themselves are employing an addictive and deadly weapon as an avoidance strategy.

There is evidence to suggest that individuals in areas with limited service options are more likely to die drug-related deaths (Monnat, 2018). Despite there being notably stronger social networks in many rural communities, treatment options matter. In fact, stronger social networks may actually increase rates of sharing prescription drugs with nonpatients. Moreover, friends are not professionals, and families are not counselors.

Treatment options in rural areas, despite rather similar rates of use, are, as we might expect, disproportionately low. Treatment facilities in rural and nonmetropolitan areas are limited in number and services offered. Many do not offer detoxification, transitional housing, or partial hospitalization options. Rural alcohol users are much more likely than city dwellers to have to depend on outpatient treatment, even though specialized providers may be unavailable in their particular community (Dixon & Chartier, 2016).

So, while the opioid epidemic may not be disproportionately affecting rural America on the whole, many rural Americans are particularly susceptible to its devastating effects (Maine Rural Health Research Center, 2016; Monnat, 2018). Opioids, designed to numb physical (and emotional) pain, are unsurprisingly common in areas that experience greater levels of psychological and economic distress. Opioids were designed by pharmaceutical researchers to provide individuals with chronic pain a refuge from their agony. Through the process of numbing, individuals whose suffering is otherwise unending experience temporary relief.

Deaths of Despair

Late in the last century, researchers noted an uptick in mortality rates from alcohol-related liver disease, suicide, and drug overdoses. As illness from cancer and heart disease and infant mortality rates fell, "deaths of despair" or "diseases of despair" were on the rise. Such deaths are believed to be the culminative outcome of long-term disadvantage (including poverty, low educational attainment, etc.). According to a study by the Brookings Institute, deaths of despair, particularly among middle-aged individuals with lower educational attainment, have risen precipitously since the early 1990s. In comparison, rates among those with some college or a college degree have risen far less steeply. The more a county experienced economic distress, the more likely they were to see higher rates of deaths of despair. Indeed, poverty and substance use often go hand in hand, with each strengthening the other's grasp. Drug misuse, which can lead to incarceration or citations (which can further poverty), can be cyclical and unending (Case & Deaton, 2017).

As stated earlier, overdose from opioids is but one of the deaths of despair, alcohol-related ailments and overdose being another. (The third, suicide, will be covered at length in the next section.) Whereas there are no general differences between rural and urban Americans in terms of alcohol use, there are subtle differences that are worth exploring. First, rural Americans tend to binge drink at higher rates than their urban and suburban peers. They are also more likely to have a diagnosed alcohol use disorder, according to the DSM-V criteria. Drinkers in the Midwest and West seem to have the highest rates of alcohol-related disorders.

In rural communities, Blacks tend to have the lowest alcohol-use rates, whereas American Indians/Alaska Natives tend to have the highest. American Indians/Alaska Natives reportedly drink the most frequently of any ethnic group in the US. American Indians living on reservations reported drinking large quantities with low frequency. That is, they are more likely to drink more in a sitting but tend to do it less often. Statistically speaking, Southerners drink the least. One reason for this may be culturally insulating factors such as religiosity, which is higher in the South and is linked to abstinence.

Economically disadvantaged areas tend to have higher rates of alcohol consumption, whereas economically advantaged areas see higher usage among minors. In general, rural areas have higher rates of underage drinking than cities. Indeed, as some of my clients would tell you, "there's just nothing else to do" in small towns and rural regions.

There were 4,935 alcohol-impaired-driving fatalities in rural areas in 2017 and 5,702 on urban roads. Given that the percentage of the US population living in rural areas is significantly less than the population living in urban areas, these numbers suggest that rural drivers tend to die more frequently from alcohol impairment. While these numbers are on the decline (and urban rates are actually rising), it still reflects a significant impact on rural communities. In rural areas, the age of the individual involved in the alcohol-impaired fatal crash is, on average, slightly younger (between 21 and 24) than urban age trends (25 to 34). These statistics are likely impacted by the greater distances between home and bar/party in rural areas, the lower age restrictions for drivers in rural areas, and increased risk-taking behavior in rural areas (National Center for Statistics and Analysis, 2019).

Deaths of despair, or really any death in a rural community, is likely to be felt with more profound reverberations than in metropolitan communities. That is not to say, of course, that the death of a rural American is more significant, objectively, than that of any city dweller, but rather that the ripples from such deaths are likely to be felt in tightly knit communities with greater intensity and with longer duration (Wuthnow, 2019). Drug deaths also affect the community's identity and threaten to demoralize the culture of a small town where many, if not all, members of a community are likely to have some tie to the individual who died. Unfortunately, in towns consistently plagued by poverty, unemployment, and low educational attainment affected by urbanization in irreversible ways, hope is a rare commodity.

Suicide

Suicide is a very real problem in rural communities.[1] Of course, suicide, one of the top ten leading causes of death in the United States, is an issue everywhere. It is also one of the aforementioned deaths of despair contributing to a rising mortality rate, particularly for men in America. For mental health professionals (outside those working with eating disordered patients), it is likely the greatest threat to our patient population. It is also one of the only leading causes of death seen as entirely preventable. As such, suicide, as a phenomenon is worthy of our attention, despite how difficult a subject it is to research, reckon with, and talk about.

Suicide rates are higher in rural areas. (See Figure 5.2.) Across all ages and nearly all races, ethnicities, and genders, people complete suicide more frequently in rural communities than in cities and suburbs. While suicide rates have been higher in rural areas for many decades, starting around the recession (2007–2008), the gap grew. In the past few decades, suicide rates have increased significantly in rural regions (as well as in the US on the whole), with

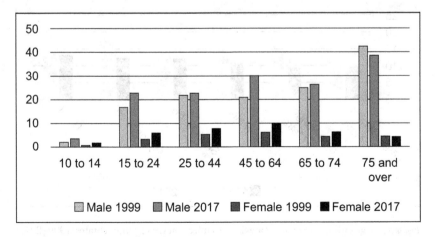

Figure 5.2 Suicide Rates, by Sex and Age Group, United States (1999–2017)

particular areas (namely, the Western US, the Ozarks, and Appalachia) seeing even greater increases than others (Steelesmith et al., 2019).

According to the Centers for Disease Control's (2018a) longitudinal, cross-sectional study of suicide trends between 2001 and 2015, non-Hispanic Whites and American Indian/Alaska Native males have the highest rates of suicide. Men die by suicide with a much higher incidence than women, and men older than 75 have the highest rates of any age group. Liz Plank (2019), in her book *For the Love of Men,* addresses the profound bind that leaves many men feeling as if they have no choice but suicide. She explains that men who are more closely aligned with masculine ideals are at a higher risk for suicide than male peers who are less bought into the myth of masculinity. According to Plank,

> Because we often conflate male independence and self-reliance with male isolation, the men who need the most help often look like the men who don't. That's because the characteristics that are associated with the highest risk of suicide for men also happen to be the ones that we put on a pedestal.
>
> (2019, p. 245)

Historical data suggests that women in the rural West die by suicide at a rate three times higher than women living in urban settings (Steelesmith et al., 2019). (See Figure 5.3.) Women ages 45 through 64 have the highest suicide rate, and girls ages 10 through 14 saw the sharpest increase in suicide between 1999 and 2017. Many theorists and researchers believe that women complete suicide at lower rates than men for several reasons. First, women are less likely to use lethal means and are more likely to have an unsuccessful attempt. Second, women are far more likely to be diagnosed and treated by a mental

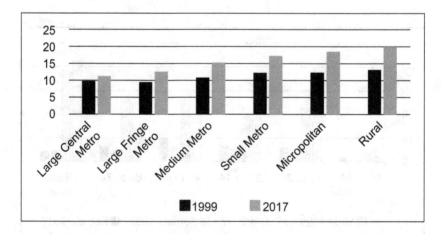

Figure 5.3 Age-Adjusted Suicide Rates by Urbanization Level, United States (1999–2017)

health professional for depression or anxiety. As a result, women are perhaps more likely to get the help they need for their suffering. Finally, women are not subjected to quite the same level of stigma around vulnerability as their male peers. This allows them to experience greater intimacy and connection, a prophylactic against suicide (National Center for Health Statistics, 2018). Some theorists have proposed that because women are more apt to use less violent means of suicide in their attempts, they may have less suicidal intent. Research conducted in 2000 (Denning, Conwell, King, & Cox, 2000) serves to dispel this myth—the type of method used by women is not indicative of any difference in suicidal intent.

One of the therapists who works in my group practice sent an email that read: "I have been working with a suicidal client who has access to lethal means and this week purchased some gun locks which I have stowed in the break room cabinet. Feel free to give them to clients as needed." Guns are the most frequently used weapon in a completed suicide.

Box 5.1

The CDC states: "Differences exist among those with and without mental health conditions. People without known mental health conditions were more likely to be male and to die by firearm."

Source: Centers for Disease Control and Prevention (2018a)

Firearms were, according to the CDC's study, the most commonly used method in successful suicides. In rural areas, the rates of suicide by firearm were nearly double those of urbanized areas. In fact, nearly 60% of all completed suicides in rural areas resulted from the use of a firearm. (The national percentage is closer to 51%.) Firearms are more than twice as likely to produce a completed suicide than the second most common suicide method: suffocation (Shenassa, Catlin, & Buka, 2003). Lethal ingestion of chemicals is the third most common method of suicide.

At least one research project, conducted in Maryland, has demonstrated that the use of firearms accounts for the difference between urban and rural suicide rates. Access to and availability of firearms in rural regions is significantly higher than in urban environs. According to a Pew Research poll, 46% of rural Americans own guns, compared to 28% of suburban Americans and 19% of urban dwellers. Individuals who reported growing up in a "rural" setting were more likely to have been raised in a home with at least one gun (72%), compared to only 39% of those raised in cities (Parker, Horowitz, Igielnik, Oliphant, & Brown, 2017). Perhaps, then, individuals in rural America die by suicide more frequently because they have greater access to lethal means. Despair and hope aside, the disparity comes down to a matter of access. In most cases, rural Americans have *less* access. When it comes to guns, unfortunately, they have more.

The frontier states see the highest suicide rates, with Wyoming, Alaska, and Montana often reporting the highest rates for any state in the country. In fact, this trend has been consistent and strong long enough to warrant many to nickname it the "suicide belt." Montana's suicide rate is 28.9 per 100,000 residents. In eight counties in Montana, between 2012 and 2016, the suicide rate was found to be over 30 per 100,000.

In fact, the most recent data show that Montana, Alaska, Wyoming, New Mexico, Idaho, Utah, and South Dakota, in that order, have the highest suicide rates in the country. West Virginia, Arkansas, Nevada, Colorado, and North Dakota are not far behind in their rates.

Countless studies have been conducted on suicide victims (using psychological autopsies), individuals who made suicide attempts, and nomothetic data studied by combing over statistics and trends. In short summary, here are some of the most significant risk factors for suicide: previous attempts; history of mental illness; lack of social support; hopelessness; intense, stressful life events; and access to lethal means. On the other hand, effective behavioral health interventions, connectedness to individuals and one's community, coping skills, meaning and purpose, and cultural or religious values that condemn suicide are believed to be primary factors protecting against suicide.

Low social capital and high social fragmentation are linked to increased incidence of suicide. Social connectedness and opportunities for civic engagement seem to protect against suicide, whereas isolation and fewer ways to be involved in one's community have the opposite effect. While one's community and the social characteristics therein affect one's propensity toward suicide, individual relationships can also affect one's likelihood of dying by suicide. Areas in which there are higher rates of single individual households, unmarried residents, and residential impermanence saw higher rates of suicide. Data repeatedly support the notion that divorced, never married, and widowed men are more likely than married men to die by suicide. In many frontier states and newly populated recreational destinations, individuals have often relocated away from their families of origin. As a result, some individuals in rural communities may have the opposite experience of what we tend to think of in rural America—fewer long-standing ties, poor family support, a weaker safety net, and fewer relatives living close by.

We know that individuals who receive mental health treatment are less likely to die by suicide. There is some evidence to suggest that suicide rates were higher in counties with greater numbers of uninsured residents. We know that rural communities tend to have higher rates of uninsured residents, lower health literacy, and stigma that prevents them from reaching out for help. Accordingly, it is possible that these factors contribute to the heightened risk of suicide evident in rural communities (Steelesmith et al., 2019).

Interestingly, nearly half of all individuals who have suicided saw their primary care provider within the previous month. A surprising 20% of suicide victims saw their primary care provider in the 24 hours preceding their suicide. We have already looked at how the de facto mental health services in a rural community may comprise individuals ill equipped or undertrained (at best) to treat mental health struggles. One of my colleagues, who is a nurse at a primary care facility, revealed that many of the nurses feel invasive and uncomfortable administering the depression screening inventory. My own experience as a patient supports their claims. While there is no awkwardness when they take my physical vitals, they become robotic in tone, avoiding my eye contact, when asking me how I have been feeling emotionally as of late. As a psychologist, I have said (on more than one occasion to a very uncomfortable nurse), "It's okay. I'm a psychologist; these questions don't make me uncomfortable." The irony of my compulsion to soothe their discomfort while they were meant to be assessing my well-being is not lost on me.

Veterans are much more likely than civilians to die by suicide. In 2017, for example, the veteran suicide rate was one and a half times higher than the civilian rate, when researchers adjusted for age and sex. The vast majority of male veteran suicides were conducted with a firearm (70.7% for males and 43.2% for females) (U.S. Department of Veteran Affairs, 2019). Nearly a quarter of all veterans reside in rural America. Recruitment rates for military service are higher in rural areas, which suggests that, at least in part, the reason that more veterans live in rural areas is because that is where they grew up. As we know, access to mental healthcare can be a challenge for all rural residents, but for veterans, who typically receive their treatment through the Veteran's Administration (VA), barriers to treatment can be even more significant. Rural veterans are more likely to be enrolled with the VA, are statistically older, are more likely to earn less than their urban peers, and are less likely to have access to broadband internet services, decreasing the chances of being able to access care through telehealth (U.S. Department of Veteran Affairs, n.d.).

As is true in urban environs, LGBTQ individuals (and particularly youth) are at heightened risk for suicide when compared with their heterosexual or cisgender peers. According to the Trevor Project, a crisis intervention and suicide prevention organization specifically geared toward LGBTQ youth, lesbian, gay, and bisexual youth are nearly five times more likely to have attempted suicide and three times more likely to have seriously contemplated suicide than their heterosexual peers. Transgender youth and adults experience some of the highest rates of suicide in the country of any marginalized group, with these numbers likely being an underrepresentation due to the stigma around reporting mental anguish and how many individuals remain closeted; 40% of transgender adults reported having made a suicide attempt. Those lesbian, gay, and bisexual youth who come from rejecting or unsupportive households are eight times more likely than their LGB peers to have attempted suicide (The Trevor Project, n.d.).

Suicide rates in Indian country are the highest of any group in the United States. Despite the fact that suicide deaths are underreported in many communities, and the US has a lengthy history of maintaining poor documentation on American Indian experiences, we know that of any group, at any age, American Indians ages 15 through 24 have the highest suicide rates (SAMHSA, 2016).

We already discussed how rates of chronic illness and disability tend to be higher in rural areas. This segment of the population is also at an increased risk for suicide. Americans living with chronic pain are three times more likely to die by suicide (Rosston, 2018). Some studies suggest that people, particularly women, living with an invisible chronic illness have a higher incidence of suicide than the general population. Whereas depression is believed to be commonly comorbid with suicidal ideation or intent, in individuals with chronic ailments, this may not be the case. Suicidality looks different in the chronically ill (Pederson, Gorman-Ezell, & Hochstetler Mayer, 2018). (See Figure 5.4.)

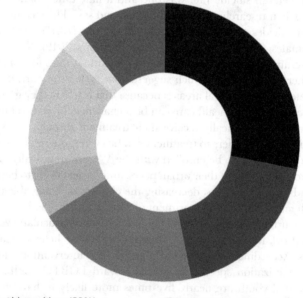

■ Relationship problem (28%)
■ Problematic substance abuse (18.67%)
■ Crisis in the past or upcoming two weeks (19.33%)
■ Criminal/legal problem (6%)
■ Physical health problem (14.67%)
■ Loss of housing (2.67%)
■ Job / financial problem (10.67%)

Figure 5.4 Factors Contributing to Suicide

Vignette: John

John is a farmer in Eastern Wyoming. His wife died several years ago, and his children both moved to Denver for university with no plans of returning to live in Wyoming. In 2008, John experienced some desperate times financially, with both his kids heading to college, and economic hardship plaguing everyone he knew. His crops—soy and corn—were negatively impacted by a particularly dry year in 2018, and fire had threatened his livestock (pigs) the year prior. John's parents died over a decade ago, and outside of the conversations he has with the clerks at the local Cenex station where he buys gasoline and feed, the store owner at the mercantile, and the waitress at the diner where he goes every Saturday for pancakes, he has few social connections and almost no intimacy. His children call every Sunday and tell him about their lives in the city, and he looks forward to their conversations, but the call always triggers grief for his wife when he recognizes how much she did to keep those relationships alive and well. He is often at a loss for what to say and finds himself unable to think of questions to keep the conversation going. John has one friend, Roy, who lives about a mile down the road. The two have been farming together for over 35 years and see one another frequently in passing. Roy's children live in homes they built on their shared property and help him with the farming and ranching responsibilities. Roy's wife often invites John to dinner, and while he accepts her invitations, he often feels uncomfortable and burdensome at their family gatherings. John attends the local church on Sundays, where he sees many of the same people he's been worshipping with for decades. John owns three rifles, which he uses for hunting, and a handgun he bought for his wife for safety purposes. In the spring of 2019, for reasons unknown, John died by suicide in his truck in his driveway.

The story of John is fictionalized, based on a conglomeration of individuals I have known and whose stories I have heard. In his story, we not only see the risk factors but can also almost imagine the inevitability of his plight. Nowhere in John's story is there a social worker or psychologist. There is very little human connection and certainly no deep connection.

If you put yourself in John's shoes and really try to imagine his perspective, as painful as it might be, you might come to understand his decision. He is alone and likely imagines that he will always be alone. Despite being able to notice the pain of losing his wife, he has no one with whom he can share that pain and certainly no professional who would help him process it. He has done one thing his entire adult life, and that one thing has grown increasingly challenging. He cannot imagine a different life for himself. He may even believe that he is worth more

> to his children dead than alive. He has a gun. For many, suicide is a way out of the pain, but it is not always thought through. Research suggests that less than a quarter of individuals who suicide spend more than five minutes contemplating and planning the act.

Note

1. I have selected to use the phrase "completed suicide" in regard to self-injurious behavior that effectively resulted in end of life. I will not use the term "committed" suicide as this is a term entrenched in a culture of shame and stigma that disparages mental illness apart far more than physical illness. If we can say that one died by a heart attack, we should use similar words for suicide.

References

Borders, T. F., & Wen, H. (2018). Illicit drug and opioid use disorders among non-metropolitan residents. *Rural & Underserved Health Research Center Publications, 3*. Retrieved December 19, 2019, from https://uknowledge.uky.edu/ruhrc_reports/3/

Case, A., & Deaton, A. (2017). Mortality and morbidity in the 21st century. *Brookings Papers on Economic Activity, 2017*(1), 397–476.

Centers for Disease Control and Prevention. (2018a). *Suicide rising across the US* [PDF file]. Retrieved December 19, 2019, from www.cdc.gov/vitalsigns/pdf/vs-0618-suicide-H.pdf

Centers for Disease Control and Prevention. (2018b). *Suicide rising across the US* [Chart]. Retrieved December 19, 2019, from www.cdc.gov/vitalsigns/suicide/infographic.html#graphic3

Denning, D. G., Conwell, Y., King, D., & Cox, C. (2000). Method choice, intent, and gender in completed suicide. *Suicide and Life-Threatening Behavior, 30*(3), 282–288.

Dixon, M. A., & Chartier, K. G. (2016). Alcohol use patterns among urban and rural residents: Demographic and social influences. *Alcohol Research: Current Reviews, 38*(1), 69–77.

Gale, J. A., & Lambert, D. (2006). Mental healthcare in rural communities: The once and future role of primary care. *North Carolina Medical Journal, 67*(1), 66.

Keyes, K. M., Cerdá, M., Brady, J. E., Havens, J. R., & Galea, S. (2014). Understanding the rural-urban differences in nonmedical prescription opioid use and abuse in the United States. *American Journal of Public Health, 104*(2), e52–e59. https://doi.org/10.2105/AJPH.2013.301709

Maine Rural Health Research Center. (2016). *Rural opioid abuse: Prevalence and user characteristics*. Retrieved October 23, 2019, from www.ruralhealthresearch.org/publications/1002

Merchant, J., Coussens, C., & Gilbert, D. (Eds.). (2006). *Rebuilding the unity of health and the environment in rural America: Workshop summary.* Washington, DC: National Academies Press.

Monnat, S. M. (2018). *Deaths of despair among non-Hispanic whites in the US: Differences along the urban-rural continuum* [PDF file]. Retrieved December 19, 2019, from https://paa.confex.com/paa/2018/mediafile/ExtendedAbstract/Paper20876/PAA2018_FullPaper.pdf

Monnat, S. M. (2019). *The contributions of socioeconomic and opioid supply factors to geographic variation in U.S. drug mortality rates.* Retrieved December 19, 2019, from www.ineteconomics.org/research/research-papers/opioid-supply-mortality-rates

Monnat, S. M., & Rigg, K. K. (2016). Examining rural/urban differences in prescription opioid misuse among US adolescents. *The Journal of Rural Health, 32*(2), 204–218.

National Alliance on Mental Illness. (2019). *Mental health by the numbers.* Retrieved December 19, 2019, from www.nami.org/learn-more/mental-health-by-the-numbers

National Center for Health Statistics. (2018, November). *Data brief 330. Suicide mortality in the United States, 1999–2017* [PDF file]. Retrieved October 23, 2019, from www.cdc.gov/nchs/data/databriefs/db330_tables-508.pdf#4

National Center for Statistics and Analysis. (2019, June). *Rural/urban comparison of traffic fatalities: 2017 data* (Traffic Safety Facts. Report No. DOT HS 812 741). Washington, DC: National Highway Traffic Safety Administration.

Parker, K., Horowitz, J. M., Igielnik, R., Oliphant, J. B., & Brown, A. (2017). *The demographics of gun ownership.* Pew Research Center Social and Demographic Trends. Retrieved December 19, 2019, from www.pewsocialtrends.org/2017/06/22/the-demographics-of-gun-ownership/

Pederson, C. L., Gorman-Ezell, K., & Hochstetler Mayer, G. (2018). *Assessing depression in those who are chronically ill.* Retrieved December 19, 2019, from https://ct.counseling.org/2018/03/assessing-depression-chronically-ill/

Plank, L. (2019). *For the love of men: A new vision for mindful masculinity.* New York: St. Martin's Press.

Reschovsky, J. D., & Staiti, A. B. (2005). Access and quality: Does rural America lag behind? *Health Affairs, 24*(4), 1128–1139. https://doi.org/10.1377/hlthaff.24.4.1128.

Rosston, K. (2018). *Suicide in Montana: Facts, figures, and formulas for prevention* [PDF file]. Retrieved December 19, 2019, from https://dphhs.mt.gov/Portals/85/suicideprevention/SuicideinMontana.pdf

SAMHSA. (2016). *Suicide prevention in Indian country* [PDF file]. Retrieved December 1, 2019, from https://store.samhsa.gov/system/files/sma16-4995.pdf

Shenassa, E. D., Catlin, S. N., & Buka, S. L. (2003). Lethality of firearms relative to other suicide methods: A population based study. *Journal of Epidemiology & Community Health, 57*(2), 120–124.

Steelesmith, D. L., Fontanella, C. A., Campo, J. V., Bridge, J. A., Warren, K. L., & Root, E. D. (2019). Contextual factors associated with county-level suicide rates in the United States, 1999 to 2016. *JAMA Network Open, 2*(9). https://doi.org/10.1001/jamanetworkopen.2019.10936

The Trevor Project. (n.d.). *Facts about suicide.* Retrieved December 19, 2019, from www.thetrevorproject.org/resources/preventing-suicide/facts-about-suicide/

US Department of Health and Human Services. (n.d.) *Mental health and rural America (1994–2005).* Retrieved October 23, 2019, from www.ruralhealthresearch.org/mirror/6/657/RuralMentalHealth.pdf

US Department of Veteran Affairs. (2019). *2019 national veteran suicide prevention annual report* [PDF file]. Retrieved October 23, 2019, from www.mentalhealth.va.gov/docs/data-sheets/2019/2019_National_Veteran_Suicide_Prevention_Annual_Report_508.pdf

US Department of Veteran Affairs. (n.d.). *Rural veteran health care challenges.* Retrieved December 19, 2019, from www.ruralhealth.va.gov/aboutus/ruralvets.asp

Wuthnow, R. (2019). *The left behind: Decline and rage in small-town America.* Princeton, NJ: Princeton University Press.

6 Healthcare in Rural America

Access

Based on their location, perhaps compounded by cultural forces, rural Americans are at some serious disadvantages when it comes to being well. As I previously stated, rural America is approximately 20% of the population of the United States. However, only 9% of America's physicians live in rural places. Nearly 60% of all counties in the US are without a single psychiatrist (New American Economy, 2017). According to this same study, there are 590 psychiatrists in rural areas serving approximately 27 million Americans. Assuming adequate distribution of these resources (which is unlikely), that means each psychiatrist is responsible for treating approximately 45,700 people. Fifteen million children live in health professional shortage areas (HPSAs), and in those areas, there is one healthcare professional for approximately every 3,500 individuals. Said another way, 60% of Americans live in these HPSAs while 90% of all psychologists and psychiatrists and 80% of all social workers and counselors work exclusively in metropolitan areas (Gale & Lambert, 2006).

Often referred to as "provider deserts" or, more specifically, "mental healthcare deserts," rural and frontier communities are not only likely to experience a dearth of providers; support services and supplemental resources crucial to the well-being of communities and individuals are often lacking too. Of all rural counties, 77% are listed as "Primary Care Health Professional Shortage Areas" by to the National Rural Health Association, and 9% lack even one physician. What's more, many of those counties lack the support services that allow physicians and clinicians to do their work effectively. In an urban center, it is likely that one might find the following:

- Community mental health center(s)
- Inpatient psychiatric treatment
- Inpatient addiction treatment
- Intensive outpatient treatment for addiction
- Intensive outpatient treatment for eating disorders
- Victim advocates
- Domestic violence shelters

- Homeless shelters
- Case managers
- Head Start programs
- Speech and language/occupational therapies
- Psychiatric care
- Therapeutic and support groups
- Grief resource centers
- Parenting classes
- Public transportation
- School psychologists
- Study centers
- Job service centers
- Legal support
- Reduced-fee clinics

In a rural community, it's possible that there might be a therapist or two, a nurse practitioner, and a school counselor. In these communities, not only are practitioners required to serve a breadth of presenting problems and personalities, but they do so with limited support from other disciplines, consultants, and peers.

In 2016, the WWAMI Rural Health Research Center illustrated the profound lack of mental healthcare in rural regions. Of nonmetropolitan counties, 65% had no psychiatrist (compared to 27% of metropolitan counties), 47% had no psychologists (versus 19% of metropolitan counties), 27% had no social workers (versus 9%), 81% had no psychiatric nurse practitioner (versus 42% of metropolitan counties), and 18% were without any counselors (versus 6% of metropolitan counties) (National Advisory Committee on Rural Health and Human Services, 2017). Community health centers, public centers that provide comprehensive and affordable treatment options in an accessible and timely manner, are limited in rural communities, particularly the farther west one travels in the United States (HHS, n.d.).

In a recent consultation group, we welcomed a new member who had moved from a coastal urban area. During her introduction, she cited her specialty and preferred clientele, reminding the forced generalists in the room of their previous fantasies of having such a luxury as a focus and forte. A few minutes into the consult, a local rural provider requested some support around working with a client who had recently been threatened with eviction from her Section 8 housing. The providers began problem solving with the concerned clinician, suggesting references and strategies. The new provider remarked on the need to go visit an agency that specialized in housing and could provide the sort of social work services necessary to address this matter of instability. The other providers in the room had to inform the new clinician that no such resources existed in our community and that our role as psychotherapists often became blurry when matters of survival and basic needs intruded on our work.

Rural people tend to seek mental health services through the path of least resistance. In many cases, the path of least resistance never even leads an individual to a trained mental health professional (HHS, n.d.). Often referred to as the "de facto mental health system," primary care providers are responsible for the provision of mental health services in a significant number of rural communities. In fact, 45% of rural Americans who do receive mental healthcare get it from their primary healthcare providers (HHS, n.d.). What's more, the "mental health crisis responder for most rural Americans is a law enforcement officer" (National Institute of Mental Health [NIMH], 2018). Anecdotally, a nurse in our local hospital's emergency department explained, "It seems like at least half of everyone who walks through that door is here because of mental health or substance abuse, maybe even more." She went on to explain,

> it's hard because they think they are having a heart attack, and it's really panic or they're seeking drugs, or they've been raped and have no one who will talk to them, and that's not really our job. So we patch them up and send them out, knowing we'll see them again in a few weeks.

Rural Americans wait longer to receive care than their urban counterparts. This well-documented trend explains why many rural mental healthcare seekers are more distraught or ill by the time they receive services (Hartley, Quam, & Lurie, 1994). Study after study has shown that symptom severity at the onset of treatment is worse in rural populations (Reschovsky & Staiti, 2005), presumably because self-imposed, cultural, or systemic barriers (Thornicroft, 2008) delay access to care.

All this contributes to the fact that rural Americans with mental health struggles are less likely to receive specialty services from a mental health professional in a timely manner (Gale & Lambert, 2006).

Affordability

In addition to matters of access, rural Americans are less likely to be insured. Health insurance premiums are higher (due to less competition), people are less likely to receive health insurance benefits from their employers (underemployment rates are higher), more people depend on Medicaid (which is less available in Southern rural areas due to political pushback against Medicaid expansion programs), and those who are insured are less likely to have providers who accept their insurance (due to provider shortages). Further, individuals who receive government aid through subsidies in the marketplace or through Medicaid are more likely, due to economic instability common to rural Americans, to experience gaps in coverage or periods of eligibility followed by periods of ineligibility. This makes continuous care challenging. This bleak outlook has certainly triggered politicians and policy wonks to attend to the crisis, but I also hope it will trigger some of you reading this book to pack your bags and move to the frontier or a rural community where opportunity awaits!

Underutilization

In my hometown of New York, New York, it is not uncommon to overhear the following: "My therapist says that he's no good for me, and I should move on" or, "How long have you and Paula been seeing a therapist?" or "My shrink told me not to do this anymore." In my chosen town of Whitefish, Montana, it seems as if people are more likely to tell you about contracting a sexually transmitted disease than attending therapy. Shame, stigma, and low mental health literacy all impact the willingness and ability of folks to get the help they need. While this topic deserves, and will get, its own chapter later, it is essential to visit as we aim to understand the bigger picture of mental health woes for rural Americans.

According to Mental Health America, underutilization is particularly salient in frontier states. Rankings based on high rates of mental illness and low rates of access to care place all the frontier states in the lower half of the United States. Particularly worthy of note is that nearly all the lowest ranked states (with the exception of the District of Columbia) are either in the West or the South regions of the US, areas known commonly to be quite rural (Mental Health America, n.d.). Indeed, according to Rural Health Quarterly (2017), the South-Central regions rank the lowest in access to mental health.

Rural Americans are less likely to "recognize mental illness and understand their care options" (Gale & Lambert, 2006). Health literacy, or the ability to access, understand, and make sense of health information in the spirit of enabling solid health decisions, is commonly lower in rural areas. Given that rural Americans on average are less educated and have less exposure to medical and mental health services, it makes sense that it is harder for them to process health information and then make informed choices. Poor health literacy has been linked, not surprisingly, to poor health outcomes. As clinicians, we are responsible for making sure that the consumers of our services understand what they are to receive. I, as a consumer of health services, have struggled to fully understand the concept of HIPAA and what it means to me as a patient, and yet I have signed no fewer than 50 forms stating that I have reviewed and understood their contents. As someone who holds a doctoral degree, I am likely among the 10% of our population considered health literate. Imagine what your patients think about your intake paperwork.

In the following chapters, we will dive more deeply into the nuances of rural culture, the barriers to effective treatment, and ethically responsible practice in rural communities and amongst rural persons.

Availability

In many rural communities, nonprofit organizations exist in far fewer numbers and with far lower budgets than in urban areas. I came upon a statistic that suggested that fewer grant dollars were spent in rural areas than in urban areas. One possible explanation for this discrepancy is that there are fewer agencies in rural regions to acquire and spend such monies. Further, rural areas tend to have less tax revenue available to spend on social service infrastructure and implementation. While rural areas tend to receive less money, their needs tend to be greater and the provision of services costlier, for the reasons outlined earlier in this chapter.

Whereas agencies and service providers in urban centers can focus on both individuals and the community, rural service provisions tend to be focused purely on the individual. A rural community, for example, may have enough resources for a social worker to help families access affordable housing, but it is far less likely that they would have advocates or even lobbyists in place to help create the sort of institutional and systemic changes that might help future families avoid similar pitfalls. As a result, social service provisions are often in the practice of supporting individuals without ever having the time, resources, or energy to support the larger need.

In summary, individuals in rural areas have more problems with fewer resources available with which to cope. We, as clinicians, regardless of our location, should be deeply concerned about this marginalized, overlooked, suffering group.

By now, you should have a general understanding of some of the common elements of rural life, a sense of what elements serve to challenge rural Americans, and some of the barriers preventing rural Americans from getting the mental health services they need. We explored common values of rural life and select populations and issues salient to rural communities and deepened our cultural understanding of and familiarity with this large cultural minority. With that foundation underneath us, we will now journey into the practice of rural psychology. In the next section, we will use clinical material to explore ethical dilemmas and expand our focus on cultural competence.

References

Gale, J. A., & Lambert, D. (2006). Mental healthcare in rural communities: The once and future role of primary care. *North Carolina Medical Journal, 67*(1), 66.

Hartley, D., Quam, L., & Lurie, N. (1994). Urban and rural differences in health insurance and access to care. *The Journal of Rural Health, 10*(2), 98–108.

Mental Health America. (n.d.). *Ranking the states 2018*. Retrieved October 23, 2019, from www.mhanational.org/issues/ranking-states-2018-0

National Advisory Committee on Rural Health and Human Services. (2017, December). *Understanding the impact of suicide in rural America* [PDF file]. Retrieved October 23, 2019, from www.hrsa.gov/sites/default/files/hrsa/advisory-committees/rural/publications/2017-impact-of-suicide.pdf

National Institute of Mental Health (NIMH). (2018). *Mental health and rural America: Challenges and opportunities*. Retrieved December 19, 2019, from www.nimh.nih.gov/news/media/2018/mental-health-and-rural-america-challenges-and-opportunities.shtml

New American Economy. (2017). *The silent shortage: How immigration can help address the large and growing psychiatrist shortage in the United States* [PDF file]. Healthcare.

Retrieved December 29, 2019, from www.newamericaneconomy.org/wp-content/uploads/2017/10/NAE_PsychiatristShortage_V6-1.pdf

Reschovsky, J. D., & Staiti, A. B. (2005). Access and quality: Does rural America lag behind? *Health Affairs*, *24*(4), 1128–1139. https://doi.org/10.1377/hlthaff.24.4.1128

Rural Health Quarterly. (2017). RHQ's 2017 rural health report card: Grading the state of rural health in America. *Rural Health Report*, *1*(4), 11–111. Retrieved October 10, 2019, from http://ruralhealthquarterly.com/home/wp-content/uploads/2017/12/RHQ.1.4_U.S.-Rural-Health-Report-Card.pdf

Thornicroft, G. (2008). Stigma and discrimination limit access to mental health care. *Epidemiology and Psychiatric Sciences*, *17*(1), 14–19.

US Department of Health and Human Services. (n.d.) *Mental health and rural America (1994–2005)*. Retrieved December 19, 2019, from www.ruralhealthresearch.org/mirror/6/657/RuralMentalHealth.pdf

Section Two
Ethics in Rural Communities

7   An Ethical Framework

Introduction

In the first section, we focused on preparing ourselves for work with rural populations by outlining how rural people and places differ from those we most commonly studied in school and training. Now that we have built a foundation of understanding from which we can deepen our cultural competency, I would like to help us move toward an ethically sound rural practice. Ethically sound practice requires the clinician not only to understand the people and the community but also to know how to navigate nuances and dilemmas as they emerge. While we cannot effectively predict any and all quandaries in which we might find ourselves, we can posit likely scenarios and dilemmas and plan accordingly.

For practitioners in the fields of psychology, social work, and counseling, ethical codes and guidelines often serve as road maps for navigating challenging situations. Anyone who has practiced in a rural setting will tell you that efforts to virtuously apply their ethics codes to their daily practice have often left them confused and disoriented. I am a member of several online forums for rural practitioners, and the number one topic of conversation concerns ethics (recruitment and retention being the second most popular subject of discussion). Though the APA, the ACA, and the NASW have received input from numerous groups representing rural populations, their point of reference remains in the dominant urban majority. Further, our educational programming, the vast majority of which takes place in urban settings, also may overlook or underrepresent the rural population of America. As rural providers or professionals working adjacent to or via telehealth in rural communities, we need an ethical code and practice that we can apply to our work.

We will start with an overview of the history and relevance of ethics, followed by a discussion of various ethical principles as they apply to rural practice. In that discussion, I will utilize clinical material to illustrate the unique elements of applied ethics in rural practice. This discussion will include specific ethical imperatives, such as confidentiality and privacy, and will also delve into ethical responsibilities such as self-care and cultural competence. I hope that by the end, you will have a firm grasp on what makes ethical practice in rural America uniquely challenging. And from that place of understanding, I will present you with a framework to understand and navigate your ethical landscape.

Why an Ethics Code?

Ethics is a branch of philosophical thought that reckons with the evaluation of human action. Because ethical determinations are a form of values judgment, one's culture, history, ideas about the world, and experiences will shape one's interpretations of morality. Ethics are ambiguous, personal, and not easily standardized, a problem for professional groups seeking to uphold a high standard of behavior. To this end, professional organizations create guidelines that do away with much ambiguity and make clear for their practitioners what exactly constitutes right and wrong. Within the context of an agreed-upon standard, actions can be categorized as right or wrong. Without such a criterion, right and wrong become undefinable, and limits blur.

Ethics codes generally seek to "establish a framework for professional behavior and responsibility" (Mabe & Rollin, 1986). The primary function of an ethics code is to preserve the public trust and protect the community from professional wrongdoing. Those who swore the Hippocratic Oath were pledging, for example, "to help the sick according to my ability and judgment, but never with a view to injury and wrong-doing" (Hippocrates of Cos, 1923). While, of course, an oath or a promise does not ensure the swearer will oblige, it provides a set of expectations of how one in a given profession should act. That is, my dentist's ethics code gives me a sense of how he should behave as a professional and allows me to know what to expect and to be clear if things are not what they should be. As Koocher and Keith-Spiegel (2008, p. 605) highlight, "If a profession is to thrive, the public must have faith in those who practice within it."

Ethical guidelines also provide an identity and a sort of group membership for those newly entering the field. By saying, we as, for example, psychologists do this and do not do this, new providers are given a set of behavioral expectations that, if followed, help them feel identified with the larger community of psychologists.

My ethics professor in graduate school taught us a saying to remind ourselves not only of the inherent goodness in people but also of the possibility of good people (such as ourselves) doing disastrous things. He said, "When you find someone engaging in behavior you find abhorrent, say to yourself, 'It seems they are good but (fill in the blank).'" The blank could be ignorant, overworked, exhausted, uninformed, or any number of other offenses that don't necessarily excuse behavior but allow us to see the humanity underlying it. The task also encourages us to remember that when we lack knowledge or are tired or burned out, we, too, may engage in behavior that others might judge harshly.

Individual morality does not automatically give rise to ethically sound behavior, and all humans are fallible; when we are compromised, we may act unethically. Consequently, there is a great need—particularly in professions that involve vulnerable people and burned-out providers—for clear, enforceable guidelines to follow.

While ethical guidelines ideally increase virtuous behavior, they also provide the professional community a standard by which to judge questionable or unethical behavior (Koocher & Keith-Spiegel, 2008). Ethical guidelines are also a specific, clear, and measurable set of expectations that allow us space to hold our brethren accountable. That is, ethical codes provide the practitioner, the professional network, and the public a set of guidelines against which we can judge the actions of the professional.

Most ethical codes include both principles and standards. Principles are aspirational in nature and serve to reflect the values of the professional organization. These core values are the foundation upon which the enforceable standards sit. Values are, typically, strongly personal. The professional committees tasked with setting forth such aspirational standards have removed the judgment, bias, and subjectivity inherent in being a human to make clear what is valued by the organization. These principles, however, do not provide clear, measurable behavioral expectations but instead outline the values upon which the profession rests. These aspirational expectations paint a picture of the supreme ethical behavior of the clinician.

The standards, enforceable by nature, are behavior specific and are much clearer about what is required of practitioners and what is prohibited. Whereas principles are vague and lofty, standards are clear, specific, and explicit. In large part, the standards stem from the principles. A nice metaphor to help guide our thinking is that the principles are like the trunk of the tree and the standards its branches. Now, let's examine the tree and how rural practice fits within.

What Is Our Ethical Duty?

Since I am a psychologist, the APA Ethics Code not only serves as my regulatory guide; it also serves as my frame of reference. However, because there are so few books on the subject of rural ethics for providers other than psychologists, I have worked to integrate a general understanding of other ethics codes. These codes include those of the Association for Marriage and Family Therapy (AAMFT), the American Counseling Association (ACA), and the National Association of Social Workers (NASW).

Mental health professions, including psychology, social work, counseling, and marriage and family therapy, have significant overlap in their ethical guidelines. Koocher and Keith-Spiegel (2008) have outlined the overlapping ethical guidelines amongst the various mental health professions (see Figure 7.1).

Further, the ethical guidelines laid forth by these organizations set forth similar aspirational guidelines for the behavior of professionals including those shown in Figure 7.2.

The APA ethics code sets forth five aspirational standards, referred to as the general principles. These principles, the trunk of the tree, are the foundational grounding from which the rest of our ethical tree grows. These are the ethical

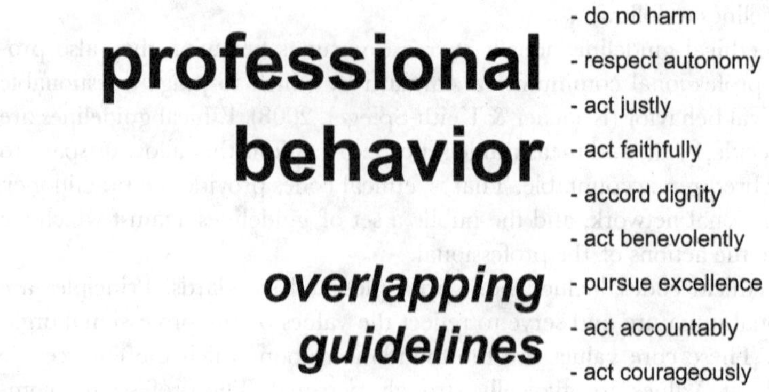

professional behavior

overlapping guidelines

- do no harm
- respect autonomy
- act justly
- act faithfully
- accord dignity
- act benevolently
- pursue excellence
- act accountably
- act courageously

Figure 7.1 Professional Behavior

ethical guidelines *for mental health* **professionals**

- integrity and competence
- acting in the best interest of those served
- maintaining and practicing within competence
- doing no harm
- confidentiality and privacy
- responsible action
- the avoidance of exploitation
- respect for those served
- exemplary conduct

Figure 7.2 Ethical Guidelines

elements to which we all should aspire. We will reference these five overarching principles as they are shared among the mental health professions and summarized succinctly for our purposes.

First, we value **beneficence** and **nonmaleficence**: psychologists should aim for good and avoid doing harm. By "good," the APA is referring to promoting the welfare of others, treating people and animals with respect, increasing knowledge and awareness, and improving the conditions of people, organizations, and society. "Harm" involves incompetence, exploitation, intrusions of privacy, ignorance, and providing services that are psychologically injurious. Rural practice is rife with opportunities to inadvertently cause harm to our clients. We must avoid harm by practicing within our scope of competence while simultaneously aiming to make services available to everyone. Doing good in rural communities can feel like a daunting, overwhelming objective.

Second, we strive for **fidelity** and **responsibility**. This includes faithfulness, professionalism, and duty. We value promise keeping; acting in the best interest of others; appropriate relationships; upholding self-standards of knowledge, competence, and integrity; and resolving situations that are in conflict. In rural practice, threats to fidelity include difficulties with confidentiality; many, many multiple relationships; and difficulties maintaining competence with such a wide scope of practice. I suspect that when it comes to responsibility, many rural practitioners (myself included) feel the weight of this resting heavily on our psyches. The need is tremendous, and we rarely can forget it.

Third, we place great import on the value of **integrity**. As psychologists, we should strive for honest communication; truth telling; promise keeping; and accuracy in science, teaching, and practice. We aim for objectivity in disseminating information and clearly communicate what we offer, don't offer, and know. This value helps us avoid exploitation, which is particularly salient given the power differential common in therapist-client relationships. In communities with lower health literacy, having integrity is essential. Because mental health providers in small communities will often be viewed as experts, we must take care to ensure we are speaking truthfully and not misrepresenting our fields.

Fourth, we value **justice**. We strive to provide all people with fair, equitable, appropriate access to treatment and the benefits of psychological knowledge. We work to safeguard against our own biases and ensure that inequities are addressed. Of course, in a rural community, with under- or uninsured citizens, low health literacy, high need, and few providers, embodying justice can be exhausting, and we must take care to safeguard against burnout, lest we find ourselves no longer able to provide the much-needed services.

Finally, we see great import in **respecting people's rights and dignity**. By engaging in informed consent, practicing privacy and confidentiality, and allowing for autonomous decision making, we provide our consumers with spaces in which they maintain their dignity. We are respectful of differences, and we familiarize ourselves with the implications of differences and reduce prejudice, discrimination, and bias (APA, 2003). Confidentiality, of course, can be a challenge to rural providers. We will dive into this topic at length in a later chapter, but for now, let me say this: confidentiality takes on new meaning and presents some unique challenges in a small community.

References

American Psychological Association. (2003). *Ethical principles of psychologists and code of conduct*. Retrieved January 10, 2019, from www.apa.org/ethics/code/

Hippocrates of Cos. (1923). *The oath*. Retrieved October 6, 2015, from www.loebclassics.com/view/hippocrates_cos-oath/1923/pb_LCL147.299.xml

Koocher, G. P., & Keith-Spiegel, P. (2008). *Ethics in psychology and the mental health professions: Standards and cases*. Oxford: Oxford University Press.

Mabe, A. R., & Rollin, S. A. (1986). The role of a code of ethical standards in counseling. *Journal of Counseling & Development, 64*(5), 294–297.

8 Ethics in Rural Practice

There are several elements of rural practice that set it apart from urban practice. I expect that, by now, you are quite familiar with the ways in which rural America is different from urban/suburban America. Our work thus far has been to develop a foundational understanding of the cultural elements relevant to rural practice. While some of the differences make things decidedly harder, others are perhaps neutral or even helpful. Regardless of their valence, these distinctions are important for us to understand generally and then apply specifically to our work.

Our next task is to apply our understanding of cultural differences, practical challenges, and professional responsibilities to ethical rural practice.

In the first section, we tackled the matter of knowledge. By now, readers should have a primary understanding of who lives in rural America and what makes rural Americans different from their metropolitan peers. We all now know that rural Americans may hold cultural values somewhat distinct from metropolitan values and often have very different historical experiences. We also know that rural Americans suffer many conditions at higher rates than the general population and have increased vulnerability to suffering due to higher poverty rates, lower educational attainment, and massive provider shortages (Thomas, Ellis, Konrad, Holzer, & Morrissey, 2009). It is also the case that rural Americans, like many other minority groups, are not a homogeneous bunch. Within-group differences are significant and should not be overlooked.

We also know that the role of the provider in a rural place may be profoundly different from that of her urban counterpart and that the demands placed on a rural provider may have implications for their applied ethics. Many of the ethical guidelines, typically understood through an urban lens, are not as easily applied to rural settings and, as a result, we must understand them and learn how to manage them in context (Roberts, Battaglia, & Epstein, 1999).

Relevant Ethics

As previously stated, due to the fact that many graduate training programs are set in metropolitan regions, many of us will have received training on ethics that were embedded in the urbancentric experience. A few specific areas of

Ethics in Rural Practice 85

ethics are particularly salient to practice in rural communities and uniquely different from ethical practice in metropolitan environs and will receive special attention in this section. Those who have trained in urban communities have likely received training on navigating the small community that is the internet. Lannin and Scott (2014) suggest that on the World Wide Web, much like in insular communities, psychologists have a heightened risk for "pervasive incidental contact, inevitable self-disclosure and unavoidable multiple relationships." Indeed, multiple relationships, privacy, and confidentiality top our list of ethical issues pertinent to rural practice. Competence and self-care are also particularly relevant, given the nature of isolation, supply, and demand. I will go into each of these in detail in later sections, but I want this section to orient you to the aspects of our ethical requirements most relevant to rural practice. (See Figure 8.1.)

Inclusively, mental health professional ethics codes require individuals to act within their realm of **competence**. Competence is defined by knowledge earned through training, supervised experience, and education. The NASW expands on this definition to also outline specific routes to competence (e.g., professional experience, certification, licensure). Competence can be thought of as one of the essential standards of behavior. Knowing and operating within the confines of one's abilities and training are foundational aspects of the ideal behavior of the provider.

Imagine, if you will, that we were to each create circles of string on the ground around us, representing our scope of practice and our areas of competence. Some of us, perhaps new practitioners or seasoned providers with a well-developed niche, would have rather small circles, not much larger than the space our feet occupy. Others, perhaps generalists, might have circles in

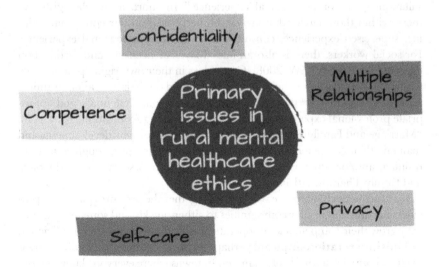

Figure 8.1 Primary Ethical Issues in Rural Mental Healthcare

which there is room to take a few steps. If we stand within that circle and plant our feet firmly, we are simultaneously grounded and restricted. We can stretch or perhaps contort our bodies to reach beyond the confines of that circle, but should we reach too far, we would easily lose our balance and perhaps come crashing down. If we had a close colleague we trusted whose circle was beyond our own, we could even imagine holding their hand to serve as a stabilizing force should we extend beyond the realm of competence. Likewise, if we piled up some resources and perhaps a wise, well-trained peer, we might be able to step even farther, balancing on the continuing education. Of course, remaining within those limits, we would not only have solid footing, but we would also eventually come to intimately know our area; its boundaries; and the movements we could freely, safely, and comfortably make therein. Should we wish to expand our circle, we would have to engage in academic, consultative, or educational pursuits that would permit us to confidently grow in our scope.

One of the ways that practitioners develop competence is by deepening their expertise in a few specialty areas. To practice as a generalist, which many rural providers must based on need, one must maintain competence in a wide range of populations, age ranges, presenting problems, and symptom severity. Further, rural practitioners often have few options when it comes to consultation and referring out (Smalley, Warren, & Rainer, 2012). Thus, the task of competence for the rural professional is significantly greater than for a clinician surrounded by colleagues to whom he may refer, training opportunities, and opportunities for consultation.

Per the APA (2003), "Psychologists provide services, teach, and conduct research with populations and in areas only within the boundaries of their competence, based on their education, training, supervised experience, consultation, study, or professional experience." In short, as psychologists, we move within those circles that are established based on our education, training, supervised experience, consultation, study, and professional experience. For social workers, there is also an added layer of licensure and certification expected from the NASW (2008). Counselors in their own right "practice only within the boundaries of their competence, based on their education, training, supervised experience, state and national professional credentials, and appropriate professional experience" (American Counseling Association, 2014, p. 8). "Marriage and Family Therapists pursue knowledge of new developments and maintain their competence in marriage and family therapy through education, training, and/or supervised experience" (American Association of Marriage and Family Therapy, 2015).

In subsequent chapters, we will explore together the pressures placed on providers in rural and insular communities to either quickly and sometimes frantically grow their competencies or operate outside the scope of their proficiency.

Multiple relationships are perhaps the most commonly identified threat to ethical practice in rural communities. In towns where everyone knows everyone, it does not take much imagination to generate some scenarios in which a practitioner might struggle to uphold the ethics code. According to the APA (1992):

> A multiple relationship occurs when a psychologist is in a professional role with a person and (1) at the same time is in another role with the same person, (2) at the same time is in a relationship with a person closely associated with or related to the person with whom the psychologist has the professional relationship, or (3) promises to enter into another relationship in the future with the person or a person closely associated with or related to the person.

A psychologist refrains from entering into a multiple relationship if the multiple relationship could reasonably be expected to impair the psychologist's objectivity, competence, or effectiveness in performing his or her functions as a psychologist or otherwise risks exploitation or harm to the person with whom the professional relationship exists.

To be clear, the ethical standards do not prohibit multiple relationships. They do, however, stipulate that should a multiple relationship impair the provider's clinical fitness or cause harm or exploitation, it should be avoided. That is to say, not all multiple relationships are unethical, but those that violate the ethical principles are. This summary belies the true complexity and hazards of this standard, particularly as it pertains to those individuals practicing within rural and/or insular communities. Accordingly, this matter will be addressed at length in a later chapter.

Per ethical standards, practitioners of psychology, therapy, social work, and counseling are bound by **privacy and confidentiality**. Here, confidentiality requires the provider "not to discuss information about a client with anyone . . . except under certain circumstances agreed to by both parties" (Koocher & Keith-Spiegel, 2008, p. 151). While the limits of confidentiality are not necessarily outlined by the ethical standards and are, instead, the purview of the law, it is required by ethical standard that practitioners review limits to confidentiality at the outset of treatment or participation in research. More than a dozen times, I have been approached by a client in a public setting, only to have my companion later ask, "Oh, how do you know so-and-so?" While I suspect this occurs in metropolitan communities, in our small town, it happens frequently, and the likelihood that my companion knows the client is great. In rural communities, threats to a client's privacy and confidentiality are amplified, so clinicians need to take certain precautions to avoid breaches and have methods for dealing with the failures. It only took one or two tries for me to realize the single best way to maintain the privacy and confidentiality of my clients was to lie outright. I have learned that saying that I have volunteered with, have a friend in common with, or know so-and-so from their place of employment may conceal their real identity as my client, provided I don't miss a beat in my presentation. While I consider integrity and truthfulness of great import, my professional obligation to confidentiality and privacy trumps these personal values. I regularly encounter such minor ethical dilemmas in the grocery store or at the gym: friction created between my personal values and my professional ethical codes.

Finally, though **self-care** is not always a stated ethical guideline, I would argue its presence is required for us to remain ethical. When we are vulnerable, burned out, overstretched, or simply tired, our ability to remain ethical is compromised. Just like my professor said, you can be "good but overwhelmed," and that overwhelm can cause you to make some very poor choices. Self-care and its nasty counterpart, burnout, are factors significant to every practitioner, no matter their setting. However, in rural communities, where the needs are tremendous, the resources limited, the professional community inadequate, and the consequences of not receiving services sometimes dire, burnout lurks in every waiting room and in every unanswered voice mail. This makes self-care even more important and, of course, its attainability restricted for some of the very same reasons it is so essential. How can you go see a therapist if you're the only therapist in town?

Applied Ethics

The reality is that ethical principles and standards provide little in the way of resolving ethical predicaments. In fact, ethics codes are not designed to solve dilemmas. Despite the early drafts of the APA Ethics Code containing dilemmas posed by psychologists in practice, the nature of an ethics code is not prescriptive, but rather a combination of aspiration and enforcement. The ethics code functions to provide a framework for conceptualizing action. It is not an answer source.

Celia B. Fisher, who has written four editions of the book *Decoding the Ethics Code*, sees psychologists as "moral agents committed to the good and just practice and science of psychology" (2009, p. 31). Ethical codes, then, do not solve our "ethical quandaries," but rather provide us with an opportunity to be simultaneously guided and kept in check by the principles and guidelines therein. There is no infallible or precise formula for solving ethical challenges. Rather, it is up to the provider to interpret and apply the code to the work they do and the practice in which they are embedded. Laws, of course, provide us with black-and-white boundaries within which we must act. Ethics are more like a puddle of grayish water—made cloudier the moment we step in. Later, I will present to you a method for evaluating ethical challenges, ethical decision making, and outcome assessment. This, I hope, will serve as a template, imperfect as it may be, that you may integrate into your regular practice of navigating the turbulent waters that are ethical practice in rural communities.

Ethics are the complicated, values-driven, socially acceptable guidelines that underpin our appraisals of right and wrong in human behavior. What is ethically sanctioned in one environment might be observed to be unscrupulous in another, and vice versa. Consequently, the cultural nuances in a rural community—particularly one that is insular in nature—may make it even harder for practitioners to behave ethically. Ethical behaviors are normed, and norms are impacted by our surroundings and our peers. Consequently, I would argue that to practice in rural communities requires heightened self-awareness, greater vigilance, and a systematic method for coping with ethical dilemmas.

References

American Association of Marriage and Family Therapy. (2015). *Code of ethics*. Retrieved October 12, 2019, from www.aamft.org/Legal_Ethics/Code_of_Ethics.aspx

American Counseling Association. (2014). *2014 ACA code of ethics* [PDF file]. Retrieved October 12, 2019, from www.counseling.org/resources/aca-code-of-ethics.pdf

American Psychological Association. (1992). *Ethical principles of psychologists and code of conduct*. Retrieved May 18, 2003, from www.apa.org/ethics/code/code-1992

American Psychological Association. (2003). *Ethical principles of psychologists and code of conduct*. Retrieved January 1, 2019, from www.apa.org/ethics/code/

Fisher, C. B. (2009). *Decoding the ethics code: A practical guide for psychologists*. Thousand Oaks, CA: Sage Publications.

Koocher, G. P., & Keith-Spiegel, P. (2008). *Ethics in psychology and the mental health professions: Standards and cases*. Oxford: Oxford University Press.

Lannin, D., & Scott, N. (2014). Best practices for an online world. *Monitor on Psychology*, *45*(2), 56.

National Association of Social Workers. (2008). *Code of ethics of the National Association of Social Workers* [PDF file]. Retrieved October 12, 2019, from www.socialworkers.org/LinkClick.aspx?fileticket=KZmmbz15evc%3D&portalid=0

Roberts, L. W., Battaglia, J., & Epstein, R. S. (1999). Frontier ethics: Mental health care needs and ethical dilemmas in rural communities. *Psychiatric Services*, *50*(4), 497–503.

Smalley, K. B., Warren, J. C., & Rainer, J. P. (Eds.). (2012). *Rural mental health: Issues, policies, and best practices*. New York: Springer Publishing Company.

Thomas, K. C., Ellis, A. R., Konrad, T. R., Holzer, C. E., Morrissey, J. P. (2009). County-level estimates of mental health professional shortage in the United States. *Psychiatric Services*, *60*(10). https://doi.org/10.1176/ps.2009.60.10.1323

9 A Road Map for Managing Ethical Dilemmas in Rural Practice

Rationale

As Archilochus said, "We do not rise to the level of our expectations, we fall to the level of our training."

Thus far, we have been discussing what ethics *are*. Now, it is time we discuss how we *do* ethics. In emergency medicine, practitioners learn a series of steps that should be followed routinely to ensure the safety of the provider and the highest level of care for the patient. They are also instructed to rehearse those steps so that when they find themselves in a crisis, the actions come as second nature, and they are not dependent on their (panicked) mind to make decisions in the moment. In psychology, we know that when we are at our most vulnerable, we are likely to make poor decisions—good, but.... As a result, we must each have a plan of action, created when we are at our best, to employ should we find ourselves compromised or at our worst.

As L.S. Brown sensibly stated:

> The goal of an ethical decision is not to avoid any and all violations and boundaries, for this is impossible. Instead, the goal is to remain on the more innocuous end of the continuum, in the position where the abuse and exploitation of the power of the therapist are minimized.
>
> (1994, p. 279)

Ergo, our goal is not perfection but to remain on this side of the beneficence spectrum whenever possible.

My practice, as with most of my clinical skills, developed in graduate school, with the help of a patient and thoughtful professor. Dr. Mike Monroe stood before the class, his hair disheveled in a way I would come to expect, and led us through a meditative exercise. This was not—I doubled-checked—a class in mindfulness. Rather, this was the sole ethics class that I would complete for my doctorate. As we moved through a body scan, he drew our attention to our toes. As instructed, we squeezed our toes tightly in our shoes while thinking about an ethical dilemma we had faced in our lives. The didactic that followed is blurred in my memory, though the outcome remains clear: he was training us to have a physiological response (squeezing our toes) when we found ourselves at an ethical crossroads or, worse, knee deep in an ethical dilemma. He believed that having such a cue might help us notice ethical dilemmas our conscious minds might otherwise attempt to keep obscured. Further, the act of squeezing our toes served to provide us budding clinicians with a moment of pause before action. More on that later. If you will, dear reader, squeeze your toes with me, and in that subtle movement of body, one not easily detected by an onlooker, let us create some neural pathways that might someday help us at least be alerted to the dilemmas in which we might find ourselves.

Now, follow me, if you will, on a brief detour. I take us on this detour to help give us a beacon in an example in otherwise murky territory. I have worked with Kathryn for several years. She is a successful woman with a deeply injured core. Raised by a mother who she describes as narcissistic, Kathryn has long struggled to feel acceptable, worthy of love, and solid in her identity. Despite creating a life for herself that, from the outside, appears quite stable and prosperous, Kathryn has known herself to regress tremendously when she visits her hometown to see her family of origin. Her husband has reported that "it's as if she's a different person" when she is around her mother, and she describes a felt sense of "wooziness" in her presence. Kathryn, despite her wishes, has found herself somewhat "required" to go home for Thanksgiving. She has purchased her ticket and is now coming to me with a sense of fear, if not desperation, about the situation.

What we do next is something that all skilled clinicians, parents, teachers, and good friends do: we help her plan for the worst, set herself up for the best, and outline how she will manage through both. I call these "crisis survival plans," and I am certain you have your own name for them. These strategies address two fundamental aspects of human behavior: first, we know that individuals tend to regress when they return to situations that were previously unhealthy. Second, we know that individuals tend to do what they have always done unless they are well practiced in the art of doing things differently.

For Kathryn, we agreed that she would pay the money for a hotel room, guaranteeing her some space and time away from the family. We also wrote down a list of names of people she could call who would support her if and when she struggled. Kathryn outlined and rehearsed several strategies she's learned over the years to manage her emotional distress, including mindfulness practice, cognitive challenging, and journaling. We also talked about self-care and the ways she can take care of herself, other than staying at a hotel, while she's visiting her family. In short, we outlined a series of steps that Kathryn could take to have the best chance of a positive outcome. These steps were concrete, her supports were listed, and her strategies well rehearsed. This is one of the best strategies I know to help my clients avoid, or at least manage effectively, the regressions inevitable in life.

Like Kathryn and all our clients, we regress. As a clinician, if I do not have an ethics crisis survival plan, I am likely to a) do what I've always done, and b) regress to old ways of being. Remember, as clinicians, the expectation is not that we uphold our own principles, values, and standards but that we uphold those of the field. If we have not practiced and do not have a plan for managing, it becomes quite challenging to do anything other than what we have always done. And inevitably, Kathryn will regress. We will stray from our ethical values and principles. The goal, to be clear, is not to never succumb to a pitfall or crisis but to have the tools and strategies necessary to notice we are in such a situation and extract ourselves with as little damage to ourselves and others as possible.

When working with Kathryn, it would have been impossible to run through every possible scenario and rehearse solutions to each specific situation. Rather, we focused on deepening our understanding of her triggers, pitfalls, desires, and limitations and working on shoring up some skills to give her the best chance of managing her emotional self in a historically complicated setting. It was only after careful introspection and the development of a rather extensive self-understanding that she could engage in this sort of work. Without knowing the hooks on which her family members placed their bait, it would be impossible for Kathryn to understand her responses and then avoid them. "It must be noted that ethical decision-making models do not make ethical decisions, counselors do" (Francis, 2015, p. 3). Kathryn's crisis survival plan would not help her successfully manage her familial dilemmas; this, of course, was up to her.

To be useful and effective, an ethical protocol must be both proactive and reactive. That is, there must be elements that are set up in advance of encountering an ethical pitfall and others designed to aid the provider in extracting themselves from, or negotiating around, an already-occurring dilemma. To do ethics well and with integrity, we should set ourselves up for success as much as possible. We should, in short, have a usable plan that is simple but also thorough. I humbly offer mine here. You will find a worksheet version at the end of this chapter for your use.

Predict, Prepare, Prevent

Indeed, if an ethics crisis survival plan is the extraction tool we may use once we have found ourselves in a dilemma, we should also hold dear a strategy for maintaining an ethically sound practice. I do not mean that we should expect the ball to change hands, so to speak, but we should have a strategy for what to do if (and when) it does. When I established my practice in Montana, I was fairly naïve as to the ethical challenges that I might face. Now, the opposite is true: I have encountered so many ethical dilemmas and have heard so many others' in workshops and consultation groups on such a regular basis that I am in danger of failing to notice their existence or properly weigh their severity. (Of course, that's a conversation for a later chapter.)

It can be difficult to accurately predict the problems one might encounter, particularly when one is new in the field. However, we need not reinvent the wheel. By reviewing the ethical standards and principles relevant to our profession, we can not only learn about our responsibilities, but we can also predict potential dilemmas.

For example, because there is an ethical standard addressing multiple relationships, it would behoove me to consider how multiple relationships in my setting, community, practice, and life might appear. Further, because there is an ethical standard addressing confidentiality, it is worth thinking about how confidentiality might create some dilemmas or challenges in my unique situation. As Kathryn generated ideas about potential pitfalls on her trip home by recounting past experiences and generating hypothetical situations based on data about her family, we, too, can develop a pretty accurate sense of what ethical challenges we might encounter. Once I have identified particular ethical dilemmas that may walk through my door, I can then create a strategy for how I might mitigate their occurrence.

If we don't set our own boundaries, someone else will. In rural communities, where the demand is high and values emphasize transparency and familiarity, providers must not only remain vigilant about their boundaries but must also maintain a solid awareness of their tendencies and vulnerabilities. All providers should come to familiarize themselves with their liabilities and blind spots, but the rural provider, whether they are part of an agency struggling to keep up with the demand of the region or in private practice working hard to make ends meet, will be at greater risk of ethical infraction should they fail to maintain a high degree of self-awareness.

Finally, the clinician would benefit from educating both herself and her clients about her ethical responsibilities. Years ago, I decided to begin running. I had never been a runner and had certainly never run very far. A good friend of mine gave me some advice: sign up for a race, and then tell everyone you know. His strategy, which I share with you here, was to create a *network of accountability*. In our practice, we have a living document on which the therapists can indicate their openings, their preferred populations, and their "refer outs." This small mechanism is in place so that our office manager does not inadvertently pressure a therapist into taking on a case beyond her scope of practice. Further, we designed our website to include each provider's areas of competence, effectively broadening our network of accountability. Now, our gatekeeper knows what we do and don't do, and so do those we serve. This strategy is also regularly employed when we inform our clients of our confidentiality practices.

These practices are designed to keep you from walking into the minefield, but, of course, sometimes we find ourselves there, intentionally or not. Let's now discuss what to do once we have landed there. (See Figure 9.1.)

Identification

The first task we have in managing an ethical dilemma is identifying the dilemma. I attended a workshop on ethics some years ago where a woman told of a time when her client saw her naked in the locker room at the local health

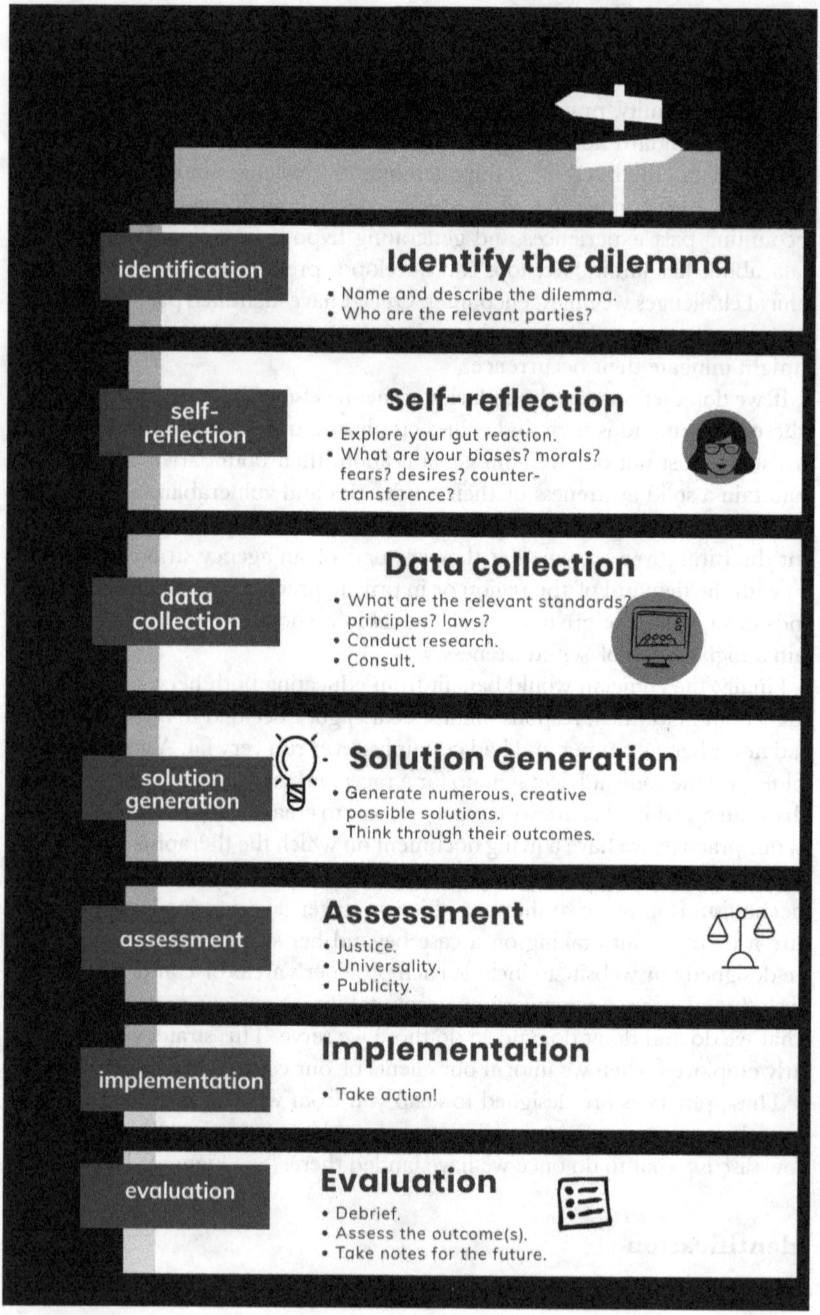

94 *Ethics in Rural Communities*

identification — **Identify the dilemma**
- Name and describe the dilemma.
- Who are the relevant parties?

self-reflection — **Self-reflection**
- Explore your gut reaction.
- What are your biases? morals? fears? desires? counter-transference?

data collection — **Data collection**
- What are the relevant standards? principles? laws?
- Conduct research.
- Consult.

solution generation — **Solution Generation**
- Generate numerous, creative possible solutions.
- Think through their outcomes.

assessment — **Assessment**
- Justice.
- Universality.
- Publicity.

implementation — **Implementation**
- Take action!

evaluation — **Evaluation**
- Debrief.
- Assess the outcome(s).
- Take notes for the future.

Figure 9.1 Resolving Ethical Dilemmas

club. I joked to the woman sitting next to me, "In rural Montana, we call that Tuesday." There are ways in which providers in rural and insular communities are so accustomed to ethical dilemmas that we can perhaps become numb to them. Looking over my caseload, there is only one client I see regularly with whom I do not have some form of multiple relationship. It is common for a rural provider in private practice to have a new patient call with a presenting problem beyond the scope of their competence. **Desensitization** occurs when an individual who is repeatedly exposed to a stimulus eventually experiences a reduction in their emotional response to it. As providers in such communities, we must remain vigilant, despite the plethora of ethical dilemmas that we encounter every week. I squeeze my toes so frequently, it is not unlikely they will fatigue.

One way to combat ethical dilemma desensitization, if you will, is to identify in advance the ethical dilemmas most likely to present. By maintaining an awareness of the ethical dilemmas most likely to impact your practice (Box 9.1), you can reduce the likelihood that you will become complacent and fail to identify an ethical dilemma sitting on your couch.

Box 9.1

Common Rural Ethical Dilemmas

- nonsexual multiple role relationships
- competency/scope of practice
- privacy + confidentiality
- referrals/limited resources/isolation
- burnout + self-care
- bartering

Further, to avoid becoming desensitized to threats to ethical action, one must be an active agent. Those of us who do cognitive behavioral, exposure, or acceptance and commitment therapies know that desensitization is a strategy to diminish an undesirable response to a stimulus. Here, when the stimulus is ethical murkiness, we must somehow avoid desensitization and instead remain vigilant and prepared. To do so, I employ and recommend a few techniques. First, enlist outside support. By talking with colleagues, or even friends who are not rural psychologists, I often gain perspective about my own realities that I struggle to see from my vantage point. I also find it helpful to reflect on, rather than avoid or ignore, my feelings of discomfort surrounding my multiple relationships, competency insecurities, and self-care. It can be easy to accept these struggles as normal and to fall victim to the pull from our community to be constantly professional and always imperturbable. However, if we ignore our emotions (our internal alarm system), we may miss out on avoiding walking right into an ethical minefield.

Before we can evaluate an ethical dilemma, we must first understand its nature. We can divide the types of ethical problems one might encounter into three major categories: *ethical distress, ethical conflict,* and *locus of authority* (Purtilo, 1987). (See Figure 9.2.) By accurately identifying which type of problem we are facing, we may gain insight into potential solutions or strategies for resolution.

Ethical distress is quite common in rural settings. As with any context, the system in which we exist exerts pressure on those within. In a rural setting, as we discussed in Section One, there are numerous forces weighing heavily on its practitioners. A long-standing ethical dilemma for me has been around the practice of neuropsychology. There is no formally trained neuropsychologist for over 100 miles, and those individuals either have extensive waiting lists or refuse to treat individuals outside their area (one way of managing the dilemma). My efforts to recruit a neuropsychologist have been unsuccessful, though the need for their services grows each year. We have, quite carefully, conducted neuropsychological screenings for individuals who would not otherwise receive services. We do not operate outside the scope of our competencies, but we do often find that clients have lingering questions at the end of our assessments due to our limitations. Further, these individuals are unlikely to receive further services due to constraints common in rural areas (gas money, time to travel, lengthy waiting lists, etc.). Evaluations of our ethical resolution suggest that we have maintained our ethical integrity despite being unable to provide the needed services.

Binds created by two conflicting standards or principles are known as *ethical conflict*. Let's examine an ethical conflict through the lens of a vignette. Dr. Martin has been working with a teenager, Jeffrey, for several months following his parents' divorce. In her last session with Jeffrey, he disclosed that he has been struggling with behaviors that to the trained ear sounded an awful lot like compulsions. Upon further investigation, it became evident to Dr. Martin that her client met the criteria for obsessive-compulsive disorder, a diagnosis outside her realm of competency. Of course, according to Ethical Standard 2.01: Boundaries of Competence, a psychologist is obliged to "provide services, teach, and conduct research with populations and in areas only within the boundaries of their competence, based on their education, training, supervised

| Ethical Distress: There is some external force or factor preventing the provider from acting ethically. | Locus of Authority: The dilemma lies in the inherent confusion as to whose morality is paramount. | Ethical Conflict: Two or more ethical imperatives (standards, principles, etc.) create a bind in which the provider, by adhering to one, compromises the other. |

Figure 9.2 The Nature of Ethical Dilemmas

experience, consultation, study, or professional experience." However, given the nature of her relationship with Jeffrey, the length of time it took him to open up to her, and the fact that she does not know anyone in her town of Silver Bay, Minnesota, qualified to work with someone with OCD, Dr. Martin may feel stuck. Further, Ethical Standard 10.10(a) outlines the psychologists' responsibilities regarding termination: "Psychologists terminate therapy when it becomes reasonably clear that the client/patient no longer needs the service, is not likely to benefit, or is being harmed by continued service" (APA, 1992). Jeffrey clearly still needs treatment, but given Dr. Martin's competencies, she cannot yet ensure that she will not cause harm or will be able to help Jeffrey, particularly in the short term, while she takes steps to increase her competence through training, supervision, reading, or consultation. Dr. Martin would, thus, find herself faced with an ethical conflict in which she is bound by two competing standards (in this case, competence and termination) as they pertain to her work with Jeffrey. Ideally, the ethical bind is resolved by adherence to the prioritized ethical standard, but such priorities are not always clear and conclusions not always so simple.

Lastly, *locus of authority*—in which the ultimate question is whose morality takes precedence—can contribute to ethical dilemmas for clinicians. In rural communities, religion is typically significant to many members of the community (Vidich & Bensman, 2000), perhaps even including clinicians. Imagine if you will, Mr. Jones is a provider in an insular community who was raised to believe that homosexuality was immoral and that conversion therapy was the treatment most likely to enable a particular individual to live a healthy and happy life. He even had some friends growing up who went to conversion camps and saw benefits in their lives. Of course, we know that not only are conversion therapies harmful to the individual (Just the Facts Coalition, 2008); they are also in violation of Ethical Standard 2.04: Bases for Scientific and Professional Judgment (APA, 1992). While the necessary follow-through is clear, it would nonetheless create some ethical itchiness for such a provider whose allegiance to his own moral beliefs would be compromised when he upholds the standards and principles of the profession. Mr. Jones might want to refer to a different provider, but if that was impossible, he would be ethically obligated to defer to the authority of the ethics code and shelve his own relevant morals.

As these vignettes illustrate, ethical dilemmas come in a variety of forms and exert different degrees of force on the professional. Some are easily settled, whereas others are messy. There are dilemmas that are easily "resolved," but the resolution does not bring peace to the clinician. In Dr. Martin's case, the resolution does not ensure an optimal outcome. Mr. Jones, of course, needed to prioritize the morals of the profession, rather than his own. Anyone who has ever had to do this knows it is uncomfortable, to say the least.

Self-Reflection

Now that we have adequately identified the type of dilemma in which we have found ourselves, we can move to the next step: noticing and naming your reaction and process. As I mentioned earlier, desensitization or habituation may impede our ability to notice ethical dilemmas, but these are not the only attributes relevant to the self that can hinder our ability to act ethically.

Several years ago, a colleague asked me if I would sit down with him to aid him in completing a graduate school assignment in which he was to speak with a provider in the field about an ethical dilemma. When recounting a dilemma, I mentioned my own personal "hero complex" and my desire to help everyone and anyone. He was quite amazed by what he saw to be a shameful disclosure and vulnerability. Of course, I am not proud that my tendency to want to be a hero might influence my decisions around issues of competence, *but it does*. To ignore this reality of self would be to set myself up for naïve engagement in ethical violations, which are—of course—abuses all the same.

In a recent workshop I facilitated, a woman shared a rather common dilemma, in which her daughter had feelings for one of her clients. Based on her work with the object of her daughter's affection, she knew that she was not a healthy potential partner for her daughter. Her motherly instincts compelled her to speak to her daughter openly and honestly, but her clinical responsibilities prohibited disclosures of any kind about her client (even the fact that she was a client). The therapist, in this case, was not only aware of how difficult it was for her not to speak openly, but also that her allegiance felt markedly stronger to her daughter than her client. Such self-awareness has led at least one of my colleagues to elect to never work with clients the ages of her children.

We mustn't forget that we are humans with strengths and weaknesses and that those weaknesses, in particular, may negatively impact our ability to do good, ethically sound work. As my graduate school professor would remind us, there are many who are "good but proud" or "good but frightened for their child's well-being." As rural clinicians, we may find ourselves in situations that stretch our ethical potential far beyond what we ever imagined. We may indeed be good, but we may have some liabilities, vulnerabilities, or biases that can compromise our action.

To bring awareness to the self, we must first start by noticing our reaction. We must notice the behaviors in which we feel compelled to engage and any urges to engage or disengage. We must, in those moments of toe squeezing, check in with our system and see what our gut is telling us to do.

Once we have understood our gut reaction, we can then identify, and perhaps explore, our own morals and values and how they relate to the dilemma at hand. Of course, this work is best done prior to encountering an ethical dilemma, but most of us working in rural (or any underserved or insular) communities are too busy responding to the needs of our people to spend time meditating on our own values. (More on burnout and self-care later!) However, any good clinician likely has an idea of where they stand on certain issues, and when a dilemma presents itself, it is a worthwhile time to dig a little deeper into the relevant aspects of our upbringing, religious beliefs, experiences, and morals.

This is also a great moment to mention time. Often ethical dilemmas can trigger our anxiety, and our anxiety can fuel a sense of urgency that may or may not be real. I have always loved the parenting phrase "If you need an answer right now, the answer is no." It allows the parent to dictate the timeline rather than a toddler's urgency. Taking time through a slow, reflective process may not only allow us the opportunity to clarify our dilemma but may actually resolve the dilemma. A therapist came to me recently and asked, "What shall I do if I am scheduled with a new client I think I know socially?" In the time it took me to respond to her request, the client had reached back out to the office and requested a different therapist, having realized the overlap himself.

One of the benefits I have found from reaching out to colleagues, reviewing written case material, or calling an ethics hotline (a free service from many liability insurance carriers) is that it provides me with a forum to think or perhaps talk through my dilemmas. In the process of outlining the issue for myself—or, even better, another person—I can reflect on my cognitive processes by hearing myself think aloud.

With some mindfulness, we can view our process with equanimity and not come to see our thoughts as truth but simply as ideas. Earlier, I stated that ethics are a deeply personal thing and that ethical codes are designed to provide anchor points that prevent us from simply leaning on our own opinions or ideas. That is to say (and this is important to note): ethical dilemmas are dilemmas because of who we are, how we think, our lived experience, or our desires and dreams. Often, our past, present, or future comingles with our client's experience, presentation, or predicament to create the dilemma. Consequently, a critical self-appraisal and careful observation of our cognitive processes will allow us to develop a clear understanding of how we contribute to, benefit from, or are negatively impacted by this dilemma.

Metacognitive processes require insight, self-awareness, and honesty. In the times of toe squeezing, can I take a moment to reflect on my immediate reactions? As I'm gathering data and generating potential solutions, might I reflect on my judgments and ideas? A benefit of metacognitive awareness is that I am less likely to fall prey to my own biases or blind spots if I am diligent about observing the ways in which my mind operates. Some questions that might be helpful to ask oneself include

- How does this affect me personally?
- How do I feel about how this affects me personally?
- Am I affected by some countertransference?
- What internal judgments, biases, heuristic traps, or personal convictions are relevant?
- What would I recommend (differently, perhaps) to someone else in a similar dilemma?
- What would someone else say if I told them about this dilemma?
- Am I influenced by any external, institutional, cultural, or financial forces?
- Are there solutions that I am avoiding entertaining?
- Is this urgent, or can I pause, reflect, and come back to it?

By exploring the process of thinking through an ethical dilemma in a systematic way, it is possible to identify and perhaps mitigate the effects of one's cognitive biases. From there, we have a greater chance of maintaining neutrality as we begin to create a solution to our dilemma.

Data Collection

Next, we need to gather data. To come to a good solution, we need to understand the elements in tension. This process will vary based on what type of dilemma you are facing. The chart in Box 9.2 reveals what questions one might ask, based on the type of ethical problem they are facing.

Once we have answered these questions, we must do our homework to better understand the power each force exerts and identify our ethical allegiance. For example, in the case of Dr. Martin from earlier, we remember that her dilemma was created between two competing sections of the ethics code (competence and termination). In this case, Dr. Martin had to identify the relevant standards and principles and the weight they each carried.

Box 9.2

Three Types of Ethical Problems

- **Ethical Distress**: What are the external forces acting upon me/ my client that are precluding me from acting ethically?
- **Ethical Conflict**: What are the ethical standards/ laws/principles that are in conflict?
- **Locus of Authority**: Who are the potential sources of authority, and what are their moral and ethical imperatives?

In the Appendix, you will find a number of resources designed to aid you in the process of making good decisions. Numerous books and articles have been written to give the provider a road map for navigating tricky ethical situations. While few of them center on work with rural and insular communities, their guidance can most certainly be generalized. Have a few of these on hand as sources for data collection during this phase of resolution.

Further, many professional liability companies and professional organizations offer consultation to members on ethical issues in their work. Often, contacting one of these hotlines can provide the clinician with resources, insight, and an outside perspective on the situation at hand.

Solution Generation

Now that we have identified our dilemma, done some digging around our immediate response, collected data, and identified the thinking patterns that arose within ourselves, it's important to start thinking about action steps and their possible consequences.

First, let's start by generating a list of possible outcomes to our dilemma using as much creativity as possible because my time practicing in rural America has taught me that the unthinkable often happens. For example, I began working with a client I knew through a friend who had long ago moved away. I did not believe this would impair my ability to serve as her therapist as I had not maintained that previous relationship. After a year of working together, she began to date a man I had dated some 15 years earlier. Awkward as that may seem, imagine me attending her wedding, with my old friend and old boyfriend both present and both curious how I know my client. Let this story serve as an example that when it comes to generating possible outcomes to ethical issues in a rural or insular setting, one can never be creative enough. This means that as we generate solutions, we must think through carefully, creatively, and fully the ramifications of our actions. Additionally, we may need to be creative in generating solutions as the pressures exerted by our community may make us feel as if we have no choice in the matter at all.

As with any good brainstorming, solution generation is best done with at least one other consultant. While it may be tempting to make haste or not to burden our colleagues, utilizing consultation during this phase of the process may mean the difference between generating a viable, ethically sound solution and defaulting to a lesser outcome, simply because your creativity failed you.

Throughout the process of generating solutions, we must draw upon the knowledge gleaned from the previous steps in this process. Now that we know the type of ethical problem we are facing, we can generate solutions applicable to that sort of dilemma.

Should we be struggling with an issue of ethical distress, we might look to see how we can resolve the distress by affecting change in the contributing forces. For example, if I am tasked with supervising a student who is my cousin, perhaps I might arrange a different placement with my institution or swap trainees with a colleague. I will reduce the external pressure creating the distress as a means of resolving the conflict. If I am attempting to reconcile an ethical conflict, as Dr. Martin was earlier, I may generate solutions based on the prioritized ethical obligation. In her case, confidentiality trumped reporting or addressing infractions of a colleague. Finally, if my own moral compass leads me into a dilemma with an ethical guideline, I can generate solutions that support me as I manage the distress that will arise from my morality taking a back seat to the ethics of my profession (Box 9.3).

Box 9.3

Three Types of Ethical Solutions

- **Ethical Distress**: Can I somehow change the external factors or reduce their influence on the situation?

- **Ethical Conflict**: Is there a way to honor both relevant ethical imperatives? Which ethical obligation has precedent?
- **Locus of Authority**: Whose morality is paramount? If I put my morality aside, does the dilemma find resolution?

Too often, when we have a dilemma, we may see only two potential alternatives. However, if we are capable of creating a third option, we may find ourselves less limited, our distress lessened as a result. Once I have generated several (creative) possible solutions to the ethical dilemma, perhaps through brainstorming with trusted colleagues, I then must evaluate those solutions to assess their impact.

Evaluation

As fallible beings, we need structured ways of evaluating our ethical decision making. To this end, Stadler (1986), the American Counseling Association (Forester-Miller & Davis, 1995), and others have provided us with some strategies for systematically evaluating our decisions. Stadler recommends evaluating our decisions by applying three simple tests to each potential solution. (See Box 9.4.)

These questions are designed to reduce the threat of bias, interpersonal dynamics, personal beliefs, and institutional forces. In essence, they aim to neutralize the humanity and generate greater objectivity.

Box 9.4

- **Justice**: Would you treat others the same way in a similar situation?
- **Universality**: Would you recommend the same course of action to another individual in your situation?
- **Publicity**: Would you want your decision written up and publicized?

As a therapist, I know myself to be loving and kind. I became a therapist, of course, to help others, and I aim to do so in all of my interactions and interventions. There are times, however, when my compassion and genuine care for my clients may interfere with my judgment. I know I am not alone in this trap. Take Emily, a 42-year-old mother of twins whose husband died several years ago. She has been coming to therapy for two years, on and off, to resolve her grief and gain coping strategies for managing her role as a single parent. Having lost my father when I was young, my compassion for Emily echoes my warmth for my own mother, who raised two children following our family's tragedy. In our last session, Emily disclosed having struck her child from a place of anger and despair last week. She was remorseful, and I sensed shame in her narrative. It wasn't until I was making dinner later that evening that my role as a mandated reporter and her behavior, which could be defined as child abuse, clicked in my mind.

I did not need to, as these are drilled into all professionals early and often, but I could have reviewed the following state statutes:

> **41-3-201, MCA. Reports.** (1) When professionals and officials listed in 41-3-201 subsection (2) know or have reasonable cause to suspect, as a result of information they receive in their professional or official capacity, that a child is abused or neglected by anyone regardless of whether the person suspected of causing the abuse or neglect is a parent or other person responsible for the child's welfare, they shall report the matter promptly to the Department of Public Health and Human Services, Child and Family Services Division's **MONTANA'S STATEWIDE TOLL-FREE CHILD ABUSE HOTLINE, (1-866-820-5437).**
> **41-3-102, MCA. Definitions.**
> (6) "Child" or "youth" means any person under 18 years of age. (7) (a) "Child abuse or neglect" means:
> (i) *actual* physical or psychological harm to a child
>
> (HHS, 2019, emphasis added)

Reporting Emily would, I suspected, trigger shame and raise questions of my adherence to the principle of beneficence. Of course, my legal obligations were, and always are, paramount, so I knew I needed to file a report with CPS. As I evaluated my solution, I realized the detrimental effects this might have on Emily—who had long struggled with depression rooted in issues with inefficacy—and our working alliance, which had been tenuous over the years as she wrestled with projections of her shame. I asked myself the questions in Box 9.4, and I came to the following conclusion: if a colleague consulted on a similar case, one in which I was not familiar with the individuals, I would have strongly recommended he file a report. Likewise, if I were somehow featured in our small-town newspaper as the clinician who failed to report parents who had abused their children, I would, myself, feel shameful and irresponsible. Finally, if I was conducting an evaluation (and, accordingly, had far less of an established relationship with the parent), I likely would have reported the case, without question. As you can see, the questions posed by Stadler allow us to move away from our biases toward greater impartiality and, accordingly, greater ethical responsibility (Forester-Miller & Davis, 2016).

As additional bits of insight, one might also elect to query: What would you think of this if a mentor had made that decision? What would you think if this decision was made regarding someone you loved and cared for? (Strom-Gottfried, 2007). If I imagined Suzy, Emily's daughter who had been on the receiving end of the strike, to be my own daughter, the path toward action suddenly became quite clear.

Implementation

For those wondering, in upholding my legal responsibilities while still maintaining a connection to my ethical guidelines, I had Emily come in the following day to make a call to the child abuse hotline with me. We preserved our relationship, and it was, to my surprise, actually a de-shaming experience for Emily to take public responsibility for her actions. All this caused her to rethink her stress and contributed to several life changes that have served her in her quest to be a better parent.

Our implementation is not always precise, nor is it always effective in producing desirable outcomes for all relevant parties. We may leave with a pit in our stomach or we may rupture therapeutic alliances irreparably. Taking note of our reactions—and the reactions of those we serve—will help us in the next phase of evaluating our decisions and their consequences.

Evaluation/Debrief

Ethical dilemmas are inevitable and, in rural situations, frequent. Of course, while our first goal should be to avoid ethical dilemmas when possible and our second to negotiate them thoughtfully and with integrity, our final goal should be to evaluate them with honest scrutiny. Through a thorough evaluation (Box 9.5), we can reflect on what went well and what went poorly and, of course, what we can do differently (or perhaps better) next time.

Box 9.5

- Process

  What did I miss?
  What could I have done differently?
  What mistakes did I make that I was lucky enough to avoid the consequences of?

We should always find things wrong with our solutions, and we should always be able to find fault in our process. In this way, we are always strengthening our ethical decision-making muscles.

In summary, we should arrange our practices to avoid ethical dilemmas in the first place. When that inevitably fails us, we should have a method for appraising our resolution and outcomes so that we can learn and apply this knowledge to avoiding future ethical dilemmas. For myself, I like to debrief my ethical decisions with my colleague (or, if I can maintain privacy and confidentiality, my spouse). Find something that works for you, that includes scrutinizing elements of the dilemma, the process, and the outcome, and use it regularly.

Now that we have a systematic process for managing ethical dilemmas, let us walk through some of the more typical ethical dilemmas faced by rural practitioners.

ETHICAL DILEMMA WORKSHEET

- What is the dilemma?
  - What is the type of dilemma?
    - Ethical distress (There is some external force or factor preventing the provider from acting ethically)
    - Ethical conflict (Two or more ethical imperatives create a bind in which the provider, by adhering to one, compromises the other)
    - Locus of authority (The dilemma lies in the inherent confusion as to whose morality is paramount)
  - Who are the relevant parties?
- Self-reflection:
  - What is my gut telling me to do?
  - What am I feeling about this (desires, fears, morals, biases)?
  - What is my countertransference?
- Data collection:
  - What are the relevant standards?
  - What are the relevant principles?
  - What are the relevant laws?
  - Review research.
  - Consult.
- Solution generation:
  - At least three possible, creative solutions!
- Assessment:
  - Justice: Would you treat others the same way in a similar situation?
  - Universality: Would you recommend the same course of action to another individual in your situation?
  - Publicity: Would you want your decision written up and publicized?
- Implementation
  - Take action!
- Evaluation:
  - Debrief:
    - What did I miss?
    - What could I have done differently?
    - Is there anything I now understand differently?
  - Review the outcomes:
  - What were the consequences?
  - Make notes for future dilemmas:
    - Could I avoid this in the future?

References

American Psychological Association. (1992). *Ethical principles of psychologists and code of conduct*. Retrieved May 18, 2003, from www.apa.org/ethics/code/code-1992

Brown, L. S. (1994). Concrete boundaries and the problem of literal-mindedness: A response to Lazarus. *Ethics & Behavior, 4*(3), 275–281.

Forester-Miller, H., & Davis, T. E. (1995). *A practitioner's guide to ethical decision making*. Alexandria, VA: American Counseling Association.

Forester-Miller, H., & Davis, T. E. (2016). *Practitioner's guide to ethical decision making* (Revised ed.). Alexandria, VA: American Counseling Association.

Francis, P. C. (2015). *A review of contemporary ethical decision-making models for mental health professionals*. Eastern Michigan University. Retrieved October 12, 2019, from https://files.eric.ed.gov/fulltext/ED565003.pdf

Just the Facts Coalition. (2008). *Just the facts about sexual orientation and youth: A primer for principals, educators, and school personnel*. Retrieved October 12, 2019, from www.apa.org/pi/lgbt/resources/just-the-facts.pdf

Purtilo, R. (1987). Rural health care: The forgotten quarter of medical ethics. *Second Opinion, 6*, 11–33.

Stadler, H. A. (1986). Making hard choices: Clarifying controversial ethical issues. *Counseling & Human Development, 19*, 1–10.

Strom-Gottfried, K. (2007). *Straight talk about professional ethics*. Chicago: Lyceum Books.

US Department of Health and Human Services. (2019). *Montana school guidelines for the identification and reporting of child abuse and neglect 2019–2020*. Retrieved December 19, 2019, from https://dphhs.mt.gov/Portals/85/cfsd/documents/SchoolGuidelinesChildAbuseandNeglect.pdf

Vidich, A. J., & Bensman, J. (2000). *Small town in mass society: Class, power, and religion in a rural community*. Chicago: University of Illinois Press.

10 Dual Roles, Multiple Relationships

No One Is a Stranger Here

Multiple Relationships, Defined

Dual, or multiple, relationships are one of the primary sources of ethical conflict for rural providers or providers in insular communities. The smaller the population, the more likely there is to be overlap in the lives of its members. In fact, rural providers are more likely than their urban counterparts to report engagement in multiple relationships (Burgard, 2013).

Ask any rural provider about their experience of multiple relationships, and they are likely to tell you that they have resigned themselves to the inevitability of such relationships. In my training, I came to believe that my task was to avoid multiple relationships; in rural psychology, the work surrounds navigating them gracefully.

Because of the ubiquitous nature of multiple relationships in rural practice, providers may become so desensitized that they fail to realize the implications of multiple relationships. A provider (particularly in a small town) can become so accustomed to overlap in their clients, social circles, and business lives that they can become desensitized to the existence and impact of multiple relationships. (See Figure 10.1.)

First, I want to take a moment to define multiple relationships, which can come in several different formats. For our purposes, I will rely on the American Psychological Association's definition:

> A multiple relationship occurs when a psychologist is in a professional role with a person and (1) at the same time is in another role with the same person, (2) at the same time is in a relationship with a person closely associated with or related to the person with whom the psychologist has the professional relationship, or (3) promises to enter into another relationship in the future with the person or a person closely associated with or related to the person.
>
> (1992)

Thus, according to the APA, professionals may find themselves in multiple relationships in three ways. First, a therapist can have a client with whom they

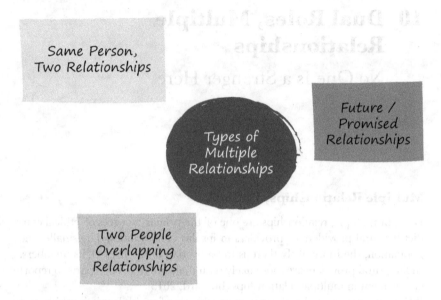

Figure 10.1 Types of Multiple Relationships

have a separate personal or professional relationship (e.g., the client is a supervisee, the client is a fellow church member, the individual client comes to them for family therapy), a therapist can be in a relationship with someone who is in a relationship with someone else they are in a relationship with (e.g., the client is dating their daughter, the client is friends with a close friend of the therapist, the client is the therapist's doctor), or there is a promise made to the client of a future relationship that would create either the first or second scenario.

Particularly in rural communities, all these relationships are common.

If my examination of ethical dilemmas had stopped when my graduate training ended, I might be left thinking that practitioners should dutifully avoid all multiple relationships. In *The Fiduciary Heart of Ethics,* Ed Zuckerman, Ph.D. (2012) writes: "We have an ethical obligation to avoid harmful multiple relationships." He goes on to explain that our duty to our client, our fiduciary responsibility, may be compromised by a conflict of interest occurring as a result of the dual role. Further, when a therapist has overlapping relationships with clients, confidentiality breaches may be more likely to occur. Indeed, while aspirational in nature, many have acknowledged the importance of avoiding dual relationships when possible (Keith-Spiegel & Koocher, 1985; Haas & Malouf, 1989; Adleman & Barrett, 1990). In rural practice and several other settings, this is simply impossible (Helbok, Marinelli, & Walls, 2006).

Upon closer inspection, though, the APA Ethics Code, as one example, does not stipulate strictly that one must avoid dual roles—instead, it invites significant nuance while providing some general guidelines.

A psychologist refrains from entering into a multiple relationship if the multiple relationship could reasonably be expected to impair the psychologist's objectivity, competence, or effectiveness in performing his or her functions as a psychologist, or otherwise risks exploitation or harm to the person with whom the professional relationship exists.

(1992)

Similar to the American Counseling Association, which suggests that counselors approach multiple relationships with "care and caution," the APA expects that practitioners will consider the ways in which a dual role will impact the client *and* the clinician (Hermann & Robinson-Kurpius, 2006). While sexual relationships are definitively off the table, multiple relationships are not inherently forbidden, though caution is advised (Lazarus & Zur, 2002).

Therapeutic Implications

The therapeutic relationship is unique. It is qualitatively different than personal or even many professional relationships insofar as there are firm boundaries, clear expectations, and guidelines established to ensure the creation of a holding environment in which a person can change or even transform. By creating a space in which a person can trust that their deepest shame, their most painful memories, and the worst parts of themselves can be shared (and perhaps even loved), the therapist creates something different from friendship. Similarly, though we may, in our professional lives, display constant equanimity, a nonjudgmental stance, and unending positive regard for our clients, we are not (shall we be honest here?) always so balanced and wholesome. Many clients need us to be all loving or all accepting as the created holding environment allows them to reveal the shameful recesses of their experiences.

Years ago, I was working in a small community and seeing a therapist (Jane) to process some childhood trauma. My employer, who triggered many old childhood wounds, sought services from my therapist. I will never forget my therapist informing me that she had refused my boss as a potential client to preserve the integrity and safety of our work. If they had worked together, it would certainly have compromised my felt sense of security, an experience vital to the healing I was undertaking. My therapist upheld a boundary that, if eroded, would have negatively affected my potential progress. Should my therapist have accepted my employer as her client and I had learned of this, it would have inevitably compromised my sense of safety and security as I would fear that my impartial therapist, who was always on my team, now had a split allegiance.

The reasons we should be cautious and careful with multiple relationships is that they have the power to cause **impairment**, **exploitation**, and **harm**. The APA (1992) advises that those that "would not reasonably be expected to cause impairment or risk exploitation or harm are not unethical." Given the ubiquity of multiple relationships in insular communities, it is essential that we evaluate each one for its potential consequences, including impairment, exploitation, and harm (Box 10.1). We would be wise to view multiple relationships as the petri dish in which a host of bacteria can grow if given the proper environment and ingredients (Schank & Skovholt, 2006).

Box 10.1

Harm: three elements to consider

- Incompatibility of expectations between client and psychologist
- Increased commitments in nontherapeutic roles
- Power differentials between psychologist and client

(APA, n.d.)

Before our next clinical example, I want to review the three elements important to avoid in a multiple relationship: impairment, exploitation, and harm.

Impairment: When we talk about impairment in this context, we are really speaking about competence, objectivity, and effectiveness. Competence is defined as "one's developed repertoire of skills, especially as it is applied to a task or set of tasks" (APA, n.d.). If a multiple relationship hinders a professional's ability to effectively apply their skill set to the work, it is likely causing impairment. An example of an impairment-causing dual role would be one in which the practitioner, because of constraints resulting from one of the relationships, cannot effectively serve as an agent of change. Multiple relationships may threaten our competence, objectivity, and effectiveness in a number of ways. Overlapping relationships may make it difficult to retain objectivity when we now have new information about a client. A fellow churchgoer may demonstrate behaviors with her children or spouse that you, as the therapist, cannot ignore as they pertain to the relational focus of your work. If a client with a desire for exploring her sexual intimacy begins dating your son, would this impair your ability to be objective and solely focus on your client's needs? It is likely. If a colleague desperately pleaded with you to see her nephew, despite his age being generally outside the scope of your competence, would this impair your work? In each of these cases, there is no obvious pathway toward right action. However, we can see how each scenario, like a petri dish, could easily grow an unethical fungus if you will, clouding our judgment or reducing our objectivity.

Exploitation: Exploitation occurs when a clinician or researcher takes advantage of a client or other individual as a result of the therapeutic relationship. Let's say a therapist is working with a client who is employed at the same place of business as the therapist's sister. Throughout the course of therapy, the therapist learns about opportunities within the company that might benefit her sister. Should she reveal these to her sister in any way, she would be exploiting the therapeutic relationship to benefit her sister. A therapist is working with a schoolteacher in whose class the therapist's son is scheduled to be next fall. Rumors lead the therapist to believe the educator to be harsh and too firm with her students. The educator is in therapy for grief related to her parents' deaths, but the therapist finds herself shifting the focus to help the client learn to better manage her frustration and understand the importance of shame-free discipline. Again, the clinician is engaging in exploitation of the client and, in both cases, is abusing the power of the therapist role to better her (or her loved one's) life circumstances. Perhaps the most devastating of all multiple relationships are the ones in which it is the therapist who gets their needs met above the client's. The flow chart in Figure 10.2 should serve as a rough guide for practitioners. Note: At no point can one proceed carefree. Caution is always recommended.

Harm: Harm is the negative impact of an inflicted emotional, psychological, or physical wound. In psychotherapy, harm can take many forms. Anyone who has been at this awhile or has done their own work knows that there are potentially harmful side effects from even the best of therapy in the form of pain, a temporary increase in symptoms, and re-experiencing of trauma. While harm

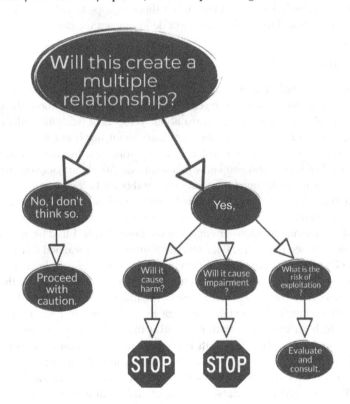

Figure 10.2 Multiple Relationship Flow Chart

along the way to positive therapeutic outcomes may be a somewhat tolerable side effect of the therapy process, multiple relationships can compromise the integrity, objectivity, or clarity of the therapist, making it possible that they inflict unnecessary harm. To this end, a therapist may cause harm by terminating treatment due to the initiation of a multiple relationship. They also may cause harm by continuing treatment despite their dual roles. Imagine a practitioner in a rural community is treating a woman for depression. Perhaps the woman's spouse requests therapy, and, because they live in a provider desert, she is the only one able to take the case. The woman may begin to feel distrustful of her therapist and unable to tell her about interpersonal problems in her marriage as a result of the dual roles served by the clinician. Perhaps the woman has had trust issues her entire life and is profoundly hurt by her therapist's perceived disloyalty, and her depression worsens.

A common value in rural communities is neighborliness and sameness (Vidich & Bensman, 2000). As we discussed in the first section of this book, therapists in rural communities are commonly expected to be embedded in the community. The more professional and boundaried a therapist is, the more likely their community members will view this as a barrier to care. The culture and values of a community may make multiple relationships unavoidable or even obligatory. And from there, it is a slippery slope to believing that they are thus harmless. This, however, is most definitely not the case.

Neutrality

One way a multiple relationship can cause harm is through a loss of therapist neutrality that comes as the result of knowledge learned about the client indirectly. Maybe your friends gossip about your client (without realizing he is your client), or your hairdresser complains about her boss's misogyny (her boss is your client), or your client is contemplating quitting her job working for a friend of yours (and you know this would negatively impact your friend). Things become murky quickly, as lines blur and boundaries overlap.

As humans it is generally impossible for us to "un-hear" things. That is, once we become privy to a bit of information, it becomes very difficult to ignore that data when making decisions or engaging with our clients. I had been working with Client B (see Figure 10.3) for several months when I learned that another client (Client D) was her direct supervisor at her place of employment. This disclosure also illuminated for me that I was a patient at the physical therapy clinic where they both worked. Of course, the following week, I would see Client D at the clinic as I was checking in for my appointment. I was thoroughly invested in both women's treatment, and it made little sense to refer either out. I soon learned that they both knew they were in therapy with me, and though I could neither confirm nor deny that reality, it gave me some relief knowing that they knew and were willful participants in this multiple relationship. The two had an amicable work relationship, and they both indicated acceptance of the multiple relationship.

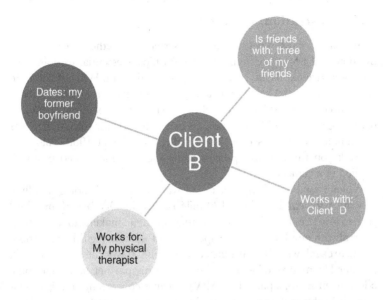

Figure 10.3 Multiple Relationships With Client B

One day, Client D, in speaking about some job-related stressors, intimated that Client B often appeared angry and hostile at work. Though remaining focused on Client D and her predicament, my brain unconsciously filed that information away. It was particularly pertinent because Client B, who appears meek in my office, had been engaging in a series of interventions designed to help her gain courage and assertiveness. On the one hand, this information was helpful in gaining a more holistic sense of Client B. In fact, I often wish I could know more about what my clients are like in the "real world." On the other hand, I now had information, gleaned from a confidential source, that I really should not be privy to and had to decide how to shift our work (or not) or how to incorporate this element of Client B's personality into my conceptualization. Gaining such knowledge from third parties (multiple relationships) circumvents the established channel of information and may compromise my client's sense of privacy and safety. Whereas many therapists wrestle with whether or not to look their clients up on Facebook, living in a small town can feel like we are wandering unintentionally through the halls of Google, inadvertently gathering information about our clients that we neither asked for nor can fairly integrate into our work (DiLillo & Gale, 2011). Multiple relationships exacerbate this dilemma tenfold, as they increase the likelihood that we will wind up knowing more about our clients than they have directly shared. Multiple relationships may also compromise our ability to see our clients accurately, may create tensions of allegiance, and may have us feeling feelings toward our clients that are not ours alone.

Case Illustration: Harmony

As we have discussed before, having a systematic method for evaluating the potential impact of multiple relationships is essential to doing our very best to avoid harm, exploitation, or impairment. When it comes to appraising potential harm done to a client, practitioners should consider these three elements: incompatibility of expectations between client and psychologist, increased commitments in nontherapeutic roles, and power differentials between psychologist and client (Kitchener, 1988). Allow me to walk you through this process using the aforementioned protocol, applied to a clinical example.

When I established my practice, I was the only psychologist willing to work with children for a 120-mile radius. In October of my third year in practice, I received a call from a colleague making an assessment referral with emphasis on the importance of completing this evaluation. My heart sank when I heard the client's name. It was the child—we will call her Harmony—of a couple for whom my partner had done some odd jobs in seasons past. The APA guideline concerning multiple relationships echoed through my mind as I listened to the voice mail. Harmony had been failing out of school, experiencing tremendous conflict with her parents and siblings, and, despite 18 months of therapy, had been making no progress. Her therapist had begun to wonder if, despite Harmony's anxious and hyperactive presentation, there wasn't some underlying depression falling below the realm of conscious awareness. Harmony had grown increasingly defensive in recent sessions and began to threaten termination. She had balked at my colleague's supposition that maybe she was depressed, and her parents had, similarly, refused the referral to a psychiatrist. The therapist, following some growing concerns of self-injurious behaviors, had gotten the family curious about my work with clients through therapeutic assessment and had finally received permission to make a referral.

This was, of course, not my first time managing the situation created when two ethical guidelines were in conflict. It was, however, the first time I saw no clear path forward. Every lesson learned in my graduate training and professional experience since was suddenly not applicable. If a multiple relationship is likely to unfold, we had learned to refer to a colleague. Alas, there were no referrals to be made. I realized, in hindsight, that the nuances of multiple relationships were rarely discussed amongst my urban-dwelling colleagues. If one appeared, the most reasonable strategy was to terminate or avoid commencing treatment.

Would it be harmful to refuse services to Harmony based on our multiple relationships? Perhaps. This young woman was struggling profoundly in school and at home, and her parents and therapist were deeply concerned that she was suffering from some undiagnosed psychological condition that was hindering her ability to thrive.

Would it be harmful to agree to services to Harmony based on our social overlap? Perhaps.

I spent the next day dissecting the previous statements into their components, searching for answers, consulting with colleagues, and searching for knowledge in books and articles. This dilemma is part of what led me to write this book.

Using the method for ethical conflict resolution proposed in Chapter 9, I will walk through this dilemma and its resolution.

Identify: The first task is to identify the ethical dilemma and the relevant parties. In the case of Harmony, our dilemma would be labeled an "ethical conflict" as there are two or more ethical imperatives that combine to create the bind: Multiple Relationships (3.05) and Principle A: Beneficence and Nonmaleficence (APA, 1992). Further, our responsibility to uphold the principle of justice is relevant as we are tasked with ensuring that everyone has equal access to treatment.

Box 10.2

In ethical matters concerning multiple relationships, very often the therapist or someone close to the therapist is an affected party. Unlike dilemmas that lie mainly in the realm of our clients, such conflict may tax the therapist or negatively (or positively) impact her family or friends and may result in a situation in which the therapist must hold distress or discomfort in the spirit of acting ethically on behalf of the client.

We know that this is a matter concerning a multiple relationship: more specifically, the sort that involves two relationships with the same client, the client in this case being the family. We also know that my ethical guidelines expect me to act with caution and care in the spirit of avoiding harm, exploitation, and impairment.

Moving forward, I want to identify the affected parties. Harmony and her parents are one of the identified parties involved, of course, and I, and my family, are the other. That is, the ethical dilemma exerts force on both Harmony and me. The situation might affect her in some profound ways but also may impact me and my family. It might influence her parents' willingness or obligation to hire (or not hire) my spouse in the future. It might also affect our relationship with Harmony's family in the future. In many ethical dilemmas, the therapist is left holding the unresolved elements of the conflict. In cases of multiple relationships in which the therapist is herself a component of the dilemma, the weight is often intensified.

Self-Reflection: Once I had identified the dilemma, I then observed my reactions, took note of any relevant values or ideals, and observed what I was initially compelled to do. I quickly noticed the desire to be a hero. As you may remember from Chapter 7, I have a tendency—as many of us likely do—to wish to help everyone. Being in an insular community has only heightened this tendency as I am often seen as the "only person capable of helping so-and-so." So it is the first thing I think of when I find myself in such an ethical conflict. To be clear, particularly to those readers to whom similar sentiments apply, this does not come from a bad or arrogant place, but rather from some combination of healthy confidence and awareness of need. It is easy to fall victim to, however, because the desire may compel a provider to trample over some important ethical boundaries en route to hero-dom.

In contrast to my desires for heroics, I noticed that I was initially reluctant to take on Harmony's case. My spouse is a very private person, and I am frequently protective of his status as my partner. Further, I foresaw future interactions with Harmony's family, which would now become awkward and possibly fraught. Experience has taught me that often child assessments become family assessments or at least carry the risk of the provider needing to give some difficult feedback to the parents. I was aware of how my previous role as acquaintance might impair my ability to assert my expertise or how our ongoing casual relationship might make Harmony's parents significantly more vulnerable. Of course, my task was to weigh whether or not the vulnerability they might experience would classify as harm and if it would be defined as more significant than what any parent being told of ways they may have contributed to their child's difficulties might feel.

As a relatively new provider, I was aware of a desire not only for business but also to establish solid referral pathways. My business and my student loans needed this referral. I was subject to "ethical fading": the phenomenon in which an ethical dilemma or moral implications move to the background, and other elements become more salient (e.g., personal gain, ease, profit) (Tenbrunsel & Messick, 2004). To counter this, I reminded myself that I had plenty of clients and a well-established relationship with the referring professional and that even if I turned down this case, I was likely to still be able to afford my mortgage payment.

Throughout the entire process, I was reminded of an aspect of the initial contact: the desperation reported by the referring professional. She was deeply concerned for this kid and family, and I found myself influenced by her anxiety. Reflecting, I noticed my desire to help not only Harmony's family but my colleague as well. When I imagined turning down the case, I was filled with guilt aimed not only at Harmony and her parents but also at the therapist, with whom I had a close professional bond.

At the time, I'd had few experiences with multiple relationships. I was still fresh, and my sensors for infractions were perhaps keener than they are today. These days, my multiple relationship alarm goes off nearly once per session. I easily lose track of the ways my life weaves into the lives of my clients. This desensitization is dangerous as it makes me likely to overlook red flags and threats to my ethical integrity.

Data Collection: I had already identified the relevant standards and began reading literature relevant to the matter. I came to identify two primary sources of harm in such circumstances: an exertion of power that resulted in exploitation and a loss of professionalism or poor decision making resulting from boundary erosion (Burgard, 2013). The first, in my assessment, was not relevant here, whereas the second was. Kitchener (1988) suggests that one of the sources of distress in clients related to multiple relationships is in disparate expectations of roles. That is, if Harmony's parents were led to view me as a consultant hired to diagnose a problem in their child and offer solutions and recommendations, they might be unduly harmed if I should suddenly suggest we explore the family dynamics relevant to Harmony's difficulties.

In addition, research shows that one of the primary subjective difficulties for rural practitioners is the feeling of being "at work" 24 hours a day. That is, because of the nature of the small community and one's role as therapist to many amongst peers and neighbors, a rural provider may never feel fully relieved of their clinical duties. Indeed, my experience has been that even when participating in fully recreational opportunities, I have a small part of my mind worrying about how professional I may or may not appear. In terms of the principle of justice, then, maintaining my sustainability and well-being is a professional obligation to my community. If I take on too many cases that blur the boundaries between my professional and personal lives, I jeopardize my ability to help my community in the long term.

As I often do, I consulted on this case with a trusted, logical colleague in an urban area. As we worked through the details and nuances, she helped me identify not only potential solutions to the dilemma but also the ramifications of those options.

Solution Generation: The conflict appeared to have only two outcomes: take the case or do not. However, through consultation, I realized that there were nuances to those solutions. If I were to take the case, I could (and should) clarify my role with the family and either elect to treat Harmony in isolation and avoid any sort of interpretations or interventions related to the parents (in the spirit of avoiding harm or role confusion), or I could, at the outset, clarify the nature of our work as inclusive of family dynamics and create some clear boundaries and expectations regarding my role and the vulnerability they might feel. Alternatively, if I elected to deny the case, I could offer to consult with the referring professional, provide psychoeducation to the parents, or speak with a colleague in a distant town and see if I might be able to convince them to somehow engage with Harmony. The tension became increasingly clear: if I were to help Harmony, I might cause harm to her parents, but if I were to attend to their needs, I might be negatively impacting Harmony, who, if you remember, was struggling significantly. A bind, indeed.

My plan became clear: I would take the case but would make clear my boundaries, the role expectations, and the potential sources of harm. In agreeing to work with the family, I would, in addition to my regular informed consent, make quite clear the discomfort and vulnerability they might experience, emphasizing that while they may not completely understand the implications, they were likely and potentially damaging. I have found that clients often underestimate or downplay the impact such things will have, particularly when they are in need of help. I also created some rigid boundaries around our future interactions outside work and ensured that I would do my best to preserve their confidentiality with my spouse (specifically that I would never bring home Harmony's case file as homework and would avoid situations in which we might engage socially, if possible).

Assessment: When I pictured my urban colleagues assessing my decision to deny Harmony treatment, I felt vindicated, but as soon as I imagined a rural counterpart judging my decision, I was clear that this was a mistake. Harmony needed care, and I was the most logical person to provide it. I believed that this would apply to anyone in Harmony's position (I was not unduly influenced by who Harmony's parents were or my particular feelings for them) and that I would recommend a similar course of action to a colleague in consultation.

Implementation: As planned, I called the referring professional and indicated my assent. I then set up a meeting with the family (half an hour longer than usual) to discuss our potential arrangement.

Evaluation: My work with Harmony ended many years ago. Indeed, her testing suggested that she was profoundly depressed and that depression existed for her as a split-off affect state as a result of her father's own long-standing and well-hidden depression. The dynamics of the assessment were trickier than I had imagined because, in order for Harmony to admit to her depression, her father had to own his. The mother, for her part, had to work through some blocks to accepting the abundant unhappiness just outside her awareness. The work was messy, and the parents, despite my efforts at informed consent, were uncomfortable with me prodding them. Ultimately, I believe I helped Harmony (though I have since lost track of her and do not know how she is functioning) and the family, but not without ample discomfort along the way. Perhaps the greatest discomfort came the following December when my spouse reported we had been invited to a holiday party, co-hosted by Harmony's parents. Unable to refuse attendance without inadvertently breaching confidentiality, I attended with my partner. To this day, he does not know that I worked with his boss or that I came to learn that his boss (who my partner always described as crotchety) was actually profoundly depressed, and I consider that a mild victory. I suspect I would do the

> same thing again if presented the opportunity and am aware that in my work with Harmony and her family, the emotional toll of navigating such a tricky relational landscape was mildly to moderately detrimental to my personal well-being. It caused significant stress and discomfort that—when I run into Harmony's parents—lingers to this day.

In summary, as stated by the American Psychological Association and other professional organizations, dual relationships are not inherently unethical, nor do they invariably lead to exploitation or harm to the client (Gutheil & Gabbard, 1993). However, when multiple relationships are likely to decrease the provider's objectivity, place undue stress on the client due to unexpected vulnerabilities resulting from role blurriness, or impair the provider's ability to do good therapy, they can be problematic (Keith-Spiegel & Koocher, 1985). In rural settings, dual relationships are not a matter of if, but when, and not simply an issue of when, but how.

References

Adleman, J., & Barrett, S. E. (1990). *Overlapping relationships: Importance of the feminist ethical perspective*. New York: Springer Publishing Company.

American Psychological Association. (1992). *Ethical principles of psychologists and code of conduct*. Retrieved May 18, 2003, from www.apa.org/ethics/code/code-1992

American Psychological Association. (n.d.). Competence. In *APA Dictionary of Psychology*. Retrieved October 1, 2019, from https://dictionary.apa.org/competence

Burgard, E. (2013). Ethical concerns about dual relationships in small and rural communities: A review. *Journal of European Psychology Students, 4*(1).

DiLillo, D., & Gale, E. B. (2011). To Google or not to Google: Graduate students' use of the Internet to access personal information about clients. *Training and Education in Professional Psychology, 5*(3), 160.

Gutheil, T. G., & Gabbard, G. O. (1993). The concept of boundaries in clinical practice: Theoretical and risk-management dimensions. *The American Journal of Psychiatry, 150*(2), 188–196.

Haas, L. J., & Malouf, J. L. (1989). *Keeping up the good work: A practitioner's guide to mental health ethics*. Sarasota, FL: Professional Resource Exchange.

Helbok, C. M., Marinelli, R. P., & Walls, R. T. (2006). National survey of ethical practices across rural and urban communities. *Professional Psychology: Research and Practice, 37*(1), 36.

Hermann, M. A., & Robinson-Kurpius, S. (2006). *New guidelines on dual relationships*. Retrieved December 19, 2019, from https://ct.counseling.org/2006/12/new-guidelines-on-dual-relationships/

Keith-Spiegel, P., & Koocher, G. (1985). *Ethics in psychology*. Hillsdale, NJ: Lawrence Earlbaum.

Kitchener, K. S. (1988). Dual role relationships: What makes them so problematic? *Journal of Counseling and Development, 67*, 217–221.

Lazarus, A. A., & Zur, O. (2002). *Dual relationships and psychotherapy*. New York: Springer Publishing Company.

Schank, J. A., & Skovholt, T. M. (2006). *Ethical practice in small communities: Challenges and rewards for psychologists.* Washington, DC: American Psychological Association.

Tenbrunsel, A. E., & Messick, D. M. (2004). Ethical fading: The role of self-deception in unethical behavior. *Social Justice Research, 17*(2), 223–236.

Vidich, A. J., & Bensman, J. (2000). *Small town in mass society: Class, power, and religion in a rural community.* Chicago: University of Illinois Press.

Zuckerman, E. (2012). The fiduciary hearty of ethics. *The National Psychologist.*

11 Confidentiality and Privacy
Small-Town Secrets

THE NICE THING ABOUT LIVING IN A SMALL TOWN IS THAT EVEN IF YOU DON'T KNOW WHAT YOU'RE DOING, SOMEONE ELSE DOES...

Figure 11.1 Small Town Woes

The terms "privacy" and "confidentiality" are sometimes used interchangeably. For our purposes, we will rely on the following definitions: privacy is the control one has over what comes in and leaves their personal world. Confidentiality, on the other hand, is an ethical principle that requires professionals to limit the amount of a client's personal information that is disclosed to a third party (see Box 11.1 for the American Psychological Association's requirements on confidentiality). Ergo, the clinician is responsible for upholding confidentiality in the spirit of ensuring a client's privacy (Keith-Spiegel & Koocher, 1985). Privacy, however, goes a step beyond confidentiality in that it also refers to the elements of the world that intrude upon a client's personal life. We will explore confidentiality as our ethical duty and the ways in which rural practice may compromise it, and then we will look at how boundaries of privacy (in both directions) are difficult to uphold for anyone practicing in rural communities.

Maintaining confidentiality is one of the greatest challenges faced by providers in rural communities. It is also one of the most essential elements to any therapeutic relationship. Indeed, the American Counseling Association (2014) states: "Counselors recognize that trust is a cornerstone of the counseling relationship. Counselors aspire to earn the trust of clients by creating an ongoing partnership, establishing and upholding appropriate boundaries, and maintaining confidentiality." I might argue that confidentiality plays a more essential role in the therapeutic relationship than in any other client-provider alliance. Most states have laws pertaining to confidentiality that govern practitioners. Likewise, all professional associations have ethical codes or statutes concerning confidentiality. It is not merely an imperative to ensure privacy for the sake of privacy, but for the sake of the therapy.

That is, therapy works because individuals come to believe that they, and their personal information, are safe. Individuals come to therapy to sort through the most complicated, vulnerable, and sometimes shameful parts of themselves. Therapy becomes a place in which the individual is free to explore their fantasies, their regrets, and all the other things they would be reluctant to share with any other sole individual. My former professor, Michael Karson, suggests:

> As much as possible, the therapy relationship should be out of time, out of place—a special world of its own that intersects only obliquely with the rest of life. (The therapist must take steps not relevant here to facilitate transfer of learning to other situations.) The patient should have an ironclad sense that nothing leaves the room. The therapist undermines that sense by taking notes and promising to report threats and child abuse, even though these intrusions are legally required. The therapist further undermines privacy by mentioning other patients, by "taking a history," and by giving advice. Anything that ties the therapy province to the rest of life (after the goals are established) reduces the patient's willingness to take off the social mask and examine the psychology of the situation.
>
> (2018, p. 121)

The importance of therapeutic confidentiality and the frame that holds it cannot be overstated in any community. In the rural context, however, it becomes, if it is possible, even more essential. Karson (2018) encourages providers to think about their own therapy. Was there something you never disclosed to your therapist? Was there a topic you glazed over or avoided repeatedly? Was there something about your explicit or implicit sense of privacy that compelled you to hide? For me, knowing even just a few things about my therapist (e.g., that she had children, which I knew from her Facebook profile picture, which popped up whenever she posted on the group of providers in our area) gave me pause when I wanted to talk about my status as a non-mother. I hope the reader will see in this example that breaches to the privacy frame not only go both ways but are often at the heart of resistance or avoidance in our clients.

In rural and insular communities—settings that fail to afford the provider the possibility of their own privacy—it is a challenge to not somehow bring the outside into the therapy room. As we discussed in the last chapter, close-knit communities rife with multiple relationships erode therapeutic boundaries. These features can compromise our ability to see clearly what lies within, and outside of, the therapeutic relationship; what is therapeutic material and what must be ignored; and what leaves and what stays in the therapeutic hour. The carefully manufactured frame, then, serves not only to keep intrusions out but also to keep confidences in.

Box 11.1

The American Psychological Association requires:

4.01 Maintaining Confidentiality

Psychologists have a primary obligation and take reasonable precautions to protect confidential information obtained through or stored in any medium, recognizing that the extent and limits of confidentiality may be regulated by law or established by institutional rules or professional or scientific relationship.

4.02 Discussing the Limits of Confidentiality

(a) Psychologists discuss with persons (including, to the extent feasible, persons who are legally incapable of giving informed consent and their legal representatives) and organizations with whom they establish a scientific or professional relationship (1) the relevant limits of confidentiality and (2) the foreseeable uses of the information generated through their psychological activities.

(b) Unless it is not feasible or is contraindicated, the discussion of confidentiality occurs at the outset of the relationship and thereafter as new circumstances may warrant.

(c) Psychologists who offer services, products, or information via electronic transmission inform clients/patients of the risks to privacy and limits of confidentiality.

Source: American Psychological Association (1992)

Individuals living in insular or rural communities are often acutely aware of the realities of privacy. They have grown accustomed to everyone knowing everything about them and their families and come to expect that of those with whom they do business. It can be off-putting or alienating for a client to encounter rigid boundaries in their therapist, even if they are there to serve them. Discussions about the purpose of that frame can serve to lessen the discomfort the boundaries may create. I have come to saying something to the effect of

> You will find that I don't reveal much about myself, and that is not only because our work is not about, or for, me, but also because the more insulated and protected our relationship is, the more you will get out of our work. I believe that the task of a therapist is to help a client uncover, reveal, and process all the hidden and shameful pieces of themselves in the spirit of becoming whole (not happy). Once a person is seen—and cherished or respected—in their whole-ness, they can live with greater authenticity, connection, and integrity. If you don't find this space to be fully private and entirely confidential, it becomes hard to reveal those shameful bits. To this end, I will work tirelessly to maintain your privacy and will also do my best to keep the outside world and myself out of it.

The conversation that can then be had allows a client a full understanding of not only what is expected of them, but also how our confidential space makes that happen.

Once the frame is set, it is up to the clinician to work to maintain it. Interestingly, Helbok, Marinelli, and Walls (2006) found that urban providers committed a greater number of breaches in confidentiality than their rural counterparts. We can speculate that this is because those of us in rural and insular communities are cognizant, and regularly reminded, of the power of the gossip network and the lack of privacy afforded its members and, accordingly, refrain from sharing even small bits of case material for fear that the client may be identified by details. Indeed, there have been several instances in our consultation group in which a therapist will begin to present a case and one, or even two, other clinicians will recognize the client though no identifying information has been provided. The side effect for maintaining privacy is often professional isolation. Further, while we, as rural providers, do our best to maintain the privacy of our clients, ours is often sacrificed by the nature of our work. (More on that later.)

The struggles to maintain confidentiality are complicated for the rural provider by the nature of the insular community. My third year in private practice, I was making a deposit at the local bank. My envelope stuffed with a mixture of cash and checks, the process was lengthy, and the teller struck up a conversation with me. She was a new teller (my regular teller, Jean, had recently moved to a different branch), and she was eager to build relationships. When she pulled up my information on her computer, she remarked "Oh you're a psychologist? That's really neat!" For many therapists this moment is dreaded—the respondent either tells you all about their uncle with mental health issues, or the conversation ends abruptly; suddenly they feel uncomfortable and shy. Then, however, it was not just a matter of discomfort but a sinking feeling that this kind young woman now knew the names of at least a dozen of my clients—revealed by their checks. Of course, the same sort of breach of confidentiality could (and probably does) happen in an urban setting, but in my small town, the likelihood that this woman knew one of my clients was significantly higher than it would be in a city. My confidentiality statement now informs clients that should they pay by check, I cannot ensure that their names will not be recognized by a bank teller. I can assure you: that was not a part of my ethics course in graduate school.

Clinical Example: Clara

Clara was a 42-year-old woman who came to therapy for relational anxiety. She and her longtime boyfriend were having some growing pains when she enrolled in therapy, and our work focused heavily on her childhood experiences, relational history, and how her attachment status influenced her unhealthy relational patterns. One day, she came in with a topic that was slightly off course but that she was desperate to resolve. Her boyfriend's daughter, previously away at college, had been living with them over the summer and was triggering my client's insecurities and desires to flee.

I validated and queried, making gentle interpretations I thought she would be able to tolerate. But I was distracted by my toes. While still listening to my client, I did a quick scan to investigate my toes' message. In the six years since Mike's lesson, I had dutifully engaged in the toe-squeezing activity whenever my ethical nerve endings were stimulated. The practice, much like he had intended, often cued me into ethical dilemmas before I was consciously aware of their occurrence. Clara's boyfriend's daughter, it occurred to me as I subtly glanced at the clock, was likely responsible for the sound of the door latch I had just heard: my next client entering my waiting area. She was, and had been since June when she returned from college, my Tuesday two p.m. client. Clara, who had just switched from Wednesdays at one to Tuesdays at one, was only a few minutes behind me in this revelation. She would certainly see Cynthia sitting eagerly on the edge of the first chair by my door, as she always did, when she left the office.

Of course, Cynthia's confidentiality limited me from sharing this with Clara. She would have to realize this for herself. All I could do was prepare for the fallout the following week when we processed my allegiance and came to understand how, or rather if, she could continue to trust me, given what would likely be perceived by her as a split alliance and by the ethical committee at the America Psychological Association as a multiple relationship.

Clara and I wound up working through the rupture, and it was Cynthia who abandoned the therapeutic work. Interestingly to me at the time, the focus of Clara's upset was her feelings of exposure, rather than worries about alliance. She explained,

> It suddenly occurred to me that you might know things about the people I talk about. It made me feel suddenly shy to share with you my ugly beliefs about people and the judgmental voice that I hate so much.

She continued,

> It also made me worried—at least for a minute—about what you might have told Cynthia about me. I then realized that you had never once shared with me something another client had said, and I tried to talk myself out of my panic. Did you tell Cynthia anything I said?

Privacy, Clara demonstrated, is at the heart of a client's ability to do good work. I can remember previous therapists of mine telling me general things about other clients or people they knew. As my consult group has taught me, even vague details can reveal an identity, and I think, on some level, our clients understand and fear this. We are not only the keepers of their secrets and their truths, but we are also a mere degree or two away from someone they love or know.

Whereas in more populous areas, individuals have great autonomy in what they reveal to their therapist, in insular communities, there are many indirect ways for therapists to learn information about their clients. In Clara's case, once I realized that Cynthia was her boyfriend's daughter, I had information (or at least one person's perspective) on her romantic partnership that she herself had not shared. Clara's boyfriend, it seemed, had a history of infidelity and was also suffering from depression. These bits of information were not only pertinent and hard to ignore; they also weren't mine to know.

In the technology era, therapists have had to—without much guidance—make sense of boundaries and limits to privacy for themselves and their clients. Ethical debates have ensued. Is it okay to "google" a client? What does one do if a client sends a "friend request" on Facebook? Rural communities faced many of these issues in the real world long before folks in urban environments encountered them on the web. Do I take into account information about a client learned from my spouse? Do I make note of a client's presence in the local police blotter for drunk driving even though they have yet to share that information with me? Do I get curious with a client about the woman I saw him at a restaurant with who was not his wife?

In certain circumstances (particularly forensic matters where truth is of great importance, the relationship secondary, and corroboration key), relying on indirect information gathering can be not only ethical but also appropriate. However, in a therapeutic relationship, it is not always ethical or proper. Some years ago, I had been treating a woman, who we will call Melissa, for ten months when I jogged by her on the country road on which I live. There are about a dozen homes in my small rural development, and it occurred to me that she must live in one of them. We smiled and greeted one another, I a little too startled to be overly professional or thoughtful. Of course, the incident intruded greatly on my run (I thought of her and her case for the remainder of the run), but that is for another chapter. Running back to my house an hour later, it occurred to me which home must be hers. The home was rundown, and the yard had cars and other articles of junk strewn about. I knew that the other person who lived there—a man we called Mean Mark—must be her boyfriend. We called him Mean Mark for a variety of reasons, the biggest being that he frequently yelled at the neighborhood kids as they rode bikes and played in the grass field behind his property. Melissa had been trying to become pregnant for months, had been struggling with self-doubt, and had talked to me repeatedly about anxiety in her relationship. I suddenly knew far more about Melissa, largely based on assumptions built on my observations and gossip network.

Privacy, dictated somewhat by confidentiality requirements, is a bit of a slippery thing. It is what keeps the outside out and the inside in and preserves the framework within which the growth and magic of therapy may transpire. In rural practice it becomes impossible to ensure, and thus, we must safeguard it as best we can and have methods in place for coping with violations when they occur.

References

American Counseling Association. (2014). *2014 ACA code of ethics* [PDF file]. Retrieved October 12, 2019, from www.counseling.org/resources/aca-code-of-ethics.pdf

American Psychological Association. (1992). *Ethical principles of psychologists and code of conduct*. Retrieved May 18, 2003, from www.apa.org/ethics/code/code-1992

Helbok, C. M., Marinelli, R. P., & Walls, R. T. (2006). National survey of ethical practices across rural and urban communities. *Professional Psychology: Research and Practice*, *37*(1), 36.

Karson, M. (2018). *What every therapist needs to know*. Lanham, MD: Rowman & Littlefield.

Keith-Spiegel, P., & Koocher, G. (1985). *Ethics in psychology*. Hillsdale, NJ: Lawrence Earlbaum.

12 The Generalist
Competencies and Necessity

One of my professors in graduate school instigated a lively ethical discussion by stating "Never refer out. You should never refer out!" He was suggesting that in order to grow as clinicians, we must not shy away from clients or situations we found complicated, undesirable, or hard. The conversation that ensued circled largely around the topic of competency. How were we to work with a client about whose issues we had no expertise? How were we, as new clinicians, to handle matters complicated and too advanced for our meager training? What were we to do when we found ourselves in over our heads?

Anyone reading this from a rural or insular community might ask themselves these questions regularly. It is not, I might add, because we do not wish to refer out, but rather because there is no one to whom we might refer. Most communities have several providers, but it is rare in such communities to have providers with specialties. Many of us practicing in communities with limited resources are generalists by necessity, even if we once dreamt of having a highly refined scope of practice.

The APA (1992) states, "Psychologists provide services, teach and conduct research with populations and in areas only within the boundaries of their competence, based on their education, training, supervised experience, consultation, study or professional experience." Dreyfus (2004) laid out five stages of development from novice to expert. The stages of adult skill acquisition as laid forth by Dreyfus are *novice, advanced beginner, competent, proficient,* and *expert*. Dreyfus hypothesized that first through instruction, then through experience, and then through practice in context, individuals can gain competency and perhaps, eventually, expertise. The American Psychological Association, in its dictionary, defines competence as follows:

> One's developed repertoire of skills, especially as it is applied to a task or set of tasks. A distinction is sometimes made between competence and performance, which is the extent to which competence is realized in one's actual work on a problem or set of problems.
>
> (APA, n.d.)

Taken as a whole, competence can be thought of as one's repertoire of relevant skills as developed through a combination of training and experience.

Graduate training programs cannot possibly instruct on any and every type of client that may walk into a consultation room. Additionally, throughout our careers, novel predicaments and presenting problems will appear. Those of us practicing in rural or insular communities are undoubtedly going to be convinced, at least on occasion, to work outside the confines of our competencies.

According to the APA Ethics Code, we are bound by our competencies insofar as we practice only within the realms in which we are formally trained, are experienced, or have consulted (APA, 1992).

This guideline aims to balance the standard requiring psychologists to work within their competencies and the principles of beneficence and nonmaleficence and justice (by providing individuals with access to services). However, the standard stipulates that psychologist are responsible for ensuring that they either have the experience or training necessary or that they make a "reasonable effort" to develop the competency by engaging in study, research, training, and/or consultation.

According to Fisher (2009), competence evolves and shifts throughout the professional lifetime. Graduate training often yields clinicians who have foundational knowledge and skills in particular areas of practice. Throughout the course of a career, there are changes in the landscape, research, trends, and understanding that must be attended to. The task of a professional is threefold. Providers must familiarize themselves with professional knowledge, research, and standards; acquire professional skills; and know the limits of their competencies.

Simply stated: maintaining one's competence is one of the greatest dilemmas for the rural provider. Rural providers often face more complex, severe, and diverse caseloads; minimal access to enrichment; limited resources; and barriers to their own mental wellness.

Hastings and Cohn (2013) conducted a survey of 40 rural providers in which the respondents revealed that rural providers are generalists as a function of the demands of their communities. Further, individuals reported working with various populations in greater numbers than they reported training in those areas. In short, rural providers are likely to be generalists and frequently find themselves working with individuals for whom they have insufficient training.

A number of factors contribute to the stretchiness of rural competence in practice. First, practitioners in rural areas are scarcer and are working with populations with greater needs. Second, trainings are infrequent in rural areas. Third, due to provider shortages, individual practitioners are less likely to be able to have thriving niche practices and, as a result, wind up practicing with broad scopes. Finally, rural practitioners, embedded in communities that tend to be worse off than urban ones, face struggles similar to those of their neighbors and may suffer more due to the difficulties in creating their own support systems.

As you learned in the first section of this book, rural Americans have higher incidence of many issues that may dictate a need for mental health treatment. Some studies have demonstrated an increased need in rural communities, whereas others have shown that while the need remains on par with metropolitan areas, rural communities often lack enough providers to keep up with the demand.

A brief internet search of some of the major conferences in the field of mental health reveals what one might suspect: most major conferences and trainings take place in urban areas. Travel to and from rural areas, particularly those far from major airline hubs, can be prohibitively costly. What's more, the travel distance is often significant, particularly for those in the rural West, where a day's drive might leave you in the same state in which you started. While it is occasionally the case that quality educators and lecturers will reach these remote places, more often, the rural provider carries the burden of travel should they decide to seek personal and professional enrichment. Increasingly, technological advances are making information accessible through webinars and distance learning opportunities. This serves to dramatically reduce the burden for the rural professional, particularly those who are comfortable with and capable of learning remotely.

Not only can urban providers expect that trainings or conferences may, at some point, come to them; they can also anticipate easily creating or finding a network of professionals with whom they may regularly consult. A study conducted in 2009 revealed widespread prescriber shortage and poor distribution of non-prescribers in rural areas (Thomas, Ellis, Konrad, Holzer, & Morrissey, 2009). Not only might there not be someone to whom a therapist practicing outside the scope of her competence might refer, there also may not be anyone with whom to consult.

In Montana, efforts have been made to improve the access of rural providers to quality supervision in their respective fields. The Billings Clinic of Montana recently launched Project ECHO, a national model focused on offering peer support to isolated providers. This project, new at the time of press, is a potential solution offered to one of the biggest problems facing rural providers. In rural communities, silos often serve as a metaphor for the way in which projects and providers tend to exist in isolation. Unlike in, say, Denver, where I trained to be a psychologist, there is no university program pumping out graduates who quickly become colleagues. When I started my practice, I was one of three psychologists in the region. I met with both of them. One was nearing retirement and was simultaneously overwhelmed professionally and thrilled to have a young person in the area to make him feel less guilty as he neared retirement. The other worked as part of a hospital and was clear about his role, boundaries, competencies, and specialties and saw our task as colleagues to divide and conquer. In other words, he saw us working in different areas to manage the need, which left little room for consultation or collaboration. My meetings, safe to say, left me feeling more alone than when I started.

For two years, I have facilitated a seminar for professionals interested in deepening their clinical skills, self-awareness, and sense of community. I have had steady enrollment and solid participation, but the group is small, and it does not seem to have shifted the culture within our profession. Like the culture in which we are embedded, practitioners often seem to lack enthusiasm about learning and growth.

What, then, can a rural provider do when an individual seeks treatment for a problem outside their areas of expertise? What's more, what can a rural provider do to maintain competence, continue to grow and learn, and somehow manage to avoid burnout despite the intense demands of a rural community with few resources?

Pathways to Competence

The three main pathways to maintaining competence are **knowledge, self-awareness**, and **professional enrichment**. While I, and others, lack a surefire or simple solution to this dilemma, much can be learned from the work of others and the successful efforts around the country designed to address some of these issues.

Competence—or perhaps, more importantly, knowing one's lack of competency—relies on accurate self-appraisal (Keith-Spiegel & Koocher, 1985). In our practice, we receive at least five phone calls a week for things we do not treat. This week, we received a call from a desperate woman whose father was being "kicked out" of his nursing home. A new facility placement had been secured, but they were requiring an "emergency neuropsychological assessment": her voice fraught, her plea desperate. The next call, a woman who was requesting CBT specifically for a sleep disorder. We do not provide "emergency neuropsychological assessments," nor is anyone in my group specifically trained on CBT for sleep disorders. It is painful—given that I joined the profession to help people—not only to say "I'm sorry, we do not" but also to then answer their next question, which invariably is "Do you know anyone who does?" with "No, I am sorry."

Now, these two cases are interesting. There is a woman in our group who is trained extensively in CBT. She has no experience, however, treating a sleep disorder with CBT. She might, after doing some research and explaining to the client the scope of her skill and the gaps in her knowledge, elect to treat this woman, knowing that without her intervention, the woman would likely go without services. In the case of the neuropsychological assessment, the boundaries of our competence are much clearer: I am not a trained neuropsychologist, and I have very limited experience working with the elderly. I am not qualified to do this assessment. Despite, and because of, my obligation to do no harm, I must decline.

Humility is perhaps one of the most essential elements of the rural practitioner. Humility allows us not only to know our limits but also to admit, aloud and often, where they lie. I have had to say, "No, I do not; I'm sorry" more times than I ever would have imagined. I have had to refer people to providers three hours away and to service providers who may be able to help the individual in certain ways but who might not be able to help them entirely. As my reputation in our small community has grown, this dilemma has only amplified. People come to me looking for help, and I must shrink back, limited by my humanness.

Knowing—and owning—one's limits might be the trickiest pieces of maintaining one's competency. The other components—professional enrichment and knowledge—only become relevant when one can, humbly, admit that they need help.

Competence rests on knowledge (Keith-Spiegel & Koocher, 1985). In the first section, I provided you with a grim but detailed summary of life in rural America and general statistics and figures about rural Americans. While the section was not exhaustive, nor did it provide the depth necessary for every practitioner in every rural area to have a complete understanding of their clients, it was a step on the path to developing cultural competency. More on this in a moment.

While it may be a lot to wade through, websites, books, and journals are a great way to continue to remain current in one's chosen profession. You will find a selection of resources in the recommended readings section of this book.

I also recommend selecting a few journals and subscribing to them. As we have discussed previously, most rural practitioners are generalists. It is important to discover and consume research and publications relevant to the work being done. The *Journal on Rural Mental Health* is a great journal that might allow the reader to feel less isolated, alone, and abnormal. In the pages of this journal, a provider may find stories, read research, and understand trends that not only enrich their professional understanding but also allow them to see their own work and life reflected in others. Subscribing to a database can be pricy but effective. Most research databases allow the user to set up alerts that will notify them of new articles relevant to their interests.

Many individuals in rural practice will have studied in a cohort or more populous region. Maintaining relationships with one's colleagues, mentors, and professors offers opportunities not only for consultation but for resources as well. I often do know people who have specialties, the lucky urban dwellers who treat a subset of the population rather than its entirety. When I am faced with a complicated problem or unfamiliar dilemma, I usually have a colleague with related skills or knowledge. If consultation isn't warranted, I can always ask for a reading list. With shipping the way it is these days, a provider can order, receive, and read an entire book on a subject before their next session with that client.

Professional Enrichment

As I said before, attending conferences or obtaining continuing education credits can prove quite challenging for the rural provider. That said, it is not impossible. The same offerings for telehealth exist for supervision, consultation, and sometimes even seminars and trainings. Here are some of the ways you can engage your community to get the collegial support we all need:

- Create a regularly occurring consultation group or seminar. Participants can rotate presenting topics based on their expertise to enrich everyone's knowledge base or share cases to receive consultation and support.

- Establish (or find and join) a local (whatever that means in your region) Facebook group. We have a group that spans about 50 miles and then another for a neighboring region. I am a member of both because often I can learn about trainings and possible referrals, share information, and, of course, feel less isolated and alone.
- Consult with colleagues from afar. In many cases, colleagues with expertise feel valued and honored when they receive consultation requests. While feeling valued is important, so is being paid. Establish early on boundaries and expectations around your working relationship as to preserve the connection and demonstrate the respect your colleagues deserve.
- Attend at least one conference or training every two years. Though these days we can get many continuing education credits online, it is important that we sit face to face with our professional community. I have learned that intensive trainings that are relevant and applicable are preferable to major conferences as I tend to be able to deepen my understanding of an area of practice, thus expanding my competence. Smaller conferences on a focused theme (e.g., psychological assessment, forensic assessment, dance and movement therapy, trauma) tend to offer opportunities not only to connect with like-minded folks, but also to gain an in-depth understanding through didactic instruction.
- Remember to list other professionals amongst your colleagues. Primary care providers, speech and language therapists, psychiatrists (if there are any), case managers, and lawyers can all be resources for collaboration and consultation. In fact, engaging with folks from varied backgrounds can enrich your understanding.
- Provide trainings to others. When I have signed up to give a lecture or lead a seminar, I have always learned a great deal in the process. I select subjects that are within my area of practice and competence and then deepen my understanding of the relevant research, current thinking, and most useful interventions. I have spoken for foster care support networks, avalanche professionals, graphic designers, lawyer groups, and university programs. I have also recently begun developing webinars and a newsletter to enrich not only my community's understanding of mental health and wellness but also my own.

References

American Psychological Association. (1992). *Ethical principles of psychologists and code of conduct*. Retrieved May 18, 2003, from www.apa.org/ethics/code/code-1992

American Psychological Association. (n.d.). *Committee on rural health vision and mission*. Retrieved December 18, 2019, from www.apa.org/practice/programs/rural/committee/mission

Dreyfus, S. E. (2004). The five-stage model of adult skill acquisition. *Bulletin of Science, Technology & Society, 24*(3), 177–181.

Fisher, C. B. (2009). *Decoding the ethics code: A practical guide for psychologists*. Thousand Oaks, CA: Sage Publications.

Hastings, S. L., & Cohn, T. J. (2013). Challenges and opportunities associated with rural mental health practice. *Journal of Rural Mental Health*, *37*(1), 37–49.

Keith-Spiegel, P., & Koocher, G. (1985). *Ethics in psychology*. Hillsdale, NJ: Lawrence Earlbaum.

Thomas, K. C., Ellis, A. R., Konrad, T. R., Holzer, C. E., Morrissey, J. P. (2009). County-level estimates of mental health professional shortage in the United States. *Psychiatric Services*, *60*(10). https://doi.org/10.1176/ps.2009.60.10.1323

13 Life as a Rural Clinician
Isolation, Impairment, and Self-Care

Rurality Complicates Mental Wellness for the Provider

In Section One, we explored the extreme deficiencies some rural communities face when it comes to achieving mental wellness. The barriers to mental wellness in rural areas exist not only for community members but for their providers as well. Clinicians are human and equally susceptible to the stresses of daily life and are certainly not immune to trauma, grief and loss, lingering effects of childhood issues, divorce, and pain (Briggs, 2005). What is more, these individuals are also often carrying the burdens of their community members with little support or consultation. So while it may be difficult or impossible for the rural provider to secure access to their own psychological care, the weight of their role in their community can compound their distress and increase the likelihood of mental anguish, impairment, and burnout. Further, their lives may not maintain the privacy often treasured by providers who can leave their offices and no longer think about their clients. I see my clients in yoga classes, naked in the gym locker room, and sometimes at intimate dinner parties among friends. For the rural provider, it can feel as if she is simultaneously terribly isolated and on full public display.

Barriers to mental health treatment exist for providers regardless of rurality. In 2009, the American Psychological Association surveyed its members to better understand the barriers to utilization of colleague assistance. Stigma, shame, guilt, embarrassment, and privacy/confidentiality concerns were high amongst the respondents' reasons. Additionally, 27% of those surveyed cited inadequate social support, and 29% cited a fear of losing their professional status (APA, 2010). Indeed, perceived threats to one's status or identity may compromise their ability to seek treatment. In some rural areas, the shortage of providers also impacts the providers themselves. Multiple relationships and complex networks amongst providers make it that much harder for a mental health professional to secure their own services (Schank & Skovholt, 2006). Similarly, whereas many states (e.g., California, Ohio) host colleague assistance programs, many rural states (e.g., West Virginia, Wyoming, Vermont) do not.

Privacy and Visibility

"The psychologist needs to be visible to build trust, but not too visible to avoid limiting whom he or she may see for treatment at a future time" (Helbok et al., 2003, p. 370).

In his chapter "Ethical and Professional Challenges of Mental Health Care Delivery in Rural Communities," James Werth (2012) recounts a day in the life of a fictitious counselor working in rural America. While the account is dramatized and contains far more ethical dilemmas and awkward run-ins than one might expect in real life, the account is not entirely factitious. The reading triggers feelings of discomfort, overwhelm, frustration with the countless intrusions, and anxiety about all the difficulties faced. For the rural reader, it will resonate.

The longer one practices in a small community, the smaller that community becomes. Between current and former clients, relations of current and former clients, and referral sources, it is rare for me to spend much time at all in public without seeing someone I know something secretive about or share something secretive with.

This can shape the rural provider's life in unexpected ways. Early on in my marriage, I accompanied my partner to a bar for a drink. Not much of a drinker, I do not frequent bars, but he convinced me to extend our dinner date with a cocktail. We arrived at the bar, ordered some drinks, and then saw his friend, with whom we sat. I excused myself, went to the restroom and returned, moments later, to find my two o'clock intake sitting at the four-person table. I sat down, and my partner cordially introduced us. I followed her lead, acting as if we had never met, and made small talk. Luckily, my partner's friend did much of the talking before I was able to feign fatigue and convince my partner to leave. On the way home, he gave me some minor grief for my unwillingness to be more social. I could not explain to him, without disclosing my client's identity, the reason for my sudden desire for retreat. By maintaining our clients' privacy, we often wind up with an entirely secretive world the intricacies of which no one can know. This is no different from the urban provider, indeed, but the rural provider's private world is smaller and the boundaries regularly pushed and blurred by everyday interactions.

The dilemma is not just one of perception. Indeed, providers in insular communities do not have the anonymity afforded to their urban counterparts. Many of my clients know where I live, what car I drive (and thus times I frequent the local health club), what my ski jacket looks like, and who my spouse is. With no active disclosure, it is easy for my clients to know more about me than I would typically like. Further, the lack of anonymity may make it difficult for the provider to feel like a fully expressed individual. In a small town with fierce, opposing beliefs on abortion rights, say, can the rural provider place a Planned Parenthood sticker on their car knowing, it might alienate entire portions of their community?

A therapist friend has remarked on several occasions the shame she feels when her child tantrums in public. Though she knows that tantrums are normal and expected, as a child and family therapist, she struggles with the burden of expectation that she somehow has parenting completely figured out. Another colleague has remarked about how she is easily embarrassed in exercise classes when she struggles to keep up or do as much as other participants. She explained, "My clients often see me as perfect, and when it's so clearly obvious that I am not, I worry they won't trust me to support them." Yet another therapist remarked, "I can't go out looking like this; what if my clients see me?" Indeed, to be a therapist in a small community is not only to be on display, but also to fear a type of exposure that may threaten the work you do.

Community Burden

As I have already reported, mental health services are in high demand and low supply in most rural areas. In my first year of practice, the waiting list that I maintained for psychological assessments grew from two to 48. As someone who places great value on self-care and sustainability, I continued to work at what I believed to be a reasonable and maintainable pace. I saw no more than 25 clients per week and worked additional hours on testing, scoring, and writing. As my waiting list grew, I found myself feeling increasingly guilty for the hours spent doing things that I enjoyed—not working. I felt this pressure, perhaps a sense of burden, that as the sole purveyor of psychological assessments to children in my region, I should be doing it around the clock, even though the wise part of me knew that was impossible and entirely untenable. Rural providers can easily feel burdened by the community in which they live and work. We know that rural communities suffer with higher rates and severity in terms of suicidality, drug use, and mental illness. With fewer providers and a greater need, it is easy for the rural provider to feel overwhelmed by the responsibility.

Impairment

While therapists generally report higher-than-average degrees of work satisfaction, they also report depression, marital discord, alcohol misuse, and loneliness just like non-therapists (Hargrove, 1986). While mental health professionals face all the same challenges as the general population, there is some evidence to suggest that psychologists may be particularly susceptible to depression, suicidal ideation, and anxiety (Kleespies et al., 2011). Physicians typically have higher suicide rates than many other populations (Andrew, 2018). While the research is inconclusive on suicide rates amongst psychologists, I came upon no evidence that mental health professionals are somehow invulnerable to mental health concerns (Kleespies et al., 2011). Indeed, despite our clients thinking that we are somehow above struggle, we belong on the couch just as much as they do.

Not only are we at risk for mental health concerns, but there are also stresses particular to our jobs (i.e., burnout, secondary trauma) that may cause clinical levels of distress and impairment (Hargrove & Curtin, 2012). Physicians, particularly in rural communities, work long hours (Weeks & Wallace, 2008), and longer work days have been associated with a higher incidence of depression (Weston, Zilanawala, Webb, Carvalho, & McMunn, 2019). Further, the greater the number of work hours, the higher the incidence of burnout (Hargrove & Curtin, 2012).

Secondary trauma (also known as vicarious or indirect trauma) is a term used to capture the phenomenon of PTSD-like symptoms occurring with exposure to indirect traumatic material, such as a client retelling a traumatic memory. Individuals may find themselves re-experiencing the traumatic material, avoiding certain emotionally arousing situations, or experiencing hyperarousal or hypervigilance (Cieslak et al., 2013). Providers working with veteran populations (remember, there are 4.7 million veterans in rural America) (Office of Rural Health, n.d.) are perhaps more susceptible to symptoms of secondary trauma (Cieslak, et al., 2013). Mental health professionals, urban and rural, experience a higher level of isolation than individuals in most other careers (Briggs, 2005). Due to the nature of our work and the high value placed on privacy and confidentiality, many of us have massive internal worlds that remain hidden from everyone we know and love. We experience profound intimacy and despair regularly in our work, and unlike intense experiences that occur outside of the consultation room, we are never to discuss them.

When it comes to psychological health, rural professionals have it harder than their urban peers in a few notable ways. First, rural Americans generally live harder lives than their urban counterparts. Mental health professionals are not excluded from this reality (Laprise, 2017). Second, there is some evidence to suggest that rural practitioners may be more susceptible to burnout than their metropolitan peers (Hargrove & Curtin, 2012). Third, rural professionals have less access to the sort of services and support that may otherwise aid in prevention or recovery (Hargrove & Curtin, 2012).

Clinicians are not immune to personal conflict or misfortune. Yes, marriage and family therapists get divorced, and child psychologists have parent-child relational problems. And, while marital discord, chronic illness, and grief and loss are no more likely for the rural provider than anyone else, personal experiences can negatively impact a clinician's capabilities (Briggs, 2005). Further, the rural provider's plight may be complicated by a lack of access to their own physical or mental healthcare and a lack of supportive colleagues to whom they can refer and on whom they can depend for accurate reflection of their capacity.

Consider this: an aging provider has served his rural community for three decades. He is beloved by his clients and valued by his town. He recently began noticing some memory loss about which he spoke to a colleague in a city three hours away. He and his colleague were keeping in touch to maintain accountability and support for the provider. His wife of 50 years unfortunately died of cancer last year, and the supportive colleague believes that he might be suffering from depression, which might be compounding his memory loss. A 14-year-old concussion victim comes for a neuropsychological screen to ensure that she is well enough to resume playing soccer. When the provider calls his colleague, the colleague gently suggests that his faculties might be compromised to the degree that such an important task may prove difficult. The provider has no one to whom he can refer.

This case example shows not only the potential professional impairment but also the burden that compounds the dilemma for the provider. It is difficult for most helping professionals to acknowledge our vulnerabilities, but it becomes even more complicated when countless others—an entire community, perhaps—are depending on our well-being.

Burnout

While distress can temporarily hinder our ability to be effective in our work, burnout threatens to eliminate our efforts for good (Cherniss, 1992; Keel, 1993). Researchers have demonstrated a strong correlation between burnout and suboptimal clinical performance (National Academy of Medicine, n.d.).

Burnout is characterized by affective, behavioral, physical, and cognitive symptoms (Cherniss, 1992). It has three primary features: physical/mental resource depletion, excessively high personal expectations, and draining personal relationships. It is often characterized by some combination of emotional exhaustion, a loss of empathy, and a feeling of failure or incompetence (Keel, 1993). Burnout can manifest as exhaustion, cynicism, or inefficacy and can affect job performance, physical and emotional health, and behavioral functioning (Maslach & Leiter, 2016).

Burnout is also commonly associated with a lack of professional choice and autonomy (Fred & Scheid, 2018). The demands of rural practice (even rural private practice) may limit a provider's experience of autonomy because they cannot develop a niche, may feel compelled to accept as a client anyone who comes to see them, and may experience a loss of privacy as a result of the insular nature of their community.

Strategies for Success

A successful resiliency plan will integrate both internal and external sources of strength and monitoring. As with our clients, we must find resources within ourselves and our communities that can support us through difficult times. While rural practice creates its own threats to the well-being of the clinician, it does not make it impossible. For effective mental healthcare, providers, particularly vulnerable ones such as those practicing in rural communities, should have a strategy that includes prevention, assessment, plan, and implementation.

Before we move forward, however, we must all agree that self-care is not just a pop-psychology buzzword but is a necessary component of our practice. It is vital that we approach this essential practice with both humility and integrity. Early in my graduate training, we paired off to do mock therapy sessions with our peers. My partner, whom we will call Allie, remarked that she had never been to her own therapy. This mock session was her first time sitting in such a format. Later, I inquired why she had never been to therapy, especially prior to embarking on a doctoral degree, and she responded, "It's just not for me." True: therapy is not for everyone. And it may not be for you. But we must be sure we do not think it isn't for us because we do not suffer in ways that therapy might address. That is, we must acknowledge our vulnerabilities and wholeheartedly believe that we need, deserve, and can attain increased insight, wellness, and engagement if we try.

Experience has taught me that while service seekers in rural and insular communities often face barriers to quality care, providers in those same areas often encounter barriers to quality personal and professional enrichment (Briggs, 2005). Indeed, individuals practicing mental health services experience the same stigma, loneliness, and accessibility issues that their clients face. Self-care, particularly for the rural provider, is an ethical imperative (Barnett, Baker, Elman, & Schoener, 2007).

Self-care helps us build resilience, deepens self-esteem and confidence, strengthens our relational capacity, and reduces the likelihood of burnout or compassion fatigue. It also models good behavior for our clients (APA Practice Organization, 2009). The last note I will make in my case for more self-care is this: we can learn a great deal about caring for others through the process of caring for ourselves. Self-care allows us to be better, healthier, more resilient clinicians. Self-care is sustainable.

Self-care entails four components: prevention, assessment, plan, and implementation. These components are cyclical and interdependent. To maintain our wellness as providers, we must attend to each.

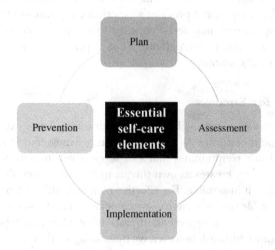

Figure 13.1 Essential Elements of Self-Care

Assessment: How Am I Doing?

There are both formal and informal methods for assessing our well-being. I recommend a strategy that encompasses both. The Maslach Burnout Inventory (MBI) is a widely accepted measure to self-assess for burnout. The MBI-Human Services Survey is geared specifically for human service professionals and includes three scales: emotional exhaustion, depersonalization, and personal accomplishment. For practitioners fearing burnout or for agencies eager to intervene at the earliest signs, such an assessment may prove useful.

Another instrument to measure well-being is the Quality of Life Inventory (QOLI). The QOLI, used by many psychologists to assess well-being and improvement in therapy clients, provides information about satisfaction with, and importance of, 16 life domains (work, relationships, etc.). It is quick, normed in a general (nonclinical) population, and allows us to track progress or regression over time (Frisch, Cornell, Villanueva, & Retzlaff, 1992).

Assessments need not rely on a formal instrument or tool. We can institute self-assessments periodically as a means of keeping ourselves apprised of how we are doing. Working an informal self-assessment into our regular lives requires intentionality and follow-through. One way to do this is to schedule monthly or quarterly check-ins. These can be done alone or with a trusted colleague. You can structure the check-in in any number of ways. You can rely on Maslach's theory and evaluate yourself on the three areas of burnout: compassion blunting, exhaustion, and feelings of efficacy. Perhaps journaling on these three areas or discussing them out loud with a colleague will clue you in to any potential threats or existing struggles. Body scans are another helpful systematic method for tuning in to our well-being. Tuesdays tend to be my longest clinical day, and though after my last client leaves, I often find myself hustling to get home, I sometimes will spend just a few moments noticing how I am feeling in my body after the day. If I do this regularly, I have a source of comparison that I can use to assess my functioning.

We can also ask others to monitor our well-being. Of course, having a therapist or professional confidant with whom one can check in can be instrumental in maintaining a sense of well-being, but of course it's not always possible. Personally, my partner is the first to notice any psychological decline in me. He will say things like "Seems like work is getting to you," or "I've noticed you bringing home your work stress." Typically, it will take me a few such cues to realize the impact my work is having on my stress levels and, subsequently, my stress levels on my relationships.

Anyone who has ever felt burnout knows that assessment is only a small piece of the self-care puzzle. Any good approach to wellness starts with prevention. Cultivating resilience entails a diversified approach that fosters balance and allows for struggle.

Prevention: Intention, Boundaries, Limits

Imagine, if you will, it is five years, maybe even ten years, from now, and you are sitting with a new clinician who reminds you an awful lot of yourself when you were just starting out. He asks, "What can I do to ensure I can live a long life and have a robust, fulfilling career?" Imagine the advice you might give him regarding boundaries, limits, ethics, training, relationships, and sustenance. I was recently asked this question by a colleague who had relocated to our small town. The first thing that popped into my head was this: "Open your practice in a community in which you do not live." Reflecting on my advice allowed me to reflect not only on how boundaries had served me but the ways in which my professional and personal integrity had been worn so thin by the nature of rural practice. As I mentioned in the second chapter, it is nearly impossible to imagine all the ripples generated by a single therapeutic relationship. In hindsight, however, I now see how I know something private about nearly every person in our community. As a mid-career psychologist, I can only imagine what this will look like when I am ready for retirement.

We have reviewed at length the needs of rural communities, particularly in terms of mental health services. If you live in a rural community, and particularly if you live in a healthcare provider shortage area, the need may significantly outweigh whatever it is that you have to give (Chipp et al., 2011). Further, practitioners in rural communities may lack anonymity amongst their peers. I would say that most everyone in our town either knows me or of me and what I do. Whereas in urban environs, the clerk at the post office or the day care director may not know your profession unless you tell them, in a rural community, mental health professionals are easily identified. The side effect of this is that professionals may find themselves "on duty" around the clock, with casual conversation turning quickly to requests for advice or understanding.

Moreover, rural professionals may easily succumb to an urge to save the community. The lack of amenities in small communities; the intense need; and cultural values such as neighborliness, familiarity, and solidarity can all compound to present the provider with a sense of urgency to which it can be very hard to say no.

It is essential that rural professionals learn to set clear, firm, and consistent limits and boundaries. Everyone knows the airline safety saying: "You must put on your own mask before you can assist others." If the rural community were an airplane it would be filled with your dentist, your child's teacher, your close friends, and your pastor. Behind you would be your neighbor, and behind them your accountant. And they would all be having trouble breathing. Putting on your own mask is no less essential in rural communities, but it can be significantly harder, psychologically, to do. This simply means that we must take extra care to ensure we do so.

The rural provider must establish clear limits around their time. Providers should have a known number that is their caseload and they should stick to that limit regardless of who the next phone call is. Hiring a virtual assistant, which can be affordable and independent of location, can be a useful strategy for those of us who have a hard time saying no. With a virtual assistant answering the phone, they can set limits you might otherwise not be able to. Of course, this is not a replacement for being able to say no. I often have people contact me directly, circumventing my office manager, because they are a friend of a friend or a relative of a client, and they will "only work with" me. Providers should also make time to be away from their email inboxes and phones. In many rural areas, cell phone coverage remains incomplete. I find this to be a benefit. We do not have cell phone coverage at our house, and there are many times in a day when I am simply unreachable. If you use a voice over internet phone provider, you may be able to schedule when your work line rings and does not ring. Further, arranging activities in such a way that bookends your work decreases the likelihood that your work hours will extend past their due. A colleague of mine enjoys Zumba (the exercise dance program) more than anything else. Zumba is offered at her gym three times weekly. Those slots (with ample time for transport and showering on either end) are permanently locked in on her calendar. For those of us with children, they may double as boundary agents, in that their requirements of us demand we leave our work at a particular time. Of course, limits set and then eroded can also be an indicator that things are not all right. If my colleague missed a few Zumba classes or another colleague's children were constantly remarking on how late he always was to pick them up, those therapists might have some data about how their prevention strategies are failing.

So, say it with me: "No!" is a complete sentence. In the world of outdoor recreation, there is a saying: "All to go, one for no." Aimed to address decision making in unsafe terrain, the phrase implies that without unanimous assent, the group will find an alternative path. Given that there are often parts of ourselves that are in disagreement, it can feel as if any decision has internal advocates and opponents. It is important for the rural provider to listen closely to those voices of opposition, even if the overall message is a resounding yes because the resistant parts of ourselves may hold wisdom easily overpowered by the eager parts. If there is a part of you that thinks entering into a multiple relationship is a bad idea or a part of you that feels reluctant to take on that new client, pause, reflect, and consider the boldest, most self-compassionate word in your vocabulary: no. Of course, such careful action requires vigilance and astute self-reflection. To have and hold good boundaries, we must know our needs, understand and appreciate our limits, have the skills to refrain from blurring those lines, and practice this stance regularly.

Mindfulness has numerous benefits. Mindfulness and meditative practices may have a prophylactic effect. Mindfulness may help us feel more resilient in difficult situations or over the course of our careers as therapists. It may also help us avoid burnout (Montero-Marin, et al., 2015) and vicarious trauma (Harker, Pidgeon, Klaassen, & King, 2016). Mindfulness has also been demonstrated to reduce emotional fatigue, thus prolonging our careers and enhancing our well-being (Poulin, Mackenzie, Soloway, & Karayolas, 2008). Mindfulness in any practiced form seems useful, but some research suggests that meditation practices that incorporate loving kindness (*metta*) have a particularly strong influence on the provider's self-compassion in addition to having a stress-reduction effect. Combined, loving kindness meditation may actually help practitioners be more effective and have longer, more enjoyable careers (Raab, 2014).

Maintenance: Having a Plan

Having good boundaries that ensure time away from work is essential. Knowing what to do with that time away from work (to receive sustaining benefits that aid our survival as good clinicians) is another essential element of our self-care plan. Nutrition and physical and spiritual health are all vital components of psychological well-being. I encourage all of my clients to generate a list of five things they can do to keep themselves well, with at least one idea from each of the areas listed earlier. For clinicians, who have a greater risk of becoming unwell, I would recommend ten. Of the ten activities you list that keep you well, make sure that some of them are things you can do alone (we cannot always guarantee we will have a running partner or someone to have lunch with), and some are done with others (we want to avoid isolation). Further, only two should be technology-related as technology can be a slippery slope when it comes to our well-being (APA, 2017).

Some have argued that self-care must be seen as an essential component in the provision of quality psychological care. That is, we need self-care just as much as our clients do (Hargrove & Curtin, 2012). Even though many of us may highlight the importance of self-care to our clients, we are not always good at implementing these strategies ourselves. Accordingly, it is important that we each have a plan in place to aid us in maintaining our well-being. Self-care plans should include, but not be limited to, physical, emotional, mental, and perhaps growth aspects. For some, self-care may also include spiritual elements. Table 13.1 provides an example of self-care plan based on the elements that I have found particularly useful.

Having five potential activities across four different areas provides me with ample opportunity to engage in a meaningful and helpful way with myself when I need it most. It is important that our self-care routines are diverse. If you are entirely dependent on physical activities to relieve stress and feel well, what happens if you sprain your ankle? Likewise, we should balance our active and challenging self-care activities with soothing ones. Take a moment and create a self-care plan similar to the one found here. List at least four activities for each area of well-being, and include spirituality if that is important to you. Reviewing it, ensure that you have both soothing or passive strategies and active, enlivening ones. I have also included a space for emergency protocol. This should include five self-care activities that can be done anytime, anywhere, that can help bring you back to baseline. These are the responses to gut-wrenching news, a curveball from a client, or a devastating scenario playing out in your business or community. The emergency protocol also includes five contacts (personal or professional) to whom you can turn when you need consultation, support, someone to help calm your nervous system, or a place to vent.

Table 13.1 Self-Care Plan

Physical Exercise	Emotional Boundaries	Mental Meditation	Growth TED Talks
Eating one nutritious meal per day	Saying no!	Listening to podcasts (that don't stress me out)	Reviewing my vision summary
Baths	Loving kindness meditation	Engaging discussion with friends	Reading one interesting book per month
Yoga	Time with my dog	Planning vacations	Training for a race/event
Monthly massage	Time with my loved ones	Time for reflection, away from my phone	Meditation training

In case of emergency:
- Count to 27
- Listen to a meditation
- Go for a walk
- Call someone
- Name colors

Emergency contacts:
- Mahlet
- Kara
- Katie
- Rachel
- Jason

Finally, it is essential that you have a strong social support network to whom you may go when you need to. I find it helpful to identify relationships that give me particular elements on my journey to wellness. Certain friends, for example, may be more adept at humor and lightness while others can really dig into painful affects and sit with struggle. As a professional, I have a short list of colleagues (five) who are part of my support network upon whom I can call for an ethical conundrum, compassion fatigue, or for a good cry after an empathic therapeutic failure on my part. I also, as I have mentioned, have (and strongly recommend) a consultation group.

Implementation: Walking the Walk

Of course, a plan is only as good as its follow-through. Self-care is a cyclical, unending process. Once you have created your plan, you now must practice and repeatedly implement, checking in with yourself regularly to see how it is going.

Our self-care plan must be sustainable and easy to implement. We do not want self-care to become burdensome or contribute to fatigue. Setting reminders, scheduling things (such as Zumba) into our workdays, and reminding ourselves that it is okay to say no are all helpful strategies for implementing and maintaining self-care plans. When I began my practice, I decided that whenever I would have a client no-show or late cancel, I would go for a walk, go get ice cream, or call a friend. I wanted to link a potentially negative experience (a no-show) with a positive experience (ice cream!) in order to reduce any potential anxiety about money, worries about the success of my practice, negative feelings and thoughts about my efficacy, and on and on. To this day, if a client no-shows, I do some form of self-care in their stead.

We all need accountability. When I began a regular meditation practice, I reached out to two friends who meditated habitually. I told them I was planning to meditate daily and asked them for some accountability. We now regularly share insights and links to podcasts or articles we have found particularly inspiring and check in with one another when we have encountered obstacles to our practice. Having someone who can lovingly remind you of your needs and practice can be a vital element in an effective self-care plan. Meditation or self-care buddies are one way we can ensure accountability.

References

American Psychological Association. (2010). *Survey findings emphasize the importance of self-care for psychologists*. Retrieved October 5, 2010, from www.apaservices.org/practice/update/2010/08-31/survey

American Psychological Association. (2017). *Connected and content: Managing healthy technology use*. Retrieved December 19, 2019, from www.apa.org/helpcenter/connected-content

American Psychological Association Practice Organization. (2009). *An action plan for self-care* [PDF file]. Retrieved December 19, 2019, from www.apaservices.org/practice/good-practice/Spring09-SelfCare.pdf

Andrew, L. B. (2018). *Physician suicide*. Retrieved October 23, 2019, from https://emedicine.medscape.com/article/806779-overview

Barnett, J. E., Baker, E. K., Elman, N. S., & Schoener, G. R. (2007). In pursuit of wellness: The self-care imperative. *Professional Psychology: Research and Practice, 38*(6), 603.

Briggs, D. (2005). *Therapist stress, career sustaining behavior, coping and the working alliance* (Doctoral dissertation). Retrieved October 23, 2019, from https://scholarworks.wmich.edu/dissertations/1018

Cherniss, C. (1992). Long-term consequences of burnout: An exploratory study. *Journal of Organizational Behavior, 13*(1), 1–11. https://doi.org/10.1002/job.4030130102

Chipp, C., Dewane, S., Brems, C., Johnson, M. E., Warner, T. D., & Roberts, L. W. (2011). "If only someone had told me . . .": Lessons from rural providers. *The Journal of Rural Health: Official Journal of the American Rural Health Association and the National Rural Health Care Association, 27*(1), 122–130. https://doi.org/10.1111/j.1748-0361.2010.00314.x

Cieslak, R., Anderson, V., Bock, J., Moore, B. A., Peterson, A. L., & Benight, C. C. (2013). Secondary traumatic stress among mental health providers working with the military: Prevalence and its work- and exposure-related correlates. *The Journal of Nervous and Mental Disease, 201*(11), 917–925. https://doi.org/10.1097/NMD.0000000000000034

Fred, H. L., & Scheid, M. S. (2018). Physician burnout: Causes, consequences, and (?) cures. *Texas Heart Institute Journal, 45*(4), 198–202. https://doi.org/10.14503/THIJ-18-6842

Frisch, M. B., Cornell, J., Villanueva, M., & Retzlaff, P. J. (1992). Clinical validation of the Quality of Life Inventory: A measure of life satisfaction for use in treatment planning and outcome assessment. *Psychological Assessment: A Journal of Consulting and Clinical Psychology, 4*, 92–101.

Hargrove, D. S. (1986). Ethical issues in rural mental health practice. *Professional Psychology: Research and Practice, 17*(1), 20.

Hargrove, D. S., & Curtin, L. I. S. A. (2012). Rural mental health practitioners: Their own mental health needs. In K. B. Smalley & J. Warren (Eds.), *Rural mental health: Issues, policies, and best practices* (pp. 113–130). New York: Springer Publishing Company.

Harker, R., Pidgeon, A. M., Klaassen, F., & King, S. (2016). Exploring resilience and mindfulness as preventative factors for psychological distress burnout and secondary traumatic stress among human service professionals. *Work, 54*(3), 631–637.

Helbok, C. M. (2003). The practice of psychology in rural communities: Potential ethical dilemmas. *Ethics & Behavior, 13*(4), 367–384. https://doi.org/10.1207/S15327019EB1304_5

Keel, P. (1993). Psychological stress caused by work: Burnout syndrome. *Soz Praventivmed, 38*(2), 131–132. https://doi.org/10.1007/bf01305364

Kleespies, P. M., Van Orden, K. A., Bongar, B., Bridgeman, D., Bufka, L. F., Galper, D. I., . . . Yufit, R. I. (2011). Psychologist suicide: Incidence, impact, and suggestions for prevention, intervention, and postvention. *Professional Psychology, Research and Practice, 42*(3), 244–251. https://doi.org/10.1037/a0022805

Laprise, J. (2017, February 22). Retrieved December 19, 2019, from https://thepolicy.us/the-lost-15-life-in-rural-america-72b7bb7d6dc7?gi=bf5f8812a8a0

Maslach, C., & Leiter, M. P. (2016). *Stress: Concepts, cognition, emotion, and behavior* (pp. 351–357). Cambridge, MA: Academic Press.

Montero-Marin, J., Tops, M., Manzanera, R., Demarzo, M. M. P., de Mon, M. A., & García-Campayo, J. (2015). Mindfulness, resilience, and burnout subtypes in primary care physicians: The possible mediating role of positive and negative affect. *Frontiers in Psychology, 6.* https://doi.org/ 10.3389/fpsyg.2015.01895

National Academy of Medicine. (n.d.). *Valid and reliable survey instruments to measure burnout, well-being, and other work-related dimensions.* Retrieved October 23, 2019, from https://nam.edu/valid-reliable-survey-instruments-measure-burnout-well-work-related-dimensions/

Office of Rural Health. (n.d.). *Rural veteran health care challenges.* Retrieved December 19, 2019, from www.ruralhealth.va.gov/aboutus/ruralvets.asp

Poulin, P. A., Mackenzie, C. S., Soloway, G., & Karayolas, E. (2008). Mindfulness training as an evidenced-based approach to reducing stress and promoting well-being among human services professionals. *International Journal of Health Promotion and Education, 46*(2), 72–80.

Raab, K. (2014). Mindfulness, self-compassion, and empathy among health care professionals: A review of the literature. *Journal of Health Care Chaplaincy, 20*(3), 95–108.

Schank, J. A., & Skovholt, T. M. (2006). *Ethical practice in small communities: Challenges and rewards for psychologists.* Washington, DC: American Psychological Association.

Vidich, A. J., & Bensman, J. (2000). *Small town in mass society: Class, power, and religion in a rural community.* Chicago: University of Illinois Press.

Weeks, W., & Wallace, A. E. (2008). Rural-urban differences in primary care physicians' practice patterns, characteristics and income. *The Journal of Rural Health, 24*(2). Retrieved December 19, 2019, from www.ncbi.nlm.nih.gov/pubmed/18397451

Werth, J. (2012). Ethical and professional challenges of mental health care delivery in rural communities. In K. B. Smalley, J. C. Warren, & J. P. Rainer (Eds.), *Rural mental health: Issues, policies, and best practices* (pp. 97–112). New York: Springer Publishing Company.

Weston, G., Zilanawala, A., Webb, E., Carvalho, L. A., & McMunn, A. (2019). Long work hours, weekend working and depressive symptoms in men and women: Findings from a UK population-based study. *Journal of Epidemiology and Community Health, 73*, 465–474. https://doi.org/10.1136/jech-2018-211309

Section Three

Innovations and Opportunities

Practical Applications
in Rural Communities

14 Clinical Practice in Insular Communities

The practice of psychology with rural populations is qualitatively and quantitatively different from working in suburban or urban settings or with urban or suburban peoples. To review, the ratio of provider to population in rural regions is much lower than in metropolitan areas. Rural populations also tend to experience higher incidences of many of the factors that tend to compromise one's mental wellness (poverty, chronic pain, etc.). Rural Americans also face stigma and other cultural forces that impede their ability to obtain mental health services. Further, providers are often not educated on the nuances of rural communities and populations, making cultural competence elusive for many practitioners.

In the first section, I gave you an overview of the rural landscape, its peoples, and the elements therein that hinder their mental wellness. In the second section, we pulled apart our ethical guidelines, in the spirit of equipping the rural provider (or budding rural provider) with the skills and strategies to maintain a rural practice with ethical integrity. Now, we will examine programs, practices, and systems unique to the rural landscape. Rural communities, because they are so often underserved, are rife with opportunity for ambitious or curious providers. Individuals seeking to establish or strengthen their practice with rural communities should find countless ways to expand or improve their work.

Partnerships

While national trends are increasingly favoring integrated care, the shifts are even more pronounced in rural areas. Integrated care is the systematic incorporation of mental health, behavioral health, substance use treatment, and primary care. Many primary care clinics are now hosting mental health service providers who not only aid in enriching primary care interventions (e.g., using motivational interviewing to address smoking cessation) but also provide easy access to mental healthcare (e.g., the individual can walk down the hall and consult with a behavioral health specialist about the anxiety they reported to their doctor). Such a partnership serves to decrease certain barriers to mental wellness. First, stigma is minimized when individuals can park in parking lots and sit in waiting areas that do not readily disclose their underlying mental health concerns. Second, cost and time may be reduced when a single round-trip drive can allow access to numerous providers. Third, individuals who might not otherwise seek out mental health services due to stigma or a lack of knowledge may be more easily convinced to talk to someone if that someone is just down the hall.

Integrated health is not the only potential path for partnership. One of the things that I quickly learned when establishing my practice was that my colleagues were not limited to psychologists. Aside from mental health professionals, there were nonprofit leaders, educators, nurses, and professionals from entirely unrelated fields (avalanche safety educators, trail builders) who were also part of the team serving the mental health needs of our community. By expanding this definition, we expand our services and our reach. Rural dwellers are more likely than their urban counterparts to utilize emergency departments at the local hospital rather than primary care facilities. Consequently, doctors and nurses in the ER might be your best intake coordinators. In our community, mental wellness has just as much to do with access to nature, civic engagement, and community participation as it does to a visit to one's therapist. The individuals working to maintain a network of trails around our small town or the person leading a center for restorative youth justice or a domestic violence hotline are essential members of the team of individuals who increase mental wellness in our community. Further, homeless shelters; community groups addressing issues of food insecurity; teachers working in schools with few, if any, mental health professionals; and volunteer organizations such as Big Brothers Big Sisters are vital components of the mental health network in rural regions.

Prevention

In addition to being a core component of the safety net in rural communities, these individuals and groups also tend to be a major force in providing preventative strategies and solutions. Head Start, for example, is a prominent fixture in approximately 86% of rural counties nationwide. This early intervention program provides not only quality early education for young people but also opportunities for childcare to income-dependent parents needing to get back to work (Malik, 2018). Head Start also ensures access to and accountability for vaccinations, wraparound services for families (including parent training and health education), and access to whole meals for the children it serves. Research is increasingly available to demonstrate the importance of early childhood education and intervention (in the case of developmental delays in particular) and the dangers of childhood poverty. Head Start is just one example of how rural communities may improve a person's mental wellness over the course of their lifetime.

While prevention addresses but one aspect of the biopsychosocial model of mental illness, it is an important component in reducing the significantly higher rates of mental illness in rural communities. It's simple math: if you have a greater need and a reduced supply, you must work to reduce the need and increase the supply if you want to find an equilibrium. This does the former. Our next topic addresses the latter.

Proximity

Sadly, recruitment of providers to rural regions remains a constant battle. Long before telehealth, mobile units served to access rural communities to provide things like routine medical care (e.g., dentistry and mammography). Mobile health centers (MHCs) are demonstrably effective at reducing barriers to treatment. MHCs allow for providers and clinics to exist in urban centers while serving those in rural communities. Likewise, telehealth allows individuals in urban communities to provide services to individuals in any geographic region, provided they meet state licensure requirements.

In the following chapters, we will take aim at issues of accessibility, affordability, and acceptability through solutions and innovations structured around partnerships, prevention, and proximity.

Reference

Malik, R. (2018). *A compass for families: Head Start in rural America*. Retrieved December 19, 2019, from www.americanprogress.org/issues/early-childhood/reports/2018/04/10/448741/a-compass-for-families/

15 Recruitment and Retention

There is a shortage of rural providers (Rural Health Information Hub, n.d.). By now, we all know that providers tend to remain where they were trained and that most of the professional training programs in America are in metropolitan areas. We also know that despite the opportunity for providers in rural and frontier regions, many rural communities do not have enough qualified professionals to address the mental health needs of their populace. For example, between Billings, Montana, and Fargo, North Dakota, there is one psychiatrist. Her service area is nearly 400 miles (Bryan, 2018). Provider deserts are common in rural regions, and those providers in rural regions are at greater risk for burnout as a result. Imagine you work full time for a salary less than half the median income of your graduating cohort, and you are tasked with the psychiatric needs of a region as large as Illinois. And let us not forget that within that area lurks the highest suicide rate of the country. Indeed, signing on to be a rural provider is a daunting task (Reel, 2019).

Despite incredible opportunities for success and tremendous need in rural regions, psychiatrists, nurses, psychologists, social workers, and mental health counselors are surprisingly not migrating from the cities in droves. I posit that the primary reason for this is a choice of comfort over risk. We know that the vast majority of Americans are raised in metropolitan areas. We also know that the majority of universities and colleges are in urban or suburban locations. Training in professional schools tends to be urbancentric. Ergo, nothing in a professional's history is likely to draw them to rural America. Individuals from rural areas are more likely to return to practice in their hometowns, but we also know that they are less likely to leave for university in the first place (Gleason, 2012). For those individuals who were raised in, and long to return to, a rural area, or for those metropolitan individuals who are curious about rural life, there are significant risks involved in taking that leap. New graduates in cities and towns may find employment at a mental health center, hospital, or group practice. Individuals seeking the rural life may have to launch an independent practice with little or no connection to their new community. Those individuals who find employment in a rural hospital or agency may face unexpected challenges such as the burden of multiple relationships, isolation, and poor access to self-care.

Federal and state governments are not oblivious to this reality. In the 1970s, the federal government established health provider shortage areas as a way of identifying medically underserved areas and allowing for grant dollars to address the growing needs in these regions. Shortages may be designated by population, geography, or facility. An HPSA may receive such designation, then, because there are not enough providers for that region, because a particular subset of the population within that region has limited access to services, or because a place of service meets particular criteria in the provision of services to underserved areas. Providers and clinics within areas designated as HPSA have access to funding, particularly in the form of loan-repayment grants, designed to incentivize providers who may not otherwise have a particular interest in serving this community ("Health Professional Shortage and Medically Underserved Designations," n.d.).

Whereas some have hypothesized that one of the primary reasons for issues with rural recruitment and retention is financial (Heneghan et al., 2005), there is no consistent agreement about whether professionals in rural communities make less than their urban peers. Some studies, highlighting cost of living disparities, suggest that rural professionals may actually make more money (Rabinowitz & Paynter, 2002).

Despite the realities, many places see financial incentives as a way of motivating individuals to relocate after school to rural areas. South Carolina, along with many other states, offers recruitment incentives to providers and employers. For example, the SC Rural Physician Incentive Grant provides a cash incentive for physicians (e.g., psychiatrists) who agree to provide services in an HPSA for four years (South Carolina Rural Physician Incentive Grant Program: Incentive Information, n.d.). In places like Virginia, the tobacco commission offers the Talent Attraction Program, which offers up to $48,000 to recent graduates who provide two years of service in the tobacco region (which includes historically underserved and rural regions) (Virginia Tobacco Region Revitalization Commission, 2019).

Maine offers tax credits for graduates who have student loans. For those with unimaginably high student loans, the offer of a tax deduction for all student loan payments made in a year can be a real incentive (Live + Work in Maine, n.d.). Kansas also started offering a tax exemption and loan repayment in 2011 (Friedenberger, 2019).

Indian reservations, which are historically underserved, also offer financial incentives for recruitment and retention. The National Health Service Corps— the same group providing funding in HPSAs—dedicates a significant portion of its funding to those serving in the Indian Health Programs, many (but not all) of which are in rural areas. Professionals can receive up to $40,000 in loan repayment when they give a two-year commitment in an American Indian or Alaska Native community (Indian Health Service, n.d.).

Physicians who participate in rural rotations during their training are the most likely to relocate to a rural region upon completion of their training (Council on Graduate Medical Education, 1998). While rural rotations are increasing in number, there are fewer than necessary to lessen the shortage of rural providers. For master's level clinicians who typically complete their training prior to degree attainment, the likelihood of a rural rotation is significantly less.

Retention

Getting people to move to a rural region is challenging; keeping them there is another task entirely. Burnout, professional isolation, overwhelm, and financial difficulties may all make it hard for professionals to remain in rural areas. Further, cultural factors may make it harder for professionals to find comfort in their rural communities. Despite all of this, rural professionals must be vigilant about retention efforts. Agencies will spend an average of nine to twelve months to recruit a physician and, over 50% of physicians leave their practices after five years (Boise State University & National Organization of State Offices of Rural Health, 2015).

Money can be an excellent motivator. Whereas the research shows that loan repayment may not be a significant enough motivator for individuals to move to rural regions, such programs may aid in retention efforts. At least one research study found that nearly three-quarters of individuals who were in rural areas and seeking loan repayment funding would live in those areas regardless of the financial incentive (Renner, Westfall, Wilroy, & Ginde, 2010).

Turnover is costly and has deleterious effects on the community. Recruitment efforts can be particularly costly in rural areas where plane and train travel may be cumbersome and expensive. In rural communities, where residents seek insiders, not outsiders, to help them with their problems, this may be particularly important. Further, institutional and local knowledge is crucial

Table 15.1 Retention and Recruitment Challenges

Modifiable Factors	*Nonmodifiable Factors*
Financial • salary • benefits • repayment/forgiveness	**Social** • opportunities for growth; personal characteristics (ambition, comfort, sociableness)
Professional/organizational • peer support • professional community/identity • nature of work • work demands • burnout • leadership • work team	**Community** • cost of living • educational opportunities • employment opportunities for spouse/children • community • climate/geography • housing • lifestyle

Source: Humphreys, Wakerman, Pashen, & Buykx, 2009

for providers, and without it, practitioners may be hindered in their output. Rural communities are often providing piecemeal services, and knowledge of the tangled and weak web of services available may be crucial to helping an individual provide adequate services (Humphreys et al., 2009).

Some research shows that a multipronged approach to rural retention is critical (Buykx, Humphreys, Wakerman, & Pashen, 2010). Indeed, programs that bundle incentives are demonstrably better than stand-alone efforts at solution. An effective strategy should address mentorship, housing and schools, community support, income growth potential, training, and professional support (see Table 15.1 for specific examples) (Boise State University & National Organization of State Offices of Rural Health, 2015).

References

Boise State University & National Organization of State Offices of Rural Health. (2015). *Toolkit for recruitment and retention of primary care physicians in rural areas* (Draft 3.18.15). Sterling Heights, MI: National Organization of State Offices of Rural Health.

Bryan, Z. (2018). *Counties lacking mental health providers turn to technology*. Retrieved October 20, 2019, from www.hcn.org/articles/the-montana-gap-counties-lacking-mental-health-providers-turn-to-technology-telemedicine

Buykx, P., Humphreys, J., Wakerman, J., & Pashen, D. (2010). Systematic review of effective retention incentives for health workers in rural and remote areas: Toward evidence-based policy. *Australian Journal of Rural Health, 18*(3). Retrieved December 19, 2019, from www.ncbi.nlm.nih.gov/pubmed/20579020

Council on Graduate Medical Education. (1998, February). *Physician distribution and health care challenges in rural and inner-city areas*. Rockville, MD: U.S. Department of Health and Human Services. Retrieved December 19, 2019, from www.hrsa.gov/advisorycommittees/bhpradvisory/cogme/Reports/tenthreport.pdf

Friedenberger, A. (2019). Move to rural Virginia, and the tobacco commission will help pay off your student debt. *The Roanoke Times*. Retrieved December 19, 2019, from www.roanoke.com/news/education/move-to-rural-virginia-and-the-tobacco-commission-will-help/article_c6302f3e-845b-57d1-ad6b-02a31ef084e8.html

Gleason, K. (2012). Rural-nonrural disparities in postsecondary educational attainment revisited. *Journalist's Resource*. Retrieved December 19, 2019, from https://journalistsresource.org/studies/society/education/rural-nonrural-disparities-postsecondary-educational-attainment-attendance/

Health professional shortage and medically underserved designations: Current approach, legislation, and rulemaking history [PDF file]. (n.d.). Retrieved December 19, 2019, from www.hrsa.gov/advisorycommittees/shortage/Meetings/20100922/currentdesignationmodels.pdf

Heneghan, S. J., Bordley, J., Dietz, P. A., Gold, M. S., Jenkins, P. L., & Zuckerman, R. J. (2005). Comparison of urban and rural general surgeons: Motivations for practice location, practice patterns, and education requirements. *Journal of the American College of Surgeons, 201*(5), 732–736. https://doi.org/10.1016/j.jamcollsurg.2005.06.262

Humphreys, J., Wakerman, J., Pashen, D., & Buykx, P. (2009). *Retention strategies & incentives for health workers in rural & remote areas: What works?* [PDF file]. Retrieved December 19, 2019, from https://openresearch-repository.anu.edu.au/bitstream/1885/119206/3/international_retention_strategies_research_pdf_10642(1).pdf

Indian Health Service. (n.d.). *Loan repayment program*. Retrieved December 21, 2019, from www.ihs.gov/loanrepayment/

Live + Work in Maine. (n.d.). *The Opportunity Maine Tax Credit reimburses student loan payments for college graduates who live and work in Maine*. Retrieved December 21, 2019, from www.liveandworkinmaine.com/opportunity-maine/

Rabinowitz, H. K., & Paynter, N. P. (2002). The rural vs urban practice decision. *Medical Student Journal of the American Medical Association, 287*(1). Retrieved December 19, 2019, from https://jamanetwork.com/journals/jama/fullarticle/1844613

Reel, M. (2019). The state with the highest suicide rate desperately needs shrinks. *Bloomberg Businessweek*. Retrieved December 19, 2019, from www.bloomberg.com/news/features/2019-08-15/the-state-with-the-highest-suicide-rate-desperately-needs-shrinks

Renner, D., Westfall, J., Wilroy, L., & Ginde, A. (2010). The influence of loan repayment on rural healthcare provider recruitment and retention in Colorado. *Rural and Remote Health, 10*(1605). Retrieved December 19, 2019, from www.rrh.org.au/journal/article/1605

Rural Health Information Hub. (n.d.). *Rural mental health*. Retrieved October 23, 2019, from www.ruralhealthinfo.org/topics/mental-health

South Carolina Rural Physician Incentive Grant Program: Incentive Information. (n.d.). Retrieved December 21, 2019, from https://southcarolinaahec.az1.qualtrics.com/jfe/form/SV_78yfKnqd1REeMVn

Virginia Tobacco Region Revitalization Commission. (2019). *Student loan repayment*. Retrieved December 19, 2019, from www.revitalizeva.org/grant-loan-program/student-loan-repayment/

16 Defining Rural Mental Healthcare

I hope by now you have come to understand that rural mental health is different than urban mental health. I want to now turn our attention to looking at the ways in which mental health treatment in rural communities does, and must, look different than its urban equivalent. Mental health models, developed in urban environs, often fail to account for or to be applicable to rural communities (Manderscheid & Henderson, 1999). Because the problems, infrastructure, resources, landscape, and culture of rural communities often differ from their urban counterparts, the systems may not be a good fit (HHS, n.d.). Consequently, how we think about service delivery in rural America should be adjusted. In rural America, stakeholders should be "concerned with the mental health needs of the entire at-risk population" (Gale & Deprez, 2003, p. 100).

Before we can shift the rural mental health treatment paradigm, we must deconstruct the urbancentric treatment models and systems that do not adequately serve rural Americans. Table 16.1, taken from Beeson, Britain, Howell, Kirwan, and Sawyer (1998), brilliantly highlights the realities of the rural-urban differences.

Due to issues pertaining to access, availability, and acceptability of mental health treatment in rural communities, our definition must be broad and inclusive and allow for possible interventions. Fewer than half of all adults with a mental illness in America received mental health treatment for their condition in 2018 (National Alliance on Mental Illness, 2019). In rural communities, estimates suggest that only one third of individuals who need mental health treatment receive it (HHS, n.d.). If we limit our thinking to individual treatment and recovery from illness, we may effectively restrict our possible impacts (Gale & Deprez, 2003).

Ratios, rates of usage, and other cultural elements make it essential that as rural providers (and urban professionals hoping to serve those in rural communities), we think beyond our traditional models of service. Rural psychology requires an appreciation for the barriers, obstacles, and possibilities; a loosening of the tightly held notion of what therapy is or isn't; and perhaps even a distinct theoretical orientation that addresses all of these nuances.

Rural psychology should include individualized treatment, preventative approaches, systems of care designed to access a broader base of the population,

Table 16.1 Mental Health in an Urban Versus Rural Setting

	Urban Presumption	Rural Experience
Mental health services	There are adequate numbers and issues concerning coordination and integration.	There are inadequate numbers and a need for coordination and integration.
Mental health providers	Mental health providers are available, and individuals just need to access them.	There are health provider shortages, and providers face challenges of self-care, competencies, and training.
Stigma	Community education can be utilized to reduce this barrier to mental health service utilization.	Stigma is embedded in the cultural norms and values, and addressing stigma often takes place on an individual level.
Specialty practice areas	Specialties are often developed over the course of a professional's career, and individuals seeking services can often find someone who specializes in their presenting problems.	A general scope of practice is required.
Ethics	Professional guidelines, boundaries, expectations, and standards are clear and applicable, and violations are believed to be generally avoidable.	Multiple relationships are common, crisp boundaries often create mistrust, and the needs of the community often require a provider to constantly stretch beyond their competencies.
The mental health service system	Numerous diverse providers with specialized training are included and can collaborate and coordinate care.	The de facto mental health service system often includes, and is sometimes limited to, primary care providers, clergy, teachers, and nonprofit entities.
In the political conversation	Urbancentric norms typically underlie the discussion around and framing of policy on the state and national level.	Rural people and providers often feel overlooked, misunderstood, and bypassed in the larger conversation, with policy often failing to adequately address the needs of their communities.
Consumers	Mental health service recipients are often more familiar with services offered, have higher health literacy rates, and are more likely to know someone in the mental health field or someone already receiving services.	Community members are more likely to have lower health literacy, are less likely to have adequate health insurance and monies available to pay for treatment, and are more likely to be skeptical of services offered.

and outreach. Rural mental health treatment cannot simply be a shrunken version of urban mental health treatment (Sawyer, Gale, & Lambert, 2006).

A Public Health Approach to Rural Psychology

A public health approach lends itself nicely as a new lens through which we might explore options for interventions. Public health includes not only diagnosis and treatment but also health promotion and disease prevention (Gale & Deprez, 2003). This approach includes "primary and secondary preventative care, acute intervention, and long-term management of chronic conditions" (Gale & Deprez, 2003, p. 101). Such programming need not focus exclusively on the reduction of mental health symptoms. A greater emphasis on social and economic determinants of mental wellness, utilizing outreach and promotion methods that are inclusive and broad in scope, and an interdisciplinary approach all serve to increase positive outcomes (World Health Organization [WHO], 2004).

There are four primary avenues through which individuals can access services that may improve their mental well-being. Regier names these as specialty mental health, general hospital/inpatient nursing home, primary care/outpatient medical sector, and the other human service sector (Regier, Goldberg, & Taube, 1978). The de facto mental health system is a series of access points and levels of care that serve complimentary functions and require coordination (Gale & Deprez, 2003). The specialty mental health sector (including private practices, mental hospitals, community mental health centers, college counseling, and other focused service providers) is often believed to be the doorway through which those without complete mental health should walk (Gale & Deprez, 2003). Indeed, while historically social work (Swenson, 1998) has emphasized social justice, often as a separate track from direct care, most graduate curricula focus on individual services to address mental illness (APA, n.d.). However, only a small portion of individuals receiving treatment for a mental disorder actually do so through this sector. Many will not receive any treatment, and a large percentage of others will receive treatment through the primary care/outpatient medical sector (Regier et al., 1993).

Nationwide, approximately half of all individuals with psychological problems will seek treatment from their medical providers. Less than a quarter will seek such support from a provider in the specialty mental health system (Kessler & Stafford, 2008). We do not have adequate data on usage patterns in rural areas (Fox, Merwin, & Blank, 1995). However, given the provider shortages common in rural regions, their inhabitants are even likelier to utilize the de facto mental health system as opposed to the specialty mental health sector for treatment of their psychological needs. Regier and colleagues believed that the psychological needs of the American community were beyond what could be provided by the mental health service community. They advocated for greater training of medical professionals and more integration of care (Regier et al., 1978).

Stigma is a barrier to mental wellness in rural communities (Smalley et al., 2010). There is evidence to suggest that informal programming may reduce the effects of such stigma. That is, classes, brief interventions in a primary care office, workshops, indirect treatment, and education may be more easily accepted by individuals who might otherwise succumb to the negative effects of mental health stigma (Polaha, Williams, Heflinger, & Studts, 2015).

We know that individuals who suicide are highly likely to have visited a medical provider within the year prior to their death. However, only 29% made a visit to a mental health professional. Of those who saw a mental health or medical provider, only half received a mental health diagnosis. Diagnoses were less likely in disadvantaged groups. Individuals who suicide are widely believed to suffer from mental illness, and yet even they are not receiving a mental health diagnosis or, by and large, treatment (Ahmedani et al., 2014).

Community development initiatives may provide an indirect pathway to mental wellness for rural community members. Community development programming offers a path to mental health in several ways: there is an increase in insulating or protective factors such as social support, social capital, coping strategies, housing, income, healthcare, education, and physical health and a decrease in destructive factors such as social isolation, discrimination, alcohol abuse, inequality, and crime. According to the World Health Organization (2004), such programming is particularly important in groups that experience social and economic disadvantage. Rural communities, of course, tend to fall into this category (USDA, 2019).

The Church

Churches have long played a vital role in rural communities. In Black communities, rural and urban alike, the church is often a central force and figure (Blank, Mahmood, Fox, & Guterbock, 2002). Historically, churches have had a central role in the support system of a small community. They are the meeting place and often a primary social service provider (Vidich & Bensman, 2000). Churches also have an extensive history of being places for those with psychological problems to receive support, treatment, and aid (Haugk, 1976). In rural Black communities, churches provide a range of mental health services, including screenings, education, support, and substance abuse treatment. Unfortunately, in many communities studied, the link between the church and professional systems was largely untapped (Blank et al., 2002).

Science, of which psychology is a branch, and religion have not always gotten along well (Argyle, 2005). Many psychology training programs overlook its importance and do not adequately train professionals to integrate it into their work with clients for whom it may be relevant. In rural areas, particularly in the Southern United States, religion plays a major role in the community and for its people. In some rural communities, churches are likely to be an integral part of the mental healthcare delivery system (Brown, Warden, & Kotis, 2012).

Rural clergy are often a major component of the de facto mental health provider network in rural communities (Voss, 1996). Mental health professionals in rural communities can and should find ways to work collaboratively with this important group of individuals and the agencies that they represent. Collaborations, similar to those with primary care providers, may be minimal or fully integrated, depending on the needs and preferences of the provider and community.

At a minimum, churches (and other religious organizations) can identify those with needs who may be beyond the purview of the mental health clinic and may serve as a source for mental health referrals (Voss, 1996). If we maintain our view that mental health is for everyone and occurs along a spectrum, we can surmise that within the walls of a congregation sit countless opportunities for intervention and mental health improvement. Further, clergy often maintain close and intimate connections with their parishioners, providing them with insight not otherwise afforded to potential referral sources. Because it is commonplace for churchgoers to speak openly to their pastors, say, it is likely that church-based therapeutic relationships are not subject to the same levels of stigma and shame as those that are outpatient mental health based.

Collaboration of this nature should be two sided. Mental health professionals should honor, support, and be curious about the work the clergy are already doing to enhance the well-being of their parishioners. Professionals should not only seek referrals but also inquire about the ways in which they can enrich the work of the clergy member. Within this trusting relationship, clergy may be tasked with helping mental health professionals identify at-risk individuals, underserved populations, or community-wide needs.

Churches may also serve a vital role in the maintenance of a mentally well community through their physical spaces. Rural practitioners often face challenges when it comes to office spaces as many small communities do not have the sort of large office buildings available in cities. Churches often have group rooms, day care facilities, and sometimes gymnasiums or large spaces to host trainings and community events. In some communities, the church may be the only public meeting space available. Similar to the experience of a patient in a doctor's office, a churchgoer may find added comfort in meeting with a new professional in a familiar space. For this reason, rural practitioners may want to consider developing such a working alliance with a prominent local church.

Mental health professionals may not only reach an extended audience through identification and referrals made by clergy; they may also find that an ongoing partnership with a local religious organization provides them with opportunities to educate and enrich their community on issues of mental wellness. Churches often provide parishioners with educational opportunities, and those mental health professionals who maintain a working alliance may find themselves called in to do in-services or lectures or lead discussion groups, thus broadening their scope of influence.

Much to my chagrin, I quickly learned that rural communities are not conducive to group therapy work. Stigma aside, individuals are often highly interconnected, making a safe, therapeutic environment free from outside influence largely impossible. However, due to the different nature of the church, support groups or even specific topic or process groups may prove possible.

Collaborating with a clergy member may make it possible for individual providers to open up this aspect of their practices.

School-Based Care

Schools, like churches, serve a massive group of community members who might otherwise not consider themselves to be consumers of mental health services. There is perhaps no better delivery system than the school for addressing the mental health needs of children, adolescents, and perhaps families. School-based programming is becoming increasingly popular both in urban and rural settings (Waguespack, Broussard, & Guilfou, 2012).

School-based mental health services tend to increase the overall rates of children engaged with mental health services (Guo, Wade, & Keller, 2008). They appear to have positive outcomes for the health and well-being of the children served (Wade et al., 2008).

School-based programming increases treatment compliance by reducing access barriers to services. The kids are seen in the school, which decreases the likelihood that they will miss their sessions due to transportation, cost, compliance, or other issues. School-based services may also make treatment more socially acceptable to teenagers (Francis, Boyd, Aisbett, Newnham, & Newnham, 2006). School-based rural youth most commonly received treatment through school-based programs designed to decrease stigma, and increase compliance and attendance (HHS, n.d.).

School-based mental health services are also a nice way to increase community participation and outreach. Schools with school-based mental health services are providing awareness to children and families therein about these services. What's more, school-based mental health workers will have regular and frequent overlap with other professionals, such as teachers, principals, and aides. This may increase the overall awareness of mental health needs and services among the broader population of an area and may reduce the threat of burnout for the professional.

School-based mental healthcare seems to work. Opportunities abound for rural professionals seeking to work with children and adolescents in this context.

Partnerships extend beyond formal institutions and should include nonprofits and smaller, community-based groups. Well-known nonprofit agencies such as Big Brothers Big Sisters and the Boys and Girls Club may not immediately come to mind as agencies dealing with mental health, but when we take a broader view of mental wellness, suddenly these operations become vital opportunities for partnerships in our communities. Rural providers may be well served by exploring the agencies providing services regionally and locally in the spirit of advancing the well-being of their communities and their individuals.

Peer Networks of Care

Peers—those with lived experiences similar to our own—are often vital to our social support networks. Even without any additional training or supervision, peers can provide us with support and assistance (Solomon, 2004). Much like our consultation group, a peer-support group can provide our clients with a variety of buffering experiences such as connection, identification, knowledge, wisdom, and empathy.

Peer-based provider programs combine lived experience and formal training to enlist the support of specialists or coaches to aid others in recovery from mental illness or addiction (SAMHSA-HRSA Center for Integrated Health Solutions, 2016). Particularly useful in areas constrained by professional shortages and financial concerns, the research on peer-based programming is quite promising. Theoretically, peer specialists "bring credibility, trust, resilience, and hope" to individuals suffering from severe mental illness (Cabassa, Camacho, Vélez-Grau, & Stefancic, 2017), and involvement in peer-based programming may increase feelings of empowerment and hope in participants (Hardiman & Segal, 2003).

Peer-based programming comes in several forms. First, peers with lived experiences can be trained to deliver services either directly (serving as peer specialists), through partnerships (not free-standing or exclusively peer-based but peer-delivered), or through programming or group opportunities with non-peer individuals functioning only at their direction (peer-run services). Second, peers can participate in mutual support groups that utilize shared facilitation or equality of group membership (self-help groups) (Miyamoto & Sono, 2012). Third, peers can lead internet support groups. Finally, peers can serve in adjunct roles in agencies in which they have peripheral functions (Solomon, 2004). Psychologists, therapists, or counselors who self-identify as having severe mental illness and who provide services are known as *prosumers* (Frese & Davis, 1997).

Peer-based interventions may provide an empathic space with compassionate connections for individuals suffering. This shared sense of community and experience may be healing for those living with mental illness (Flegg, Gordon-Walker, & Maguire, 2015). Research findings suggest that the presence of peer-support specialists or inclusion in peer-led programming results in feelings of respect, humanity, trust, and understanding (Miyamoto & Sono, 2012).

Quantitative findings also support the efficacy of models of peer-based support (Miyamoto & Sono, 2012). The positive effects of peer-based programming appear to be bidirectional, with individuals giving support reaping benefits such as self-efficacy, confidence, competence, and group membership while the individuals receiving the support experience effects similar to or better than treatment effects from therapy with professionals (Solomon, 2004).

Of note, particularly to rural groups, is a finding by Mowbray, Moxley, and Collins (1998) that participants in peer-based programming found comfort in the collective sharing of frustrations regarding the mental health system. Peers involved in the system, aside from those tasked with mental health service provisions, may prove useful in helping those with lower health literacy navigate complex systems of care. Case management, done by a peer, can involve an empowered approach that enables access to resources with less stigma, frustration, and confusion (Solomon, 2004).

166   Innovations and Opportunities

In rural communities, peer-based programming offers some unique, important potential outcomes. (See Figure 16.1.) First, the cost savings of peer-based programming has been demonstrated. Second, peer-based programming offers a workaround to provider shortages. Third, peer participation in informal care, referral networks, and initial client contact may increase treatment compliance and positive outcomes (Solomon, 2004).

Careful attention to training, supervision, and management is essential to ensure efficacy in peer-based programming (Repper & Carter, 2011). Peer-delivered service is not simply the dispersion of those with lived experiences into communities to aid in recovery, though this may have some benefit. Peer programming is a thoughtful and carefully constructed model that requires three major elements: service elements, peer characteristics, and system principles. Peer services rely on an experiential learning process in which the peer shares aspects of his or her experience in the spirit of aiding the recovery of the client. The process must be voluntary in nature, with the client selecting the peer programming, and should be directed by the peer to preserve the integrity of the therapeutic alliance, maintaining boundaries of influence. Through this process, a natural system of support will emerge while stigma and shame are reduced. This benefits both provider and client. The peers should be carefully selected and must have had previous struggles with the relevant mental health/substance use issues and relevant treatment but should no longer be unstable or dependent on treatment for their well-being. Finally, the system should ensure that the peer-based offerings are diverse in culture and content so that those seeking such services can find their likeness in the issues addressed by the services and providers (Solomon, 2004).

When I reviewed the literature surrounding peer programming, I found very little regarding its efficacy specific to rural communities. Several findings suggested that peer-based programming might be useful in rural areas. Peer support can be particularly useful in augmenting social support in vulnerable populations. It can also be a method of filling gaps in service in areas without adequate professional support (Gray, Davies, & Butcher, 2017). Specifically, individuals from underserved or historically oppressed groups, such as LGBTQ youth and ethnic minorities living in rural regions, may find particular comfort in peer programming (Schwinn, Thom, Schinke, & Hopkins, 2015). Peer-to-peer support networks in rural communities may most easily occur through the

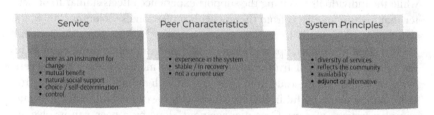

Figure 16.1 Peer-to-Peer Service Requirements

internet. Limited research exists on the validity and efficacy of online peer-to-peer support groups (Ali, Farrer, Gulliver, & Griffiths, 2015). Though research appears to be limited on the efficacy and applicability of peer programming in rural communities, the outlook suggested by the data is hopeful.

Mental Health First Aid

Mental health first aid (MHFA), a community-based public health approach to mental health, was designed to simultaneously educate and empower community members to be good consumers and referrers of psychological services. Based on the similar medical first aid model, MHFA aims to increase the public's response to mental health issues by increasing mental health literacy (Kitchener & Jorm, 2002). Trainers attend a three- or five-day training that enables them to offer MHFA training programs in their community. MHFA has both adolescent and adult tracks. Individuals can and do attend trainings, but schools, businesses, police forces, and other public servants are frequent participants (Mental Health First Aid USA, n.d.).

An MHFA course is typically a nine-hour training program, and the curriculum covers five steps for administering first aid to those who are either experiencing a mental health crisis or in the early stages of mental health problems: (1) assess risk, (2) listen nonjudgmentally, (3) provide information and reassurance, (4) provide paths to professional help, and (5) offer and encourage the use of self-help techniques (Kitchener & Jorm, 2002).

Research supports the efficacy of MHFA courses. Findings have demonstrated that, upon completion, participants were less likely to hold stigmatized views of mental illness, more knowledgeable and confident in their perceived ability to help those in a mental health crisis, and more willing to help others (Hadlaczky, Hökby, Mkrtchian, Carli, & Wasserman, 2014). They were slightly less likely to encourage others to seek professional care, though those findings were not significant.

Mental health first aid courses might be an excellent way to supplement those services offered by professionals in a rural community. Coupled with the finding that MHFA helps reduce stigma, MHFA's public health approach to utilizing friends, neighbors, classmates, and coworkers to raise awareness and get folks tied in with services seems like an excellent fit for a rural community.

Mobile Therapy: The "Psych Mobile"

Mobile health clinics (MHCs) are an increasingly popular way to address treatment disparities in rural (and urban) areas. MHCs are mobile offices, typically in vans or trucks, outfitted for a specific purpose, such as mental health, mammography, prevention, or prenatal care. By bringing services to the community members, rather than requiring the individuals to come to the services, MHCs increase patient trust, decrease logistical barriers to treatment, and provide much-needed services to historically underserved communities (Population Health Advisor, 2017).

MHCs have been popping up for decades with estimates citing thousands now serving communities across the country (Mobile Health Map, n.d.). MHCs provide services in areas where there historically has not been access. Mobile units are an increasingly common way to provide health services to the chronically underserved. In recent years, such programs have opened up services to rural Americans (Carmack, 2010). Mobile units are built on tenets of both visibility and accessibility. Individuals in historically underserved areas may see a mobile unit more often than they would a therapy clinic. Further, mobile units, which are designed to go to the person or people, by definition make care significantly more accessible (Stephanie, Hill, Ricks, Bennet, & Oriol, 2017). Mobile units may also serve to garner increased trust as a result of the demonstrated willingness to literally meet the client where he or she is at (Stephanie et al., 2017).

Historically, MHCs focused on preventative care (Hill et al., 2012), such as prenatal healthcare (Edgerley, El-Sayed, Druzin, Kiernan, & Daniels, 2007) and mammography services (Kann, Bradley, & Lane, 1998). MHCs have also addressed the healthcare needs of the homeless (McGee, Morgan, McNamee, & Bartek, 1995) and other health concerns of inner-city populations (Hill et al., 2012).

Mobile healthcare provides a cost savings to the community as a whole. In a preventative care model in Boston over 16 years, a mobile unit provided a 36:1 return on investment (Oriol et al., 2009). MHCs, by expanding preventative care services to underserved populations, often reduce the use of emergency medicine services—including initial admissions and readmissions (Stephanie et al., 2017).

The MHC model is a natural fit, in some ways, for the rural setting. Mobile health requires community building and buy-in (Stephanie et al., 2017). MHC providers must conduct a needs assessment, build community partnerships, and address the requests of the community they aim to serve. On the other hand, MHCs may trigger apprehension or mistrust in rural community members who might see MHC providers as outsiders.

The concept is simple: build or retrofit a van or truck to resemble a healthcare space, travel to a location selected for its population and need, provide services, repeat. The implementation, however, can be challenging.

Despite saving the system and people money, mobile healthcare units are often run at a loss or face serious financial hardship. Research demonstrates that a significant portion of mobile health units struggled to meet their financial goals, due in part to high costs and periods of inactivity due to weather and vehicular damage/repairs (Stephanie et al., 2017).

Additionally, unless embedded in a larger network of care, mobile health units may contribute to the fragmentation of the healthcare system insofar as individuals may be less likely to follow up with referrals or subsequent appointments (Stephanie et al., 2017).

The Veteran's Administration has been using mobile units to expand its reach, particularly to rural locations, for over ten years. There are approximately 80 mobile vet centers nationwide, designed to meet the needs of communities that do not have brick-and-mortar vet centers or VA clinics (Office of the First Lady, 2015).

Though there have been limited research studies on the subject, the initial research is quite favorable (Stephanie et al., 2017). Mobile health clinics may be one effective answer to the question of how we serve rural communities. Those interested in developing or learning more about mobile healthcare should inquire with the Mobile Health Map or the Mobile Healthcare Association.

References

Ahmedani, B. K., Simon, G. E., Stewart, C., Beck, A., Waitzfelder, B. E., Rossom, R., . . . Operskalski, B. H. (2014). Health care contacts in the year before suicide death. *Journal of General Internal Medicine, 29*(6), 870–877.

Ali, K., Farrer, L., Gulliver, A., & Griffiths, K. M. (2015). Online peer-to-peer support for young people with mental health problems: A systematic review. *JMIR Mental Health, 2*(2), e19.

American Psychological Association (APA). (n.d.). *APA accreditation.* Retrieved May 1, 2020, from https://www.accreditation.apa.org

Argyle, M. (2005). *Psychology and religion: An introduction.* London: Routledge.

Beeson, P., Britain, C., Howell, M., Kirwan, A., & Sawyer, D. (1998). Rural mental health at the millennium. In R. W. Manderscheid & M. J. Henderson (Eds.), *Mental health, United States* (8th ed., pp. 82–97). Washington, DC: U.S. Government Printing Office.

Blank, M. B., Mahmood, M., Fox, J. C., & Guterbock, T. (2002). Alternative mental health services: The role of the Black church in the South. *American Journal of Public Health, 92*(10), 1668–1672.

Brown, F. F., Warden, S. P., & Kotis, A. B. (2012). Providing mental health services for women in rural areas. In K. B. Smalley, J. C. Warren, & J. P. Rainer (Eds.), *Rural mental health: Issues, policies, and best practices* (pp. 253–266). New York: Springer Publishing Company.

Cabassa, L. J., Camacho, D., Vélez-Grau, C. M., & Stefancic, A. (2017). Peer-based health interventions for people with serious mental illness: A systematic literature review. *Journal of Psychiatric Research, 84,* 80–89.

Carmack, H. J. (2010). "What happens on the van, stays on the van": The (re) structuring of privacy and disclosure scripts on an Appalachian mobile health clinic. *Qualitative Health Research, 20*(10), 1393–1405.

Edgerley, L. P., El-Sayed, Y. Y., Druzin, M. L., Kiernan, M., & Daniels, K. I. (2007). Use of a community mobile health van to increase early access to prenatal care. *Maternal and Child Health Journal, 11*(3), 235–239.

Flegg, M., Gordon-Walker, M., & Maguire, S. (2015). Peer-to-peer mental health: A community evaluation case study. *The Journal of Mental Health Training, Education and Practice, 10*(5), 282–293.

Fox, J., Merwin, E., & Blank, M. (1995). De facto mental health services in the rural south. *Journal of Health Care for the Poor and Underserved, 6*(4), 434–468.

Francis, K., Boyd, C., Aisbett, D., Newnham, K., & Newnham, K. (2006). Rural adolescents' attitudes to seeking help for mental health problems. *Youth Studies Australia*, *25*(4), 42.

Frese, F. J., & Davis, W. W. (1997). The consumer–survivor movement, recovery, and consumer professionals. *Professional Psychology: Research and Practice*, *28*(3), 243.

Gale, J. A., & Deprez, R. D. (2003). A public health approach to the challenges of rural mental health service integration. In B. H. Stamm (Ed.), *Rural behavioral health care: An interdisciplinary guide* (pp. 95–108). Washington, DC: American Psychological Association.

Gray, M., Davies, K., & Butcher, L. (2017). Finding the right connections: Peer support within a community-based mental health service. *International Journal of Social Welfare*, *26*(2), 188–196.

Guo, J. J., Wade, T. J., & Keller, K. N. (2008). Impact of school-based health centers on students with mental health problems. *Public Health Reports*, *123*(6), 768–780.

Hadlaczky, G., Hökby, S., Mkrtchian, A., Carli, V., & Wasserman, D. (2014). Mental Health First Aid is an effective public health intervention for improving knowledge, attitudes, and behaviour: A meta-analysis. *International Review of Psychiatry*, *26*(4), 467–475.

Hardiman, E. R., & Segal, S. P. (2003). Community membership and social networks in mental health self-help agencies. *Psychiatric Rehabilitation Journal*, *27*(1), 25.

Haugk, K. C. (1976). Unique contributions of churches and clergy to community mental health. *Community Mental Health Journal*, *12*(1), 20–28.

Hill, C., Zurakowski, D., Bennet, J., Walker-White, R., Osman, J. L., Quarles, A., & Oriol, N. (2012). Knowledgeable neighbors: A mobile clinic model for disease prevention and screening in underserved communities. *American Journal of Public Health*, *102*(3), 406–410.

Kann, P. E., Bradley, C., & Lane, D. S. (1998). Outcomes of recommendations for breast biopsies in women receiving mammograms from a county health van. *Public Health Reports*, *113*(1), 71.

Kessler, R., & Stafford, D. (2008). Primary care is the de facto mental health system. In *Collaborative medicine case studies* (pp. 9–21). New York: Springer.

Kitchener, B. A., & Jorm, A. F. (2002). Mental health first aid training for the public: Evaluation of effects on knowledge, attitudes and helping behavior. *BMC Psychiatry*, *2*, 10. https://doi.org/10.1186/1471-244X-2-10

Manderscheid, R. W., & Henderson, M. J. (Eds.). (1999). *Mental health, United States, 1998*. Rockville, MD: Diane Publishing Company.

McGee, D., Morgan, M., McNamee, M. J., & Bartek, J. K. (1995). Use of a mobile health van by a vulnerable population: Homeless sheltered women. *Health Care for Women International*, *16*(5), 451–461.

Mental Health First Aid USA. (n.d.). *About*. Retrieved November 30, 2019, from www.mentalhealthfirstaid.org/about/

Miyamoto, Y., & Sono, T. (2012). Lessons from peer support among individuals with mental health difficulties: A review of the literature. *Clinical Practice and Epidemiology in Mental Health: CP & EMH*, *8*, 22.

Mobile Health Map. (n.d.). *What is Mobile Health Map?* Retrieved December 2, 2019, from www.mobilehealthmap.org/what-is-mobile-health-map

Mowbray, C. T., Moxley, D. P., & Collins, M. E. (1998). Consumers as mental health providers first-person accounts of benefits and limitations. *The Journal of Behavioral Health Services & Research*, *25*(4), 397–411.

National Alliance on Mental Illness. (2019). *Mental health by the numbers*. Retrieved December 19, 2019, from www.nami.org/learn-more/mental-health-by-the-numbers

Office of the First Lady. (2015). *Fact sheet: VA vet centers and administration progress on mental health*. Retrieved December 19, 2019, from https://obamawhitehouse.archives.gov/the-press-office/2015/04/17/fact-sheet-va-vet-centers-and-administration-progress-mental-health

Oriol, N. E., Cote, P. J., Vavasis, A. P., Bennet, J., DeLorenzo, D., Blanc, P., & Kohane, I. (2009). Calculating the return on investment of mobile healthcare. *BMC Medicine, 7*(1), 27.

Polaha, J., Williams, S. L., Heflinger, C. A., & Studts, C. R. (2015). The perceived stigma of mental health services among rural parents of children with psychosocial concerns. *Journal of Pediatric Psychology, 40*(10), 1095–1104. https://doi.org/10.1093/jpepsy/jsv054

Population Health Advisor. (2017). *Mobile health clinics: Improving access to care for the underserved* [PDF file]. Retrieved December 19, 2019, from www.mobilehealthmap.org/sites/default/files/uploads/PHA_Mobile%20Clinic%20Brief_0317_General.pdf

Regier, D. A., Goldberg, I. D., & Taube, C. A. (1978). The de facto US mental health services system: A public health perspective. *Archives of General Psychiatry, 35*(6), 685–693.

Regier, D. A., Narrow, W. E., Rae, D. S., Manderscheid, R. W., Locke, B. Z., & Goodwin, F. K. (1993). The de facto US mental and addictive disorders service system: Epidemiologic Catchment Area prospective 1-year prevalence rates of disorders and services. *Archives of General Psychiatry, 50*(2), 85–94.

Repper, J., & Carter, T. (2011). A review of the literature on peer support in mental health services. *Journal of Mental Health, 20*(4), 392–411.

SAMHSA-HRSA Center for Integrated Health Solutions. 2016. *Peer providers*. Retrieved December 19, 2019, from www.integration.samhsa.gov/workforce/team-members/peer-providers

Sawyer, D., Gale, J. A., & Lambert, D. (2006). *Rural and frontier mental and behavioral health care: Barriers, effective policy strategies, best practices*. Waite Park, MN: National Association of Rural Mental Health.

Schwinn, T. M., Thom, B., Schinke, S. P., & Hopkins, J. (2015). Preventing drug use among sexual-minority youths: Findings from a tailored, web-based intervention. *Journal of Adolescent Health, 56*(5), 571–573.

Smalley, K. B., Yancey, C. T., Warren, J. C., Naufel, K., Ryan, R., & Pugh, J. L. (2010). Rural mental health and psychological treatment: A review for practitioners. *Journal of Clinical Psychology, 66*(5), 479–489.

Solomon, P. (2004). Peer support/peer provided services underlying processes, benefits, and critical ingredients. *Psychiatric Rehabilitation Journal, 27*(4), 392–401. https://doi.org/10.2975/27.2004.392.401

Stephanie, W. Y., Hill, C., Ricks, M. L., Bennet, J., & Oriol, N. E. (2017). The scope and impact of mobile health clinics in the United States: A literature review. *International Journal for Equity in Health, 16*(1), 178.

Swenson, C. R. (1998). Clinical social work's contribution to a social justice perspective. *Social Work, 43*(6), 527–537.

US Department of Health and Human Services. (n.d.). Mental health and rural America (1994–2005). Retrieved from www.ruralhealthresearch.org/mirror/6/657/RuralMentalHealth.pdf

United States Department of Agriculture. (2019, August 20). *Rural poverty & well-being*. Retrieved December 19, 2019, from www.ers.usda.gov/topics/rural-economy-population/rural-poverty-well-being/

Vidich, A. J., & Bensman, J. (2000). *Small town in mass society: Class, power, and religion in a rural community*. Chicago: University of Illinois Press.

Voss, S. L. (1996). The church as an agent in rural mental health. *Journal of Psychology and Theology, 24*(2), 114–123.

Wade, T. J., Mansour, M. E., Guo, J. J., Huentelman, T., Line, K., & Keller, K. N. (2008). Access and utilization patterns of school-based health centers at urban and rural elementary and middle schools. *Public health reports, 123*(6), 739–750.

Waguespack, A. M., Broussard, C., & Guilfou, K. (2012). School and home-based interventions in rural communities. In K. B. Smalley & J. Rainer (Eds.), *Rural mental health: Issues, policies, and best practices* (pp. 173–190). New York: Springer Publishing Company.

World Health Organization. (2004). *Promoting mental health: Concepts, emerging evidence, practice: Summary report* [PDF file]. Retrieved October 23, 2019, from www.who.int/mental_health/evidence/en/promoting_mhh.pdf

17 From Collaboration to Colocation

Integrated, Whole-Person Care in Rural America

Rural communities are ripe with opportunities for professional partnerships and cooperation. Many rural practitioners will find some form of collaboration to be essential to their viability. Others may view integrated care as an ambitious goal that would solve many problems in their work. Along a continuum of collaboration, integrated models can take many forms. Systems of integration vary based on layers of collaboration, location, and information shared.

Models may be informal, coordinated, based on a partnership, collaborative, or integrated. Informal partnerships require an awareness of the services offered and communication on an as-needed basis. Coordinated efforts require an established connection with some standard protocol for teamwork. Partnerships entail networks of professionals who work between their respective agencies. Agencies may also collaborate in sharing or merging both resources and responsibilities. Finally, providers may fully combine and complement services in a fully integrated partnership (Sears, Evans, & Kuper, 2003).

Such collaboration can happen with medical professionals, schools, churches, nonprofit agencies, and individuals within the community, with healthcare partnerships being the most prominent and, perhaps, popular.

Individuals in rural areas are even more likely than their urban counterparts to depend on medical professionals to address their mental health needs (Riding-Malon & Werth, 2014). Stigma, privacy concerns, low health literacy, and numerous other factors all make it easier for rural Americans to seek out care from doctors and nurses rather than therapists and counselors. Historically, medical doctors, likely due to undertraining and time constraints, are not particularly effective at diagnosing mental health disorders. Rural individuals are more likely to have somatic presentations of mental health distress and to experience stigma (and subsequent denial of mental health issues) and are less likely to receive services from a mental health professional, in part because so few of them are practicing in rural areas. Medical professionals, those most likely afforded the opportunity to effectively diagnose and treat a mental health concern, are ill equipped for this demand and ill prepared for the process. Rural Americans, then, are potentially trapped in a cycle that leaves them unable to get what they need to achieve complete (or even partial) mental health (Riding-Malon & Werth, 2014).

Integrated Care

Much attention has been paid to the integration of mental and physical healthcare in recent years (Gale & Lambert, 2006). Integrated care refers to the combined efforts of mental health professionals, dentists, medical doctors, and specialists in the spirit of addressing the inclusive health needs of the whole person (Sears et al., 2003). Due to the lack of specialty service professionals, rural America is an excellent place for integrated care (Gale & Lambert, 2006). Of course, it also poses challenges.

Integrated care is neither simple nor easy. Rather, integrated care requires collaboration and planning on both the part of the provider and the process (Sears et al., 2003). To be effective, then, integration must be more than simply structural; it must be functional.

Integrated care often provides a bridge between physical and mental healthcare. Primary care—the "accessible, comprehensive and continuous" care occurring along bio, psycho, and social domains (Sears et al., 2003, p. 114)—is a reasonable starting point for our collaboration given the similar approach to the whole person. Further, primary care providers are more common in rural settings where, again, specialties are prohibitive. Finally, primary care office visits account for half of all medical office visits in the United States, with this percentage likely being higher in rural areas (Robert Graham Center, 2018).

The various methods of integrative collaboration occur along a spectrum. These can range from full integration to complete autonomy:

- System and facilities remain separate, shared referrals and cases, separate functioning
- System and facilities remain largely independent with some shared resources, cases, referrals, or basic collaboration; separate functioning
- Shared facilities, separate systems, minimally integrated functioning
- Shared facilities and some overlapping systems, partially integrated functioning
- Shared facilities and systems, fully integrated functioning

(Sears et al., 2003)

Integration can happen in four distinct ways: diversification, linkage, referral, and enhancement (Bird, Lambert, Hartley, Beeson, & Coburn, 1995).

Diversification entails the hiring and training of a particular individual to fulfill duties not previously provided within a facility or entity. Perhaps a cancer center hires a social worker to provide therapeutic services, or a primary care facility hires an addictions counselor to provide substance use screenings (Bird et al., 1995). In rural communities this model may be effective insofar as mental health providers are available for hire by the agencies requiring their services. In severe shortage areas, a hospital or clinic may not be able to secure these resources. This type of integration involves shared location, shared systems, and shared functionality. A client may experience a full level of integrated care within one space or even office visit.

Many practitioners may choose colocation (or **linkage**) with independent systems. The independence of both professions remains intact, but individuals can access services more easily due to the physical proximity. Professionals often refer to one another in a manner that can provide clients or patients with some sense that they are being looked after in a holistic way (Riding-Malon & Werth, 2014). The colocation or linkage model sometimes allows for what is known as a "warm handoff" in medicine, in which the patient is introduced to their supplemental provider by their primary medical person (Sears et al., 2003). This approach allows for mild collaboration while remaining functionally independent, for better or worse. Without a release of information and informed consent, colocation providers cannot speak openly about patients' needs, status, symptoms, or treatment, thus limiting the scope of continuity of care.

This model is a good starting point and may address issues surrounding access insofar as patients may utilize a shared parking lot and waiting area, thus potentially reducing stigma and shame. Linkage efforts may also increase patient trust and hasten rapport building, which may increase treatment effects and follow-through (Sears et al., 2003). To date, we have participated in linkage efforts with primary care offices, a physical therapy clinic, and a women's wellness center. By and large these efforts, anecdotally, have increased our reach to include patients who may not otherwise have sought or received our services. An unintended consequence has been the education of other professionals simply through proximal contact and perhaps a de-stigmatization effect as a result of our presence in these facilities.

Linkage also provides professionals an opportunity to consult outside their areas of expertise. Working through preestablished channels of communications, medical doctors can consult with autism experts, and psychologists can consult with a physician assistant on chronic pain. In this way, linkage helps address issues of comorbidity in a holistic way. The patient is not simply bumped from one provider to the next, but care is taken to treat the whole person, to the degree that it is possible (National Institute of Mental Health, n.d.).

Referrals are a common, often overlooked, form of integration. With a formal agreement in place, practitioners of different modalities (e.g., mental health and medical) agree to a particular method for referring clients to one another (Bird et al., 1995). For the overworked practitioner, referrals may be cumbersome as they now have the responsibility of communicating and arranging with a client and reporting back to the primary referral source. Further, clients may not have a cohesive experience in care. Depending on the arrangement, the onus may be on the client or the practitioner to ensure follow-through, leaving room for a breakdown in the process. Anecdotally, our clinic has the lowest rates of attendance for first and subsequent sessions under this model of integration. We believe that medical professionals are not always adept or allowed time for proper explanation of the treatment needs and process, and clients may experience internal and external barriers in the process, such as shame, lack of information, uncertainty, and stigma.

Enhancement integration occurs when the primary care provider receives specialized training in the provision of mental health services (Bird et al., 1995). This may entail the administration of a screening tool by a nurse or specific training aimed at assisting the practitioner in identifying autism in children. A common, often overlooked, method of enhancement, particularly useful in rural communities, is the practice of medical professionals providing psychotropic medications (typically the purview of a psychiatrist). Because there are so few rural psychiatrists and psychiatric nurse practitioners, primary care providers often find themselves tasked with this responsibility. This model of integration rests on the assumptions that medical professionals have the time and resources to engage in training and that education is the only barrier to the provision of quality mental health services. Indeed, like mental health professionals, medical providers in rural communities are often overworked, overburdened, and forced to practice general (rather than specialized) medicine (Rabinowitz & Paynter, 2002). Further, when psychiatric conditions are complex or patients fail to respond well to psychiatric treatment, medical providers may not have the skills or training to further the treatment (Lambert & Gale, 2014). Behavioral health, which addresses risk factors and encourages behaviors that promote physical health and prevent disease, is commonly integrated into primary care medicine because of its relevance to health outcomes (Sears et al., 2003).

While integration can happen in any of these four ways, in rural practices, it is common for integration to include more than one of these strategies. Lambert and Gale (2014) recommend that practitioners carefully evaluate their goals, the available resources, existing services, and possible outcomes prior to initiating integration. As I have previously mentioned, rural America is not a homogenous place, and its people and their needs are as diverse as its landscape. Consequently, each rural professional must take careful stock of his or her community and the unique cultural elements, subgroups, and needs therein.

Considerations for Rural Integration

In an urban center where specialty care and primary care need only a simple connection, integrated medicine comes perhaps more naturally and easily than in rural communities where integration is limited by scarcity. In rural communities where there is no psychiatrist, say, it is not merely a matter of linking a family nurse practitioner with a child psychiatrist but figuring out how to create systems that address the needs of the community with the resources available. There are three primary elements to consider when integrating medical services in rural communities.

First, particularly in areas with sparse resources, **flexibility** is essential (Rygh & Hjortdahl, 2007). In a small town without a psychiatrist, general practitioners must prescribe psychotropic medications, or community members won't get them. Such flexibility is vital and also problematic. Many states have addressed this particular shortage by providing a pathway for psychologists (who appear in higher numbers in the US than psychiatrists) to obtain prescription privileges.

Iowa has approximately 7.9 psychiatrists for every 100,000 people. Compared to Massachusetts, which has 30 psychiatrists for every 100,000 people, states like Iowa, Montana, Nevada, Wyoming, Alabama, and Idaho have a profound shortage of psychiatrists (Beck, Page, Buche, Rittman, & Gaiser, 2018). As you might expect, there are far fewer psychiatrists in rural areas than in urban ones (Jameson & Blank, 2007). Iowa, Idaho, and New Mexico (APA, 2008), among other states with high rural populations and few psychiatrists, have implemented legislation granting prescriptive authority to psychologists (Lavoie & Fleet, 2002). Evidence suggests that in rural places where psychologists have prescription privileges, there is an increase in services received by community members (Linda & McGrath, 2017).

Similarly, nurse practitioners and physician assistants are increasingly able to practice independently, particularly in rural areas. When nurse practitioners are allowed to practice independently, access to primary care is expanded (Kuo, Loresto Jr, Rounds, & Goodwin, 2013). Indeed, allowing nurse practitioners to practice independently is one way to reduce urban-rural health disparities (Ortiz et al., 2018). By expanding the breadth of services offered by any one provider, communities see an increase in access to care (Linda & McGrath, 2017).

To increase access to care, we must not only expand the limits of what services providers can provide; we must also expand our definition of who service providers are. **Substituting** trained lay people for professional service providers may also expand the reach of the mental health community in rural areas (Rygh & Hjortdahl, 2007). Rural communities can enlist the help of nonprofessionals in health promotion, self-help programming, or referrals. We have already explored specific programmatic opportunities such as Mental Health First Aid and how to utilize peers in reducing stigma, increasing access, and raising awareness of mental health services.

Due to the patchwork nature of many rural resources, having trained, locally based **case managers** is vital to ensuring that those who need mental health services have access and experience integration. Given the fact that many traditional resources do not exist in many rural communities, case managers will need to be creative and flexible in their interventions (Meyer & Morrissey, 2007; Rygh & Hjortdahl, 2007). Research has highlighted the importance of case management in rural areas when working with families with developmentally disabled children (Fiene & Taylor, 1991), children in kinship placements (Myers, Kropf, & Robinson, 2002), veterans (Mohamed,

Neale, & Rosenheck, 2009), individuals with schizophrenia (Drake et al., 1991), individuals with substance use issues (Vaughan-Sarrazin, Hall, & Rick, 2000), and others.

References

American Psychological Association. (2008). *Prescriptive authority in the states*. Retrieved December 19, 2019, from www.apa.org/monitor/feb08/prescriptive

Beck, A. J., Page, C., Buche, M. J., Rittman, D., & Gaiser, M. (2018). Estimating the distribution of the US psychiatric subspecialist workforce. *Population, 600*, 47–46.

Bird, D., Lambert, D., Hartley, D., Beeson, P., & Coburn, A. (1995). Integrating primary care and mental health services in rural America: A policy review and conceptual framework. *Administration and Policy in Mental Health and Mental Health Services Research, 25*, 287–308. Retrieved December 19, 2019, from https://link.springer.com/article/10.1023/A:1022291306283

Drake, R. E., Wallach, M. A., Teague, G. B., Freeman, D. H., Paskus, T. S., & Clark, T. A. (1991). Housing instability and homelessness among rural schizophrenic patients. *The American Journal of Psychiatry, 148*(3), 330–336.

Fiene, J. I., & Taylor, P. A. (1991). Serving rural families of developmentally disabled children: A case management model. *Social Work, 36*(4), 323–327.

Gale, J. A., & Lambert, D. (2006). Mental healthcare in rural communities: The once and future role of primary care. *North Carolina Medical Journal, 67*(1), 66.

Jameson, J. P., & Blank, M. B. (2007). The role of clinical psychology in rural mental health services: Defining problems and developing solutions. *Clinical Psychology: Science and Practice, 14*(3), 283–298. https://doi.org/ 10.1111/j.1468-2850.2007.00089.x

Kuo, Y. F., Loresto Jr, F. L., Rounds, L. R., & Goodwin, J. S. (2013). States with the least restrictive regulations experienced the largest increase in patients seen by nurse practitioners. *Health Affairs, 32*(7), 1236–1243.

Lambert, D., & Gale, J. A. (2014). Integrated care in rural areas. In J. C. Warren & K. B. Smalley (Eds.), *Rural public health: Best practices and preventative models* (pp. 67–84). New York: Springer Publishing Company.

Lavoie, K. L., & Fleet, R. P. (2002). Should psychologists be granted prescription privileges? A review of the prescription privilege debate for psychiatrists. *The Canadian Journal of Psychiatry, 47*(5), 443–449.

Linda, W. P., & McGrath, R. E. (2017). The current status of prescribing psychologists: Practice patterns and medical professional evaluations. *Professional Psychology: Research and Practice, 48*(1), 38.

Meyer, P. S., & Morrissey, J. P. (2007). A comparison of assertive community treatment and intensive case management for patients in rural areas. *Psychiatric Services, 58*(1), 121–127.

Mohamed, S., Neale, M., & Rosenheck, R. A. (2009). VA intensive mental health case management in urban and rural areas: Veteran characteristics and service delivery. *Psychiatric Services, 60*(7), 914–921.

Myers, L. L., Kropf, N. P., & Robinson, M. (2002). Grandparents raising grandchildren: Case management in a rural setting. *Journal of Human Behavior in the Social Environment, 5*(1), 53–71.

National Institute of Mental Health. (n.d.). *Integrated care: Overview*. Retrieved November 30, 2019, from www.nimh.nih.gov/health/topics/integrated-care/index.shtml

Ortiz, J., Hofler, R., Bushy, A., Lin, Y. L., Khanijahani, A., & Bitney, A. (2018). Impact of Nurse Practitioner Practice Regulations on Rural Population Health Outcomes. *Healthcare (Basel, Switzerland), 6*(2), 65. https://doi.org/10.3390/healthcare6020065

Rabinowitz, H. K., & Paynter, N. P. (2002). The rural vs urban practice decision. *Medical Student Journal of the American Medical Association, 287*(1). Retrieved December 19, 2019, from https://jamanetwork.com/journals/jama/fullarticle/1844613

Riding-Malon, R., & Werth Jr, J. L. (2014). Psychological practice in rural settings: At the cutting edge. *Professional Psychology: Research and Practice, 45*(2), 85.

Robert Graham Center. (2018). *The state of primary care in the United States: A chartbook of facts and figures.* Retrieved December 19, 2019, from www.graham-center.org/content/dam/rgc/documents/publications-reports/reports/PrimaryCareChartbook.pdf

Rygh, E. M., & Hjortdahl, P. (2007). Continuous and integrated health care services in rural areas. A literature study. *Rural & Remote Health, 7*(3). Retrieved December 19, 2019, from www.ncbi.nlm.nih.gov/pubmed/17650058

Sears, S. F., Jr., Evans, G. D., & Kuper, B. D. (2003). Rural social service systems as behavioral health delivery systems. In B. H. Stamm (Ed.), *Rural behavioral health care: An interdisciplinary guide* (pp. 109–120). Washington, DC: American Psychological Association.

Vaughan-Sarrazin, M. S., Hall, J. A., & Rick, G. S. (2000). Impact of case management on use of health services by rural clients in substance abuse treatment. *Journal of Drug Issues, 30*(2), 435–463.

18 Telehealth
Advances, Advantages, and Limitations

Discussions about improving rural mental health often include enthusiasm about the prospect of telehealth or telemedicine (Lambert, Gale, Hartley, Croll, & Hansen, 2016). Whereas rural communities are frequently dated in their approaches to medicine, science, and technology, rural communities are currently, by necessity, at the forefront of advances in utilizing technology for the purposes of providing mental healthcare (Lambert et al., 2016).

Simply stated, telehealth is using videoconferencing to provide healthcare to people in a different location. Though more complex than video calling your mother on your phone, telehealth has long been viewed as a viable option for the historically underserved rural communities of our country. Telehealth is growing in popularity, and usage and developments in research and policy are following close behind (APA, 2010).

Telehealth includes any and all electronic and telecommunications (including training, meetings, continuing education) that pertain to remote clinical services.

Telemental Health: Treatment Through Technology

Telemedicine (translated literally as "healing at a distance") is defined by the World Health Organization (2004) as

> The delivery of health care services, where distance is a critical factor, by all health care professionals using information and communication technologies for the exchange of valid information for diagnosis, treatment and prevention of disease and injuries, research and evaluation, and for the continuing education of health care providers, all in the interests of advancing the health of individuals and their communities.

At first glance, telehealth appears to be a panacea for the underserved rural communities. Telemedicine, particularly telemental health therapy, provides a close approximation to in-person mental health treatment and offers great promise (Velasquez, Duncan, & Nelson, 2012). Telemedicine provides an answer to one of the greatest dilemmas in rural communities as it helps overcome geographic and cost barriers as well as issues pertaining to provider shortages (WHO, 2009). In particularly rural states, telehealth may not solve matters of supply so simply. Licensure requirements still limit practices that span state lines. As a result, in states that have significant provider shortages, telehealth may extend services to more remote communities but may not add to the overall numbers of providers in the rural communities (Stamm, 2003).

Increasingly, we have good evidence to suggest that telemental health services are equivalent to in-person, face-to-face care (Lambert et al., 2016). However, telemental health, as with in-person mental health services, requires highly trained clinicians, effective at their trade. Further, for telehealth to adequately address the needs of rural America, given the shortages in rural communities, providers in metropolitan regions will have to broaden their scope of practice to include rural peoples.

There is limited data on the cost effectiveness of telemedicine (De La Torre-Díez, López-Coronado, Vaca, Aguado, & de Castro, 2015). Practitioners have consistently reported funding as a major barrier to telemental health service provision. Start-up costs, particularly in areas with limited broadband internet and other technological impediments, can be great. Whereas third-party payers are increasingly reimbursing for telehealth services (with Medicaid and Medicare both offering reimbursement), requirements and standards for technology and training require additional funding, which can make the entire effort cost prohibitive (Lambert et al., 2016). The Centers for Medicaid and Medicare services, a federal agency with administrative power that sets many of the requirements and billing standards for health and mental health services, requires that individuals receiving telehealth be housed within a health facility within a health professional shortage area (HPSA). Further, CMS (2019) does not allow providers to bill for a psychiatric diagnostic interview, the first step for many in establishing care.

Research on telemental health, though still limited, shows promise. One study in the Black Belt demonstrated promising findings, with the researchers concluding the telemedicine networks had the potential for improving access and service provision in rural regions (Ishfaq & Raja, 2015). Another study, exploring the effects of integrated telemedical care in federally qualified health centers (FQHCs) (nonprofit, federally funded health facilities providing primary care to low-income populations), concluded that while telemedicine was more expensive, it was perhaps more effective in treating depression from an integrated care model (Harju, 2018).

Minimal research has been done on the acceptance of telemental health provision with indigenous populations. One qualitative study in Canada found significant ambivalence regarding the use of telemental health. While many viewed it as a suitable intervention that may reduce costs, increase services, and offer a private and secure method for receiving care, others highlighted several concerns. Some participants expressed concerns that it might be difficult to build trust—an essential component in any healing relationship—through video conferencing. Others expressed concerns about the nature of working with individuals not embedded in their community. Issues surrounding security and privacy related to cybersecurity as well as within the facility that housed the origination site concerned some interviewees. Others expressed concerns surrounding limitations of the telehealth relationship when it came to matters of safety and crises (Gibson et al., 2011).

Given what we have covered regarding rural communities, you might suspect that the qualitative data obtained from research with the First Peoples in Canada could apply to individuals in other insular communities. Ambivalence toward outside help is consistent with evidence of rugged individualism, stoicism, and favoring independence over dependence. Further, rural communities with intense poverty, low health literacy, and mistrust for outsiders may hold negative views of telehealth providers and the telehealth system. At least one study hypothesized, based on their findings, that internet-based mental health programming is particularly well suited for rural mental healthcare (Griffiths & Christensen, 2007).

One of the largest barriers to widespread use of telemedicine in rural communities has to do with internet capabilities. In a phenomenon known as the "digital divide," rural areas lag behind urban centers in connectivity (Magana-Rodriguez, Villarreal-Reyes, Galaviz-Mosqueda, Rivera-Rodriguez, & Conte-Galvan, 2015). While, in recent years, tremendous innovations have taken place, government funding has been allocated for such improvements, and urbanization has transformed not only the physical rural landscape but the technological one as well (Velasquez et al., 2012).

Though promising, telemedicine has yet to be widely embraced by the medical or patient communities (WHO, 2009). It has, generally speaking, received mixed reviews from users and potential users (Simms, Gibson, & O'Donnell, 2011). Some studies have demonstrated that individuals still hold a preference for face-to-face services, with a slight bias against telehealth, viewing it as potentially less effective (Grubaugh, Cain, Elhai, Patrick, & Frueh, 2008). Other studies have found that professionals who had not yet provided telemental health services were more skeptical and negative in their views of their effectiveness. Similarly, those who had not yet provided services via telehealth technologies feared difficulties with ease of utilization. Those who had provided such services had more positive experiences and beliefs about its functionality and ease. Not surprisingly, individual overall comfort with technology influenced provider's comfort with telehealth technology (Gibson, Simms, O'Donnell, & Molyneaux, 2009). Maine, a state with many rural residents, has demonstrated significant success with its massive telemedicine system. It has been widely accepted with great institutional, provider, and consumer support and has been demonstrated to have great clinical and financial benefits. There, with tremendous support, the program has received great acceptance and has reached rural and remote people who would not otherwise be served (Edwards & Patel, 2003). Those interested in learning more about telemedicine program development would be well served by seeing what Maine has done.

Though individuals seem to favor face-to-face interventions when possible, telemental health seems to be an increasingly accepted, viable service for those in rural and remote areas (Gibson et al., 2009). Telehealth also offers tremendous promise to ensuring provider support, competence, and growth in rural areas.

Telehealth: Expanding the Clinician's Network

Telehealth is not merely directly beneficial for rural clients; it may bolster rural clinicians in several ways. Telehealth provides opportunities for individual clinicians in rural and remote areas to obtain support, training, and supervision, potentially reducing the impact of professional isolation, training, and competency issues. Telehealth may thus help with retention issues in rural communities (WHO, 2009). Telehealth can be synchronous or asynchronous with trainings, often in the form of webinars happening either live or recorded. Telehealth also offers the possibility for rural clinicians to experience a lesser burden of care insofar as remote clinicians may serve as additional resources to clientele, reducing the feeling of overwhelm to the rural provider. Of course, this may also create fear for the rural provider that they will lose business to remote providers, making their practice unsustainable.

Project ECHO (Extension for Community Healthcare Outcomes) is an innovative initiative that is gaining traction in the medical community. Initially developed at the University of New Mexico Health Sciences Center to enhance provider knowledge and interventions with underserved populations with chronic and complex presentations (Arora et al., 2016), Project ECHO uses "ongoing telementoring to equip primary care practitioners in rural areas with the knowledge they need to provide high-quality specialty care" (Robert Wood Johnson Foundation, n.d.). Project ECHO is a model that emphasizes didactic training, case presentations, and case-based learning to enhance specialty service provisions among primary care providers (Socolovsky et al., 2013). Project ECHO serves to reduce the gap in care between urban and rural regions by decentralizing knowledge and skills training (Arora et al., 2014). As of 2019, the program had been established in 229 locations, with 520 programs operating in 48 states. Initially focusing on physical health conditions many ECHO programs have developed around autism, substance use, chronic pain, and behavioral health issues (Project ECHO, n.d.). Project ECHO utilizes technology to bolster and enrich the professionals practicing with little support or resources. Preliminary research findings suggest that Project ECHO has the potential to influence patient outcomes by increasing provider self-efficacy and knowledge (Anderson et al., 2017), changing provider behavior and competence, and increasing access to patients in rural communities (Zhou, Crawford, Serhal, Kurdyak, & Sockalingam, 2016).

Informal Telecare

Televideo interventions are not the only use for technology in rural communities. Technology can be used to support individual and community well-being outside telehealth services. Increasingly, people are accessing mental health resources through social media, email campaigns, emails with their providers, blogs, webinars, and videos related to mental wellness. Many mental health provider groups and professional organizations have a presence on social media (Velasquez et al., 2012). Increasingly, Facebook has become a place for clinicians to share information about their services, expand their reach, and provide mental health tidbits to their community (Lukes, 2010). Many practitioners are utilizing webinars or newsletters to educate the public on mental health–related topics, treatment options, and even specific interventions. My brief internet search for such items yielded more than six million results.

Given the nature of stigma, issues with access, and low health literacy often found in rural communities, indirect educational campaigns and nontraditional therapeutic mediums may serve to increase services to a community without necessarily increasing the number of in-office therapy visits. Of course, therapists should take care to ensure that their content is not perceived as a treatment or an intervention.

Pocket Mental Health

Given the ubiquity of smartphones and the increasing acceptance of their functionality in our daily lives, it is no surprise that mental health has found its way into our pockets. There are over 1,400 apps geared toward mental health available for download (Larsen et al., 2019). App function varies, with some providing a mental healthcare experience. Others aid users in tracking data about mental wellness (Daylio, n.d.), and others teach mental wellness skills, such as meditation (Headspace, n.d.), sleep improvement (Calm, n.d.), and stress management (Happify, n.d.). Therapy apps such as Betterhelp and Talkspace merge the practice of telemental healthcare with emerging technological advances and app development. These apps are not limited to synchronous video conferencing but may include texting and other forms of communication.

App-based therapy is an emerging market with limited research to back its efficacy and safety. Some concerns regarding this modality include its inappropriateness for the treatment of severe symptoms, lack of knowledge about who and where the individual is should they require immediate assistance, and lack of a relational connection (Novotney, 2017) demonstrated and understood to be essential in therapeutic growth (Barber, Khalsa, & Sharpless, 2010).

There is a profoundly limited amount of data regarding the safety and efficacy of such programs (Leigh & Flatt, 2015). One ethical consideration surrounds privacy. Apps that store large amounts of personal data can pose a threat to an individual's privacy, particularly as it pertains to mental health information. Free apps, which rely on advertisements for financing, may reveal personal health data in exchange for money. Other apps may not utilize sufficient security measures to ensure protection from data breaches (Giota & Kleftaras, 2014).

Further, research into efficacy of app-based mental health treatment is seriously lacking (Giota & Kleftaras, 2014). Some apps, such as Australia-based

MyCompass, claim to "address mild-to-moderate symptoms of stress, anxiety, and depression through personalized treatments delivered entirely online." Findings published in a peer-reviewed journal suggest that MyCompass's delivery of cognitive behavioral therapy shows promising outcomes in short-term symptom reduction in depression, anxiety, and stress (Proudfoot et al., 2013; Harrison et al., 2011). One small meta-analysis revealed that computerized treatments hold promise in the treatment of depression (Andersson & Cuijpers, 2009). As with most apps, designers are typically technophiles creating in the spirit of innovation and business growth. Mental healthcare apps, then, are not likely to be designed exclusively by mental health clinicians and may lack some of the properties commonly associated with a mental health practice.

App-based mental healthcare may have significant benefits for specific groups. Younger individuals in particular may be drawn to app-based treatment options.

References

American Psychological Association. (2010). *Telehealth resources for psychologists*. Retrieved October 23, 2019, from www.apaservices.org/practice/update/2010/08-31/telehealth-resources

Anderson, D., Zlateva, I., Davis, B., Bifulco, L., Giannotti, T., Coman, E., & Spegman, D. (2017). Improving pain care with Project ECHO in community health centers. *Pain Medicine, 18*(10), 1882–1889.

Andersson, G., & Cuijpers, P. (2009). Internet-based and other computerized psychological treatments for adult depression: A meta-analysis. *Cognitive Behaviour Therapy, 38*(4), 196–205.

Arora, S., Kalishman, S., Thornton, K., Komaromy, M., Katzman, J., Struminger, B., & Rayburn, W. F. (2016). Project ECHO (Project Extension for Community Healthcare Outcomes): A national and global model for continuing professional development. *Journal of Continuing Education in the Health Professions, 36*, S48–S49.

Arora, S., Thornton, K., Komaromy, M., Kalishman, S., Katzman, J., & Duhigg, D. (2014). Demonopolizing medical knowledge. *Academic Medicine, 89*(1), 30–32.

Barber, J. P., Khalsa, S. R., & Sharpless, B. A. (2010). The validity of the alliance as a predictor of psychotherapy outcome. In J. C. Muran & J. P. Barber (Eds.), *The therapeutic alliance: An evidence-based guide to practice* (pp. 29–43). New York: Guilford Press.

Calm. (n.d.). *Find your calm*. Retrieved December 22, 2019, from www.calm.com

Centers for Medicare and Medicaid Services. (2019). *Telehealth services*. Retrieved December 19, 2019, from www.cms.gov/Outreach-and-Education/Medicare-Learning-Network-MLN/MLNProducts/Downloads/Telehealth-Services-Text-Only.pdf

Daylio. (n.d.). Retrieved December 19, 2019, from https://daylio.webflow.io/

De La Torre-Díez, I., López-Coronado, M., Vaca, C., Aguado, J. S., & de Castro, C. (2015). Cost-utility and cost-effectiveness studies of telemedicine, electronic, and mobile health systems in the literature: A systematic review. *Telemedicine and e-Health, 21*(2), 81–85.

Edwards, M. A., & Patel, A. C. (2003). Telemedicine in the state of Maine: A model for growth driven by rural needs. *Telemedicine Journal and e-Health, 9*(1), 25–39.

Gibson, K., Simms, D., O'Donnell, S., & Molyneaux, H. (2009). *Clinicians' attitudes toward the use of information and communication technologies for mental health services in remote* and rural areas. Paper presented at Canadian Society of Telehealth Conference, Vancouver, British Columbia.

Gibson, K. L., Coulson, H., Miles, R., Kakekakekung, C., Daniels, E., & O'Donnell, S. (2011). Conversations on telemental health: Listening to remote and rural First Nations communities. *Rural & Remote Health, 11*(2).

Giota, K. G., & Kleftaras, G. (2014). Mental health apps: Innovations, risks and ethical considerations. *E-Health Telecommunication Systems and Networks, 3*(3), 19.

Griffiths, K. M., & Christensen, H. (2007). Internet-based mental health programs: A powerful tool in the rural medical kit. *Australian Journal of Rural Health, 15*(2), 81–87.

Grubaugh, A. L., Cain, G. D., Elhai, J. D., Patrick, S. L., & Frueh, B. C. (2008). Attitudes toward medical and mental health care delivered via telehealth applications among rural and urban primary care patients. *The Journal of Nervous and Mental Disease, 196*(2), 166–170.

Happify. (n.d.). *Overcome stress and negative thoughts: Build resilience*. Retrieved December 22, 2019, from www.happify.com

Harju, A. (2018). Cost-effectiveness of telemedicine-based integrated care for treating mental illness in rural FQHCs. *Public Health Review, 1*(1).

Harrison, V., Proudfoot, J., Wee, P. P., Parker, G., Pavlovic, D. H., & Manicavasagar, V. (2011). Mobile mental health: Review of the emerging field and proof of concept study. *Journal of Mental Health, 20*(6), 509–524.

Headspace. (n.d.). Retrieved December 19, 2019, from www.headspace.com

Ishfaq, R., & Raja, U. (2015). Bridging the healthcare access divide: A strategic planning model for rural telemedicine network. *Decision Sciences, 46*(4), 755–790.

Lambert, D., Gale, J., Hartley, D., Croll, Z., & Hansen, A. (2016). Understanding the business case for telemental health in rural communities. *The Journal of Behavioral Health Services & Research, 43*(3), 366–379.

Larsen, M. E., Huckvale, K., Nicholas, J., Torous, J., Birrell, L., Li, E., & Reda, B. (2019). Using science to sell apps: Evaluation of mental health app store quality claims. *npj Digital Medicine, 2*, 18. https://doi.org/10.1038/s41746-019-0093-1

Leigh, S., & Flatt, S. (2015). App-based psychological interventions: Friend or foe? *Evidence-Based Mental Health, 18*(4), 97–99.

Lukes, C. A. (2010). Social media. *AAOHN Journal, 58*(10), 415–417.

Magana-Rodriguez, R., Villarreal-Reyes, S., Galaviz-Mosqueda, A., Rivera-Rodriguez, R., & Conte-Galvan, R. (2015). Telemedicine services over rural broadband wireless access technologies: IEEE 802.22/WRAN and IEEE 802.16 WiMAX. In *Mobile Health* (pp. 743–769). Cham: Springer.

Novotney, A. (2017). A growing wave of online therapy. *Monitor on Psychology, 48*(2), 48.

Project ECHO. (n.d.). Retrieved December 19, 2019, from https://echo.unm.edu/

Proudfoot, J., Clarke, J., Birch, M., Whitton, A. E., Parker, G., Manicavasagar, V., Harrison, V., Christensen, H., & Hadzi-Pavlovic. (2013). Impact of a mobile phone and web program on symptom and functional outcomes for people with mild-to-moderate depression, anxiety and stress: A randomised controlled trial. *BMC Psychiatry, 13*, 312.

Robert Wood Johnson Foundation. (n.d.). *Project ECHO connects specialists with on-the-ground practitioners to bridge health gaps in rural communities*. Retrieved December 19, 2019, from www.rwjf.org/en/how-we-work/grants-explorer/featured-programs/project-echo.html

Simms, D. C., Gibson, K., & O'Donnell, S. (2011). To use or not to use: Clinicians' perceptions of telemental health. *Canadian Psychology/Psychologie canadienne, 52*(1), 41.

Socolovsky, C., Masi, C., Hamlish, T., Aduana, G., Arora, S., Bakris, G., & Johnson, D. (2013). Evaluating the role of key learning theories in ECHO: A telehealth educational program for primary care providers. *Progress in community health partnerships: Research, education, and action, 7*(4), 361–368.

Stamm, B. H. (2003). Bridging the rural-urban divide with telehealth and telemedicine. In B. H. Stamm (Ed.), *Rural behavioral health care: An interdisciplinary guide* (pp. 145–155). Washington, DC: American Psychological Association.

Velasquez, S. E., Duncan, A. B., & Nelson, E. L. (2012). Technological innovations in rural mental health service delivery. In K. B. Smalley, J. C. Warren, & J. P. Rainer (Eds.), *Rural mental health: Issues, policies, and best practices* (pp. 149–172). New York: Springer Publishing Company.

World Health Organization. (2004). *Promoting mental health: Concepts, emerging evidence, practice: Summary report* [PDF file]. Retrieved December 19, 2019, from www.who.int/mental_health/evidence/en/promoting_mhh.pdf

World Health Organization. (2009). *Telemedicine: Opportunities and developments in member states*. Retrieved December 19, 2019, from www.who.int/goe/publications/goe_telemedicine_2010.pdf

Zhou, C., Crawford, A., Serhal, E., Kurdyak, P., & Sockalingam, S. (2016). The impact of project ECHO on participant and patient outcomes: A systematic review. *Academic Medicine, 91*(10), 1439–1461.

19 Creating a Culture
Decreasing Stigma, Increasing Wellness

> Stigma is a quintessentially social psychological topic: a phenomenon rooted in the individual psyche, yet constantly mediated by . . . material, political, institutional and symbolic contexts.
>
> (Campbell & Deacon, 2006, pp. 411–417)

Stigma is a toxic societal force perpetuated by myths and beliefs about what is and isn't acceptable in one's culture or group. Stigma is a status, attribute, or behavioral pattern that's existence somehow disqualifies the individual from full society acceptance (Stangor & Crandall, 2000).

Stigma can be destructive to the psyche, and the effects of stigma, particularly when it pertains to mental illness, can last even beyond effective treatment (Link, Struening, Rahav, Phelan, & Nuttbrock, 1997). We have already reviewed the ways in which stigma can negatively impact help seeking and how a culture that stigmatizes mental illness can perpetuate mental illness. You may remember from this text, or you may know from lived experience, that there can be a deleterious effect of gossip in a small town (namely, shame and stigma).

Stigma serves to simplify social perception (e.g., I know X about this person; therefore, I know Y must also be true) (Stangor & Crandall, 2000). Stigma spreads quickly and easily in small towns where anonymity is virtually impossible, and values such as sameness and stoicism are embraced. Stigma around mental illness is substantial and problematic. Stigma spreads easily through a small town, using gossip networks and social contagion.

Stigma around mental illness usually derives from misattribution. Often, beliefs about the origins of mental illness create thinking that erroneously leaves the victim of mental illness to blame. Further, when individuals are seen as not responsible for their own problems, they receive more help and experience less stigma (Turner DePalma, Madey, Tillman, & Wheeler, 1999). There is lower mental health literacy in rural communities. Mental health is not easily understood, and its causes are not entirely agreed upon by scientists, researchers, and theorists. It is not difficult to conclude, then, that many individuals in rural communities may lack the knowledge and understanding to attribute mental illness to its accurate causes. When individuals believe that someone has control over their struggles, they are at risk of taking a blaming or judgmental stance, rather than a helping one (Corrigan, 2000).

Belief in a just world, simply stated as the theory that good things happen to good people and bad things happen to bad people, also reduces helping behavior when the victim is perceived to have had some power, control, or responsibility (Ottati, Bodenhausen, & Newman, 2005).

Stigma, or judgment about mental illness, may in part be blamed on misattributing responsibility to the sufferer as if, somehow, they could simply just not be depressed or anxious. We know stigma is a grave barrier to accessing mental healthcare, and we know that it produces shame and has the potential to lead to discrimination for our clients. As a rural provider, I implore you to consider the stigma in your community and your role in perpetuating it or not.

The good news is that stigma can change. I would like to suggest that stigma surrounding mental health in small towns can be changed, perhaps more easily than in more densely populated areas. I believe that the very same things that make a small town more susceptible to stigma make it more possible for that community to change.

There are three main approaches to changing stigma in communities: education, contact, and protest. **Education** challenges assumptions and inaccurate stereotypes with factual information. These can entail public service announcements, books, flyers, advertisements, etc. **Contact** includes personal interaction with members of the stigmatized group. **Protest** entails public strategies to point out injustice and rebuke offenders. Contact and education, based on research, have the most significant impacts on reducing stigma. Meeting and interacting with a person with mental illness is perhaps the single best way to reduce stigma. Face-to-face contact has the greatest destigmatizing effects when it occurs between people of similar status who can find some common ground and has an interaction that is, or is linked to something, rewarding (Corrigan & Shapiro, 2010). When it comes to stigma and adolescents, education seems to play a huge role in stigma reduction (Corrigan, Morris, Michaels, Rafacz, & Rüsch, 2012).

Despite national campaigns and efforts by large-scale organizations to address mental health stigma, it turns out de-stigmatization occurs best on a local, personal level (Byrne, 2000). What's more local and personal than a small, rural community?

Contact may occur simply as a biproduct of small-town psychology, but providers may also elect to take a more proactive approach to exploiting this naturally occurring phenomenon for good. Over the past five years, our group practice has sponsored local non-mental-health-related events, advertised on public radio, and encouraged participation in social media campaigns (honoring confidentiality, of course). Several years ago, I was asked to give a talk at a local avalanche awareness symposium. In the weeks following my lecture, we noticed an uptick in initial client calls, with many individuals citing their exposure to the topic of mental health and a professional as reasons behind their contact.

Other individuals reach out for therapy simply because they have passed our clinic on their way to work, the gym, or home. They see our advertisements on the public shuttle and meet our clinicians at school pickup. They come to us because our presence—somewhat abundant in this small community—reduces the metaphorical distance they must travel to seek services.

What I have noticed is that we have moved the needle ever so slightly away from the pole of stigma. Many of the people who come to our clinic know a client or a therapist who practices therein. This is a common phenomenon in many settings, and one interpretation is that it is triggered by an increase in comfort and familiarity and a decrease in the sense of the unknown. Perhaps, too, our visibility and presence in the community have led to the suggestion that mental illness is not something that happens in hospitals or windowless buildings in cities but right here, on Main Street, in your town.

References

Byrne, P. (2000). Stigma of mental illness and ways of diminishing it. *Advances in Psychiatric Treatment*, *6*(1), 65–72.

Campbell, C., & Deacon, H. (2006). Unravelling the contexts of stigma: From internalisation to resistance to change. *Journal of Community and Applied Psychology*, *16*(6), 411–417.

Corrigan, P. W. (2000). Mental health stigma as social attribution: Implications for research methods and attitude change. *Clinical Psychology: Science and Practice*, *7*(1), 48–67.

Corrigan, P. W., Morris, S. B., Michaels, P. J., Rafacz, J. D., & Rüsch, N. (2012). Challenging the public stigma of mental illness: A meta-analysis of outcome studies. *Psychiatric Services*, *63*(10), 963–973.

Corrigan, P. W., & Shapiro, J. R. (2010). Measuring the impact of programs that challenge the public stigma of mental illness. *Clinical Psychology Review*, *30*(8), 907–922. https://doi.org/10.1016/j.cpr.2010.06.004

Link, B. G., Struening, E. L., Rahav, M., Phelan, J. C., & Nuttbrock, L. (1997). On stigma and its consequences: Evidence from a longitudinal study of men with dual diagnoses of mental illness and substance abuse. *Journal of Health and Social Behavior*, *38*, 177–190.

Ottati, V., Bodenhausen, G. V., & Newman, L. S. (2005). Social psychological models of mental illness stigma. In P. W. Corrigan (Ed.), *On the stigma of mental illness: Practical strategies for research and social change* (pp. 99–128). Washington, DC: American Psychological Association.

Stangor, C., & Crandall, C. S. (2000). Threat and the social construction of stigma. *The Social Psychology of Stigma*, *87*, 62.

Turner DePalma, M., Madey, S. F., Tillman, T. C., & Wheeler, J. (1999). Perceived patient responsibility and belief in a just world affect helping. *Basic and Applied Social Psychology*, *21*(2), 131–137.

Closing Thoughts

Writing this book has underscored that, as rural providers and researchers, we have a long way to go in terms of fully understanding this large minority group. One thing is clear: our urbancentric methods and thinking are insufficient frameworks for understanding and working with rural Americans. If you are practicing in a rural community, it is essential that you familiarize yourself with the histories, experiences, norms, and values that are relevant to the population you serve. Further, because of the nature of rural life and rural practice, you are likely to encounter predictable ethical dilemmas, including multiple relationships, competency issues, matters of privacy and confidentiality, and self-care. I have learned, not always gracefully, that our best strategy combines individualized treatment embedded in a community-based approach that honors both the individual and the culture in which they are embedded.

What I hope you have realized by now is that practicing psychology in rural America is challenging and satisfying. The need is great, and the rewards are limitless. Perhaps you are already interested in returning to your rural roots or looking to trade in the urban grind for something more sustainable. Maybe you live in suburbia and realize that rural Americans are coming to you because you are the closest provider to them. Or maybe you are entertaining the possibility of building bridges between your metropolitan practice and the rural communities in your state through telemental health. Whatever your motivation, I hope that this book has served to provide you with more hope than despair and a pathway toward possibility.

It all began for me in Babb, a small town perched on the Blackfeet Indian Reservation in Northwest Montana. Sitting at 4,500 feet, it borders Glacier National Park and is home to approximately 200 year-round residents. In the summer, the population swells with tourists, hikers, mountaineers, and college students hungry for summer work. The economic bump resulting from the seasonal tourist swell is not enough to sustain the residents through the cold, windy, harsh winters, which last from about October to April or May. At times, snow drifts make it impossible for some residents to leave their homes, let alone travel to the nearest grocery store, some 40 miles away. Traveling east from Babb, one finds oneself on the Hi-Line, the northern route for the Great Northern Railway. Havre, the crown jewel of the Hi-Line, is the closest developed area, though it still does not qualify as an urbanized area. There are, however, several practitioners serving the community. From Babb, one can drive west for about 120 miles over Mariah's Pass (the lowest point along the Continental Divide, a formidable obstacle in any weather) to Columbia Falls, a small town that was populated as a hub for the railroad, sustained by an aluminum plant long closed. There, a hospital extension, several practitioners, and a Head Start exist. While driving from Babb to services is certainly possible, it is unlikely to be the answer to the mental health needs of the community. Similarly, those in Selbyville, West Virginia; Bakersfield, Vermont; Glen Elder, Kansas; and Silver Bay, Minnesota, are likely to face more obstacles than opportunities when it comes to accessing mental health services. They are less likely to have specialized mental health service providers and are more likely to be considered provider shortage areas.

Driving distances and provider deserts aside, these communities are also likely to face cultural barriers to seeking mental health services. With lower mental health literacy; lower rates of viable health insurance; and pressures from stigma, self-reliance, and resilience, individual members of these communities are more likely to wait longer to receive services, often making them worse off when they finally do receive services than their urban counterparts. Further, when they do finally obtain the care, they are more likely to be treated for a mental health condition by a clergy member or primary care provider than a specialized mental health provider.

These people and their respective communities need services. They need more providers who understand their culture, are equipped to deal with the ethical dilemmas such work will present, receive ongoing consultation and support, and regularly engage in self-care behaviors to ensure their competency and longevity. They also need innovative solutions to address the very real barriers to access. They need treatment options that don't always look like treatment options and providers who will come to them. They need outreach and education, de-stigmatizing efforts and community-wide solutions. In short, they—and all the other rural areas of this country—need you.

Appendix
Recommended Reading and Resources

Books

Brown, D. L., & Swanson, L. E. (Eds.). (2004). *Challenges for rural America in the twenty-first century*. Penn State Press.

Crosby, R. A., Wendel, M. L., Vanderpool, R. C., & Casey, B. R. (2012). *Rural populations and health: determinants, disparities, and solutions*. John Wiley & Sons.

Keefe, S. E. (Ed.). (2005). *Appalachian cultural competency: A guide for medical, mental health and social service professionals*. University of Tennessee Press.

Rothschild, B. (2006). *Help for the helper: The psychophysiology of compassion fatigue and vicarious trauma*. WW Norton & Co.

Skovholt, T. M., & Trotter-Mathison, M. (2014). *The resilient practitioner: Burnout prevention and self-care strategies for counselors, therapists, teachers, and health professionals*. Routledge.

Smalley, K. B., & Rainer, J. (2012). *Rural mental health: Issues, policies, and best practices*. Springer Publishing Company.

Strom-Gottfried, K. (2014). *Straight talk about professional ethics*. Oxford University Press.

Warren, J., & Smalley, K. B. (Eds.). (2014). *Rural public health: Best practices and preventive models*. Springer Publishing Company.

Witko, T. M. (2006). *Mental health care for urban Indians: Clinical insights from Native practitioners*. American Psychological Association.

Wodarski, J. S. (1983). *Rural community mental health practice*. Baltimore: University Park Press.

Journals

The Journal of Rural Health, National Rural Health Association
The Journal of Rural Mental Health, American Psychological Association
Rural and Remote Health Journal

Web-based resources

Amber Waves, monthly publication of the Economic Research Services
Rural Health Information Hub: www.ruralhealthinfo.org
APA Rural Program: www.apa.org/practice/programs/rural/

Rural Information Center: www.nal.usda.gov/ric

Rural Horizons Magazine, National Rural Health Association: www.ruralhealthweb.org/news/content-hub/rural-horizons-magazine

Western Interstate Commission for Higher Education: Cultural Competence standards in managed care mental health services for Native American populations: Provider competencies: www.wiche.edu/archive/mh/culturalCompetenceStandards/na/provider

Index

Note: Page numbers in *italics* indicate figures and page numbers in **bold** indicate tables on the corresponding pages.

access to healthcare 70–72, 153
acculturation 51–53
adolescent health 56
affordability of healthcare 72
African Americans *30*, 31
alcohol misuse 57–59, *58*; deaths of despair and 60
Amazon.com 52
American Community Survey 25, 26
American Counseling Association (ACA) 13, 16, 79, 81, 102, 109; on confidentiality 122
American Indians and Alaska Natives 33–35; health of 35–37, *36*; Indian Health Service (IHS) and 20, 34–35
American Psychiatric Association (APA) 13–14, 16
American Psychological Association (APA) 13, 16, 49, 79, 86, 119; on competence 128; on confidentiality 123; Ethics Code 81–83, 88, 108–109, 129; on generalist practice 128; on multiple relationships 107, 109–110; on utilization of colleague assistance by clinicians 135
anti-Semitism 47
applied ethics 88–89
apps, mental health 184–185
Archilochus 90
Association for Marriage and Family Therapy (AAMFT) 81
availability of healthcare 73–74

Babb, Montana 1–2, 10, 191–192
beneficence 82
Berry, J. W. 52

Betterhelp 184
Blank, M. 15
Brokeback Mountain 32
Brookings Institute 60
Brown, L. S. 90
burnout 139; assessment of 141

Camacho, F. T. 45
case managers 177–178
Census Bureau, US 7, 8–9
Center for Native American Youth 35
Centers for Disease Control 57, 62, 63
Centers for Medicaid and Medicare services 181
child health 56
chronic illness 57; suicide and 66
clinicians *see* rural clinicians
codes of ethics 80–81
Cohn, T. J. 129
collaboration *see* partnerships
Collins, M. E. 165
colonialism 37
Committee on Rural Health 16
community 43
competence *85*, 85–86, 128–132
confidentiality *85*, 87–88, 121–127
conflict, ethical *96*, 96–97
Connolly, C. 32
conservatism 46–48, *47*
crime 36
cultural competence 3, 13–14
cultural dimension, rurality as 14–15
culture, rural 42

data collection 100
deaths of despair 56, 59–61

debrief 104–105
Decoding the Ethics Code (Fisher) 88
deprivation 28–29, *29*
desensitization 95
Diagnostic and Statistical Manual of Mental Disorders, Fifth Edition (DSM-V) 13
digital divide 182
disability and suicide 66
distress, ethical 96, *96*
diversification 174–175
Dreyfus, S. E. 128
drug and alcohol misuse 57–59, *58*; deaths of despair and 60
dual relationships 86–87, 107–109, *108*

economic indicators 25–26
Economic Research Service 11, 26, 27
education: competence and 128–132; race and ethnicity and 31; of rural Americans 25; and training in rural social work 15–20
enhancement 176
ethical conflict *96*, 96–97
ethical dilemmas: data collection and 100; evaluation and 102–103; evaluation/debrief and 104–105; identification of 93–97, *94*, *96*; implementation and 104; predict, prepare, prevent 92–93; rationale 90–92; self-reflection and 97–100; solution generation and 100–102; worksheet for 105–106
ethical distress 96, *96*
ethics: applied 88–89; codes of 80–81, 108–109; dilemmas in 90–106; ethical duty and 81–83, *82*; introduction to 79–80; relevant 84–88
evaluation 102–103; debrief and 104–105
exploitation 109, 110–111

Federal Office of Rural Health Policy 15
fidelity 82
Fiduciary Heart of Ethics, The (Zuckerman) 108
Fisher, C. B. 129
flexibility 177
For the Love of Men (Plank) 62
frontier areas 10–11

Gale, J. A. 176
generalists 128–133
Glacier County, Montana 9–10
Google 2
Great Depression 26

Great Migration 31
Great Recession 25

harm 109–112
Hastings, S. L. 129
Head Start 19, 152
healthcare in rural America: access to 70–72, 153; affordability of 72; availability of 73–74; integrated 151–152, 174–176; underutilization of 73
health in rural America 55; deaths of despair and 56, 59–61; drugs and 57–59, *58*; prevalence rates of illness and 55–57; suicide and 56, *61*, 61–68, *62*, *66*
Helbok, C. M. 124
Hill, G. J. 32
Hispanic and Latino Americans *30*, 31
Hoover, H. 46

identification of ethical dilemmas 93–97, *94*, *96*
impairment 109, 110; of clinicians 137–139
implementation 104
Improving Cultural Competence 15
Indian Health Service (IHS) 20, 34–35
indices of deprivation 28–29, *29*
individualism, rugged 45–46
Industrial Revolution 29
informal telecare 183–184
integrated care 151–152; components of 174–176; considerations for 176–178
integrity 83

Jameson, J. 15
Johnson, L. 34
journaling 141
Journal on Rural Mental Health 132
Juang, L. 13
justice 83

Karson, M. 122
Keith-Spiegel, P. 80, 81
Koocher, G. P. 80, 81

Lambert, D. 176
Lannin, D. 85
Leedy, G. 32
Left Behind, The: Decline and Rage in Rural America (Wuthnow) 44
Lengerich, E. J. 45
LGBTQ individuals 32–33, 166; suicide among 65–66

linkage 175
locus of authority 96, *96*, 97

Marinelli, R. P. 124
Marlboro Man 49
masculinity 49–50
Maslach Burnout Inventory (MBI) 141
Matsumoto, D. 13
Medicaid 72
meditative practices 143–144
Mental Health America 73
mental health first aid (MHFA) 167
mindfulness 143–144
minority groups in rural America *30*, 30–32
mobile health centers (MHCs) 153, 167–169
Monroe, M. 90
Mowbray, C. T. 165
Moxley, D. P. 165
multiple relationships *85*, 86–87; defined 107–109, *108*; neutrality and 112–119; therapeutic implications of 109–112
MyCompass 185

National Alliance on Mental Illness 55
National Association of Social Workers (NASW) 13, 14, 16, 79, 81, 86
National Rural Health Association 10, 70
neighborliness 43–44
neutrality 112–119
nonmaleficence 82

obesity 57
Office of Management and Budget (OMB) 8
opioids 57–59

partnerships 151–152, 173; with churches 162–164; with schools 164
peer networks of care 164–167, *166*
Phantom, D. 33
Plank, L. 45, 62
pocket mental health 184–185
population of rural America 24–25
poverty: deprivation and 28–29, *29*; educational attainment and 25; in Native communities 35–36; rates of rural 26–28, *27*
predicting ethical dilemmas 92–93
preparation for ethical dilemmas 92–93
prevalence of mental illness in rural America 55–57
prevention 141–144; in clinical practice 152–153; of ethical dilemmas 92–93

privacy: client *85*, 87–88, 121–127; clinician 136–137
professional enrichment 132–133
Project ECHO 130, 183
Proulx, A. 32
proximity in rural practice 153
public health approach to rural psychology 161–162

Quality of Life Inventory (QOLI) 141

race and ethnicity in rural America *30*, 30–32
Rainer, J. P. 14, 15
rape 36
rationale 90–92
recruitment and retention of rural clinicians 154–157, **156**
referrals 175–176
Regier, D. A. 161
relevant ethics 84–88, *85*
religion 37–38, 162–164
respect for people's rights and dignity 83
responsibility 82
rugged individualism 45–46
rural America 23–24; American Indians and Alaska Natives in 20, 33–38, *36*; defining 7–8, *8*; deprivation in 28–29, *29*; economic indicators on 25–26; education of 25; frontier areas and 10–11; LGBTQ individuals in 32–33, 166; minority groups in *30*, 30–32; population of 24–25; poverty in 25, 26–28, *27*; religion in 37–38; rurality and 8–10; termed "flyover country" 24; as under-studied, misunderstood, and underserved 1–3; workforce of 29–30; *see also* healthcare in rural America; health in rural America; values, rural
rural clinicians: assessment of 141; burnout in 139, 141; community burden on 137; impairment in 137–139; implementation of self-care plans by 145–146; maintenance for 144–145, **145**; prevention for 141–144; privacy and visibility of 136–137; recruitment and retention of 154–157, **156**; rurality complicating mental wellness for 135; self-care by 139–140, *140*, 144–146, **145**; strategies for success of 139–140; *see also* rural practice

rural culture 42
Rural Health Information Hub 15
Rural Health Quarterly 73
rurality 8–10; complicating mental wellness for providers 135; as cultural dimension 14–15; in policy, education, and training 15–20
rural practice 191–192; application of ethics in 84–89; churches and 162–164; compared to urban setting **160**; competence in *85*, 85–86, 128–132; confidentiality and privacy in 121–127; defining rural mental healthcare 159–169; education and training for 15–20, 128–129; ethical dilemmas in 90–106; generalists in 128–133; integrated care in 151–152, 174–176; mental health first aid (MHFA) and 167; mobile health clinics (MHCs) in 153, 167–169; multiple relationships in *85*, 86–87, 107–109, *108*; neutrality in 112–119; peer networks of care in 164–167, *166*; prevention in 152–153; professional enrichment for 132–133; proximity in 153; public health approach to rural psychology and 161–162; school-based care and 164; telehealth in 180–185; therapeutic relationship in 109–112; *see also* partnerships; rural clinicians
rural psychology, public health approach to 161–162
Rural-Urban Commuting Area (RUCA) codes 8

school-based care 164
Scott, N. 85
self-care *85*, 88, 139–140, *140*, 144–146, **145**
self-reflection 97–100
self-reliance 44–45
sexual assault 36
Shepard, M. 32
Slama, K. 1, 3, 15
Smalley, K. B. 14, 15
solution generation 100–102
Spleen, A. M. 45
Stadler, H. A. 102
Stewart, E. G. 15

stigma and shame 50–51, 162, 175; reducing 188–190
stoicism 48–49
Substance Abuse and Mental Health Services Administration (SAMHSA) 15
substituting 177
suicide 56, *61*, 61–68, *62*, *66*

Talkspace 184
telehealth: expanding the clinician's network 183; informal 183–184; pocket mental health 184–185; treatment through 180–183
terror management theory 48
therapeutic relationship 109–112
Thompson, J. H. 23
training *see* education
trauma 36–37, 109; in clinicians 137–139
Trevor Project 65

Uber 2
underutilization of healthcare 73
unemployment rates 29–30
US Indian Reorganizations Act 34

values, rural *42*, 42–43; acculturation 51–53; community 43; conservative 46–48, *47*; masculinity 49–50; neighborliness 43–44; rugged individualism 45–46; self-reliance 44–45; stigma 50–51; stoicism 48–49
Vanderpool, R. C. 45
veterans 65, 169
violence 36

Wakefield, M. 57
Walls, R. T. 124
Warren, J. C. 14, 15
Werth, J. 136
Westboro Baptist Church 32
Wienke, C. 32
workforce, rural American 29–30
World Health Organization 162, 180
Wuthnow, R. 44, 46
WWAMI Rural Health Research Center 71

Zuckerman, E. 108